Reprint Publishing

For People Who Go For Originals.

www.reprintpublishing.com

THE

ETHICS OF JOHN STUART MILL

THE

ETHICS OF JOHN STUART MILL

EDITED

WITH INTRODUCTORY ESSAYS

BY

CHARLES DOUGLAS, M.A., D.Sc.

LECTURER AND ASSISTANT IN MORAL PHILOSOPHY
IN THE UNIVERSITY OF EDINBURGH

WILLIAM BLACKWOOD AND SONS
EDINBURGH AND LONDON
MDCCCXCVII

PREFACE

THIS edition of Mill's chief ethical writings is designed for the use of those who are beginning the study of moral science, and has been prepared in the belief that there is no better introduction to this subject than an accurate knowledge of Mill's ethical theory. Mill's writings are useful, not only because they mark a period of change in English Philosophy, but also because they possess qualities of thought and expression which give permanent weight to their speculative freedom and precision. To study them is an education in ethics, both because they treat the chief topics of the science in a broad and vigorous way, and because they evoke the mood of mind which is appropriate to the whole subject. It is very important that the student should approach the problems of moral experience in a treatment of them which maintains the human interest of the subject, rather than in purely technical discussions, in which this interest may not appear to those who have not learned their importance; and Mill's simplicity, his seriousness, the fervour of his appreciation of morality, and his largeness of outlook, help to make his work a real introduction to ethical studies. That his errors are not the least instructive part of his writings is one of the many good results of his singular and unfailing candour.

It has been very usual for students to confine their reading of Mill's ethics to his 'Utilitarianism'; and this book is, of course, his principal exposition of his ethical opinions; but I think it unfortunate that the theory of morality which is conveyed in it should be divorced from the conception of the method of ethical science by which Mill's work as a moralist is determined; and I have therefore prefaced the 'Utilitarianism' by the chapters from his 'System of Logic' in which that conception is chiefly set forth. It has also seemed desirable to give an opportunity of supplementing the knowledge of Mill's ethics which is to be gained from a study of these chapters, and of 'Utilitarianism,' by quoting, as footnotes and appendices, passages from his other writings, which corroborate, supplement, or correct the statements of the text. It is hoped that in this way a reasonably complete account of Mill's ethical theory is presented. The editions of Mill's works referred to in the notes are the most recent Library Editions, except in the cases of the 'System of Logic,' 'Principles of Political Economy,' and 'Liberty,' in which it seemed best to use the People's Editions.

The introductory Essays, on Mill's theory of method, are intended to guide the student in his interpretation and criticism of the ethical writings, and to connect these writings with Mill's philosophy as a whole, and with his place in the development of speculation. I have to thank the Rev. A. Halliday Douglas, of Cambridge, for revising the proof-sheets of these Essays.

I am indebted to Miss Helen Taylor for a most generous permission to reprint the 'Utilitarianism,' and to make use of the other writings from which I have quoted.

CHARLES DOUGLAS.

UNIVERSITY OF EDINBURGH,
February 1897.

CONTENTS

INTRODUCTORY ESSAYS

	PAGE
I. ETHICS AND INDUCTION	xiii
II. ETHICS AND PSYCHOLOGY	xxxvii
III. ETHICS AND MORALITY	lxi

ANALYSIS

ON THE LOGIC OF THE MORAL SCIENCES	lxxxiii
UTILITARIANISM	xcix

From the ETHICAL WRITINGS OF JOHN STUART MILL

I. ON THE LOGIC OF THE MORAL SCIENCES—

CHAP. I. INTRODUCTORY REMARKS	3
,, II. OF LIBERTY AND NECESSITY	9
,, III. THAT THERE IS, OR MAY BE, A SCIENCE OF HUMAN NATURE	26
,, IV. OF THE LAWS OF MIND	34
,, V. OF ETHOLOGY, OR THE SCIENCE OF THE FORMATION OF CHARACTER	54

CONTENTS

II. UTILITARIANISM—

    CHAP. I. GENERAL REMARKS . . . 79
        " II. WHAT UTILITARIANISM IS . . 89
        " III. OF THE ULTIMATE SANCTION OF THE PRINCIPLE OF UTILITY . . 128
        " IV. OF WHAT SORT OF PROOF THE PRINCIPLE OF UTILITY IS SUSCEPTIBLE . . 146
        " V. OF THE CONNEXION BETWEEN JUSTICE AND UTILITY 161

APPENDIX

A. CAUSALITY AND INDUCTION 203
B. MILL'S THEORY OF THE SELF 206
C. MILL'S THEORY OF THE RELATION OF MORALITY TO NATURE 209
D. MILL'S ESTIMATE OF BENTHAM 214

INDEX 223

INTRODUCTORY ESSAYS

ESSAY I

ETHICS AND INDUCTION

ESSAY I

ETHICS AND INDUCTION

THE method of the science of ethics must be considered in any careful study of moral questions; for most of the variations which occur in the definition of the moral life are the issue of differences in the method by which the facts of morality are approached; and there is no result of moral science that does not bear traces of the way in which it has been discovered or established.

For the student of John Stuart Mill, the subject of ethical method has a peculiar interest: it may even be said to form the central topic of Mill's philosophy. His investigation of it connects his work as a logician with those practical interests to which his mind was most constantly directed;[1] and his idea of the way in which morals and politics are to be studied has a very direct influence upon all the more important parts of his theory of those subjects. It was his interest in the logic of ethics which chiefly brought about his rejection of the unsystematic views of morality which were pre-

[1] Pp. 3 ff.

valent in his day. It was this interest, too, which first made him sensible of the importance of Bentham's work as a moralist, and which afterwards served to maintain Bentham's influence over his mind, in spite of many changes in his philosophical opinions.[1]

It was because Mill was a logician no less than a moralist that the question of method assumed for him the proportions in which he saw it; and the tendency of his idea of ethical method appears in those of his opinions which are most affected by his logical interest. His attempt to create a logic of ethics issued, on the one hand, in his utilitarian view of morality, and, on the other hand, in his deterministic idea of human conduct; and, quite apart from the way in which Mill sought to elaborate them in the detail of a theory of conduct and morals, these two conceptions have a common meaning: they both express the idea of morality by which Mill's work is inspired—the idea that it is a matter of reasoning and experience, our account of which must answer to concrete facts, and be capable of consistent statement and reasoned defence.

Mill's "Utilitarian" view of the morality of actions —that it consists in the pleasure-value of their consequences—must be understood as a criticism of the intuitional philosophy of morals. His argument is chiefly directed against the idea of morality which is set forth by Whewell. Whewell, indeed, affirms that "there must be *reasons* why actions are right and good";[2] but these reasons are found in self-evident

[1] Pp. 214-216.   [2] Elements of Morality, Preface, p. 3.

"principles," which are not shown to give effect to any single or ultimate ground of judgment, and which merely define certain opinions about morality that are generally held. Such reasons depend both for their authority and for their interpretation upon the moral feelings which they express; and Mill regards the attempt to explain morality by them as the mere opposite of sober theory. He sees in Whewell's 'Elements of Ethics' "nothing better than a classification and systematising of the opinions which he found prevailing among those who had been educated according to the approved methods of his own country; or, let us rather say, an apparatus for converting those prevailing opinions on matters of morality into reasons for themselves."[1] Mill's contempt for the "mere deification of opinion and habit"[2] leads him to demand an experiential science of moral issues; and he rightly conceives such a science to be foreign to the temper of moralists like Whewell. This is the ground of his antagonism to the intuitional theory. That morality should "be referred to an *end* of some sort, and not left in the dominion of vague feeling or inexplicable internal conviction, that it be made a matter of reason and calculation, and not merely of sentiment, is essential to the very idea of moral philosophy; is, in fact, what renders argument or discussion on moral questions possible."[3] It is Mill's intellectual seriousness that is responsible for his austere refusal to make speculative concessions to sentiment or custom. He is convinced of the

[1] P. 84 note 1. [2] P. 123 note 1. [3] P. 83 note 1.

necessity for deriving a theory of conduct from discoverable circumstances of human activity and desire rather than from shifting imaginations and vagrant prejudices, even if these be dignified by more august titles. It is not enough, in his view, merely to say that the ground of morality is in man's own nature. Morality cannot be verified, and ethics cannot be a science, unless the facts on which moral obligation rests are accessible to knowledge. If the morality of actions consists in their conformity to rules, while both the ground of these rules and the relation of acts to them are left unexplained, a science of ethics is out of the question. Mill desired to find an objective verifiable criterion of right and wrong in conduct, and his demand for such a criterion could hardly have expressed itself otherwise than in that appeal to the consequences of actions which Utilitarianism makes.[1] This was a method of ethical science—a way of explaining the moral consciousness—which lay ready to his hand, and in the use of which he had been originally trained. That unity of moral action with its consequences, which it has been the virtue of Hedonism to assert, offered a ready escape from mere dogmatism on moral subjects. Since consequences can be known and can be estimated by their pleasure-value, the acts to which they belong can be criticised in virtue of their tendency to produce pain or pleasure.

This method of judging the morality of conduct was not, of course, discovered by Mill: it was a heritage

[1] P. 83 note 1.

from English moralists who went before him. It has, indeed, never been found possible entirely to ignore the relation of the effects of conduct to its morality; and the attempt to make light of this relation has been apt to provoke an exaggerated estimate of its importance, and even a fictitious isolation of consequences from the conduct which produces them. It is only natural, however, that the significance of the effects of action should have been perceived with special clearness in England; since English philosophy has chiefly been the creation not of academic specialists, but of men of affairs, whose practical interests it continually reflects. The consequences of action were never wholly forgotten by any of the earlier English moralists, in their attempts to explain the nature and ground of the moral judgment; and, more than a century before the publication of Mill's 'Utilitarianism,' Hume's 'Inquiry into the Principles of Morals' (1751) had argued that acts are judged to be right because they are found to be "useful or agreeable to ourselves or others." Impelled by the same interest which actuated Mill — the desire to find a single ground for the approval and disapproval which moral judgments express—Hume had made an inductive comparison of the judgments in question; and his inquiry led to the result that actions need only be useful or agreeable in order that they may be called virtuous.

The view which Hume arrived at in this inductive and psychological way became an important part of Paley's 'Principles of Moral and Political Philosophy'

(1785). Paley's doctrine of moral obligation makes morality consist in obedience to a divine command; but, while he thus understands virtue as action which is done "in obedience to the will of God, and for the sake of everlasting happiness," he yet maintains that, in itself, it is "the doing good to mankind."[1] Paley's main work as a moralist was not so much to define the idea of "general happiness" as to show its application to moral and social conditions, and the rules of conduct that can be derived from it. While the motive of his ethics is mainly theological, the chief interest of his system is political. It cannot indeed be denied that Paley's use of the utilitarian principle is very carefully limited. He is deeply attached to the *status quo* — the institutions and moralities of his day; and his utilitarianism is little more than an accidental weapon by which to defend conclusions already present to his mind. He is intent rather upon finding "utilitarian reasons by the way" for existing practices which he desires to support, than upon constructing a system of ethics to give effect to the utilitarian principle: his motive is practical, conservative, and apologetic. But, in so far as his work has a constructive character, it is a study of the moral and social consequences of utilitarianism.

This political use of the utilitarian principle is carried

[1] Paley's 'Principles of Moral and Political Philosophy,' Book I. chap. iii.

further in Bentham's system. Bentham gives consistent effect to the idea that acts are made good or bad by their relation to general happiness: he makes this the whole, and not merely a subordinate part, of the meaning of virtue; and his argument is thus free from the embarrassments in which Paley had been involved by his theological doctrine of obligation, and by the necessity, which this doctrine had laid upon him, of showing a correspondence between the elements of a definition made up of such diverse material as "the will of God," "everlasting happiness," and "the doing good to mankind." The fact that he made "the greatest happiness of the greatest number" a complete definition of the standard of morals gave Bentham's work its peculiar significance in the development of English ethics; and the consistency with which he repudiated all other grounds of judgment, and made the utilitarian principle a foundation for actual law and actual morality, gave to his system that logical coherence which was the secret of its power.

It was this coherent unity of Bentham's system of ethics—the degree in which it made a single principle determine all the variety of moral rules—that recommended it to Mill. In sharp contrast to the unsystematic speculations by which the application of moral rules to conduct and the foundation of these rules themselves were left obscure, this system offered a definite principle of judgment, derived from experience and fitted both to be the ground of moral rules and to determine their application.[1] Mill finds in Bentham the true moralist, the scientific student of morals who analyses the facts, and does not make general or abstract statements of them do duty for the real details.[2]

This way of explaining morality, then—this judgment of acts by their consequences alone—was Mill's most obvious escape from the difficulty in which he found himself; and his adoption of it was, for him, the necessary issue of his demand for a scientific theory of ethics. In this direction, and in no other, he saw a possible explanation of moral judgments—a single and objective reason for them. The appeal to consequences brought the grounds of morality within reach of experience, and introduced that possibility of verification without which scientific knowledge cannot exist. It thus made induction—which is, for Mill, the only ground of real knowledge—applicable to the moral aspect of conduct; and it offered a test of the worth of ordinary moral opinion.[1]

The same interest in an inductive science of human conduct which disposes Mill to adopt the utilitarian standard of morality, appears also in his determinism. This part of his theory does not arise from any failure, on Mill's part, to appreciate the reality or worth of the individual human mind. It is not, with him, a consequence of any disposition to make little of the human will in comparison with the universal order

[1] Pp. 83 note 1, 123 note 1, 214.   [2] Pp. 215, 216.

of which it is a part. Mill sees, indeed, that man's life is bound up with the order of nature, from which he comes, and to which he must perpetually adapt himself;[1] but this does not prevent him from acknowledging that man's relation to his world is partly the product of his own will, nor from finding in human personality the chief factor in social development as well as the end in relation to which alone conduct and social arrangements and the natural order itself can be criticised.[2] His interest in the free development of the individual human being is so great that he has laid himself open, in more than one argument, to the charge of political individualism; and it is characteristic of his mind to conceive all interests and problems wholly in relation to individual persons and their needs. Mill's deterministic account of volition is thus not the outcome, in his case, of that unwillingness to admit the reality of personal life which has sometimes been responsible for similar opinions.

The very terms in which Mill states his theory of the determination of conduct point to the source of his interest in it. He expressly rejects the idea of a compulsion of voluntary acts, and he declines to use the word "necessity," on the ground that it conveys a misleading view of the whole question. What he argues for is simply the existence, in human conduct and character, of the causal relation which obtains in the non-human or natural world. He does not understand causality to involve any "necessity" or

[1] P. 209. [2] P. 154 note 1.

"bond," but regards it merely as a relation of "unconditional sequence"; and he maintains that this "unconditional sequence" obtains between human volitions and their antecedents. If we examine this doctrine, we find that it means for Mill neither more nor less than that it is possible to form inductions about human conduct. The idea of unconditional relation, which is Mill's only positive notion of causality, has, for him, a merely logical use. He means no more by it than the possibility of inferring one member of the relation from the other with complete certainty. Causality is a relation that exists only between elements in the world of our experiences, and not between these experiences as a whole and anything else. It is a category that determines individual objects of experience, and it belongs only to our knowledge of them.[1]

Mill never treats the causal relation as more or other than the condition or postulate of induction; and when he affirms the existence of this relation in human conduct, he expressly disclaims any other meaning than this which has been indicated. He means only "that, given the motives which are present to an individual's mind, and given likewise the character and disposition of the individual, the manner in which he will act might be unerringly inferred."[2] The "abstract possibility of being foreseen"[3] is all that he means to attribute to conduct, when he says that it is subject to causal connection. To regard it as caused

[1] Pp. 7 note 1, 203-205.   [2] P. 10.   [3] P. 10 note 1.

is simply to make it a possible object of inductive or scientific study—not a series of unrelated occurrences, but a part of the mental process, subject to its laws and influenced by all the elements which go to make the unity of mind or character. Even the view which Mill takes of the way in which volitions are caused—that "will is the child of desire"[1]—means only that acts of will do not exist in that complete independence which libertarian theories are apt to suggest, but are in vital relation to the whole mental life of the agent. Mill's determinism is thus chiefly interesting to him as the postulate of a "science of human nature." Volition can only be made an object of scientific knowledge, if it exhibits those invariable and unconditional uniformities of sequence which it is the office of induction to investigate, and if its causes are to be sought in the structure of a character whose elements exist in relation to each other.[2]

Both in Mill's Utilitarianism, then, and in his deterministic account of volition, we can trace the influence of a theory of method from which his conception of the moral life and of social relations takes its distinctive character. He considers the method of ethics to be induction. He regards conduct as an object to the study of which the inductive methods can be applied with the same propriety as to any other set of phenomena; and he uses the same methods to discover the principle by which moral judgments are determined and the relation of actions to this principle.

[1] P. 159. [2] Pp. 7, 26.

We have seen that the way was partly prepared for this theory of the method of ethics by the course which the study of morality had already taken in England. But it is probable that Mill was also influenced, in favour of such a conception of the subject, by other elements in his intellectual heritage.

We learn from Mill's own statement that his early "Philosophical Radicalism" was nourished by "a combination of Bentham's point of view with that of the modern political economy, and with the Hartleian metaphysics";[1] and while there can be no doubt that Bentham's influence was decisive in forming his idea of the method of moral science, it is impossible to ignore the presence of the other factors which he names.

The economic theory of Bentham and Ricardo had incurred considerable obligations to Bentham's utilitarian theory of morals and politics;[2] and though the individualism and the hedonistic ethics and psychology which political economy derived from this source are not essential to its methods and purpose, it can hardly be denied that they have influenced its development; but the growth of economic science reacted in turn upon the utilitarian theory of ethics. Political economy studies human conduct in the same relation to its effects which utilitarianism considers. The utilitarianism of Paley, and still more definitely

[1] Autobiography, p. 105.
[2] Cf. Mr Bonar's Philosophy and Political Economy, Book III. chap. ii.

that of Bentham, is essentially a political system of ethics: it is a system in which the idea of the social consequences of action plays a leading part; and political economy, which is the scientific study of certain social effects of conduct, develops the idea of these effects, and so contributes to the utilitarian conception of ethical method.

The development of the theory of knowledge follows rather than precedes the growth of knowledge itself, for it is never possible to give a reasoned account of a scientific method until the method has actually been made use of. Bentham had practised, and economic science had developed, the judgment of actions according to their social consequences; and this made it possible to define a method of ethical science founded upon this way of judging conduct.

An effect of economic studies, which is even more evident, is the increased knowledge which they give of the consequences of actions. Every advance in the precision or the extent of our knowledge of economic laws tends to connect conduct with a wider range of effects; and in proportion as the results of actions are seen to be bound up with them, these actions cease to be imagined or considered in abstraction or isolation. The intention is weighted with the foresight of consequences which become part of itself; and it is judged as an intention or consent to produce the effects which obviously issue from it. In this way economic science, tending as it does to make the idea of every action include an increasing range of social consequences, renders the neglect of these consequences in the judgment of conduct a violent and impossible abstraction.

It appears, then, that the habit of judging actions according to their consequences, and the knowledge of these consequences in detail, grew with the growth of economic theory, which thus contributed to the development of an experiential method of ethical science. It is a natural result of Mill's relation, not only to the work of Bentham, but also to the tradition of political economy, that he should give a more systematic expression to the view of ethical method which he inherited; and that, while his predecessors had for the most part merely adopted, without argument, this method or another, he should perceive the necessity of defining it and showing its propriety and usefulness.

While Mill's economic studies connect themselves, in this way, with his application of inductive method to the problem of the moral standard, they also affect his theory of the determination of conduct. It is an important aspect of economic science that it is a purely objective study of human life. Apart from its practical application, it regards man merely as one of the factors in the production, distribution, and consumption of wealth; and it omits all consideration of his actions, except in so far as it is possible to forecast them and to estimate their consequences. If the conception of human conduct expressed in Ricardo's economic theory was hypothetical or abstract, rather than a result of inductive study, Malthus at all events, in his theory of population, had returned to a consideration of real motives, and had affirmed the dependence of man upon the natural order and its laws; and certainly Mill's account of the economic process does not give consistent effect to the abstract conception of motives from which he professedly reasons. In his use of the idea of a "standard of comfort," Mill makes character—regarded as the concrete unity of desires and active tendencies —the determining element in the production and distribution no less than in the consumption of wealth; for the standard of comfort represents the economic effect of character; and it serves to determine both the "energy of labour," which forms so important a condition of production, and also the way in which wealth is distributed and used. Human conduct and character thus become an important part of the subject-matter of political economy, as Mill understands it; and, in point of fact, it is largely by his interest in social science that Mill is led to formulate his deterministic account of personal life. According to his view of social science, it can only be constructed on the basis of a science of individual character; for society is essentially a community of individual persons, and there can be no well-founded theory of it which does not depend upon knowledge of the individuals who compose it.[1] But a science of individual human persons — of conduct and character — postulates that existence in human life of the causal relation which is asserted by Mill's determinism. Mill is interested in deter-

[1] Pp. 32, 39 note 1, 60.

minism chiefly because it is the postulate of a "science of human nature," and because an "ethological" account of individual personality is the only true foundation of economic and social science. Accustomed by his economic studies to the external view of human activity which disposes the mind to lay stress upon uniformities and to neglect differences in the conduct of individuals, he is the more ready to suppose that changes of conduct and character occur in uniform ways, and to make use of his deterministic postulate — that conduct can be inductively known. Political economy, as he conceives it, implies the deterministic postulate, and constitutes a real application of the method of studying conduct which determinism warrants.

If Mill's economic studies are partly responsible for his idea of an inductive science of character, it is impossible to ignore a like tendency in another influence of which he speaks. "The Hartleian metaphysics" formed an important part of Mill's early training; and his study of Hartley's account of mental life could hardly fail to intensify his determinism. Not only is Hartley's investigation of human consciousness a professedly inductive study; but at least two of his most characteristic doctrines tend to corroborate the determinism which he frankly avows. In his 'Observations on Man, his Frame, his Duty, and his Expectations' (1748), he explains the whole of experience as a development of its simpler elements, and connects changes of consciousness with organic and specially with nervous functions.

Hartley's was the earliest systematic attempt to explain the whole development of experience by the Association of Ideas. He accounted for the more complex feelings—even such feelings as "the moral sense" and "theopathy"—as developments of simpler mental conditions; and association was the principle by which he explained their origin. Since his day the "association" theory has been developed so far beyond the point to which he brought it that his early attempt is now apt to be forgotten. But Hartley's work is significant not only on account of his conclusions, important as these are, but also because his is practically the earliest attempt to furnish a complete analysis of mental function. Encumbered as it is with ethical and theological reflections, his philosophy is primarily an inductive study of human consciousness, designed to show what its elements are, and by what process they are combined; and his problem itself is hardly less significant, in relation to Mill's view of moral science, than the solution which he offers. The theory of mental association, as Hartley explains it, is not only a statement of the mode in which states of consciousness succeed one another; it contains also a fairly definite account of the process by which the mental complex acquires the character which it exhibits in our experience. The doctrine that our more complex ideas reflect the mode in which our simpler experiences have actually been combined in the past represents the content of consciousness as the product of circumstances: it implies a complete subordination of mental development to the order of external events; and such a conception of the way in which our mental dispositions arise makes them the direct continuation of the environment in which we have grown up. To say that we may expect to find these same relations in the mental or internal process which we have observed in the outer world of spatial existence is merely to state this view of mental life in a slightly altered form of words; and it is therefore worthy of note that, although Mill does not always appear to be quite satisfied with the account which the Association Psychology gives of mental functions,[1] he never doubts the complete dependence of these functions upon the course of external events, or the possibility which that dependence confirms of studying conduct by the methods proper to natural sciences.[2]

But, in relation to the method of moral science, even the extent of Hartley's use of the principle of mental association is less important than the interpretation of that principle which is offered by his physiological conception of it.

The basis of Hartley's system of psychology and ethics is a revised idea of nervous action. The earlier physiology had followed without question the lead of those physicists who explained light and heat and magnetism as imponderable fluids; and it had conceived the function of nerves to be the transmission of such a fluid. Hartley, on the other hand, accounts for nervous action by a doctrine "taken from the hints concerning the

[1] P. 45. [2] Pp. 18 note 1, 45 note 1.

performance of sensation and motion, which Sir Isaac Newton has given at the end of his Principia, and in the questions annexed to his Optics."[1] We need not here examine in detail an hypothesis which, so far as its physiology of nervous action is concerned, has long been obsolete; but it is worth remarking that Hartley's starting-point is a physiological adaptation of Newton's doctrine of ethereal vibrations. Hartley affirms that "external objects impressed upon the Senses occasion, first in the Nerves on which they are impressed, and then in the Brain, vibrations of the small and, as one may say, infinitesimal medullary particles;"[2] and he supposes that, when these vibrations are repeated, they tend to produce "a Disposition to diminutive Vibrations,"[3] or "Vibratiuncles," which correspond to them, or are their "Miniatures." It is by the connection which frequent concurrence of definite vibrations establishes between their miniatures that the association of the ideas or movements corresponding to these miniatures is determined.

This idea, that mental association corresponds to nervous habit, is of considerable interest in relation to the method of mental and moral science. Hartley, it must be observed, although his whole theory turns on the answer to the question how "vibration" and "association" are related, has nothing more convincing to say than that "the doctrine of *vibrations* may appear at first sight to have no connection with that of associa-

---

[1] Observations on Man, Part I. chap. i.
[2] Ib., Prop. IV.   [3] Ib., Prop. VIII.

tion; however, if these doctrines be found in fact to contain the laws of the bodily and mental powers respectively, they must be related to each other, since the body and mind are. One may expect that *vibrations* should infer *association* as their effect, and *association* point to *vibrations* as its cause."[1] But, however little Hartley may justify or even define his assumption of a correspondence or a causal relation between mental and organic events, his suggestion of a psycho-physical theory connects itself with the question how far inductive method, as Mill conceives it, can be applied to conduct. Physical events are the only phenomena in which we can hope to discover a complete continuity: they alone consist of changes which form a causal series. Consciousness is essentially discontinuous; for not only is its course perpetually interrupted, so that intervals of time elapse between its states; but, even when there is no break of this sort, the mental process does not exhibit the orderly progress which is found in physical phenomena. We see that mental conditions generally succeed one another in a certain way; but between stages of the mental process, as we know it, there is never any self-evident connection. Now, the causal connection for which we look in vain between the stages of our mental life is sought there because it is suggested by the kind of knowledge which we have of physical facts; for it is in our experience of physical changes that we discover the unconditional relation which is the only ground, according to Mill, for the

[1] Observations on Man, Part I. chap. i.

application of inductive method. It is thus of no small importance for our knowledge of mental and moral subjects if we can connect them with that physical order which reveals causal connections, and which can be made the object of induction and scientific knowledge.

It must be remembered that Mill himself adopts a critical attitude towards the use of physiological principles in the explanation of mental states. He is both too well aware of the difficulties of the method and too little intent upon system at any price to accept Hartley's artificially simple solution; and he argues, against Comte's similar reduction of psychology to physiology, that introspection is the essential method of our knowledge of mind, and that only the direct knowledge of mental facts which introspection gives can impart psychological meaning to physiological data.[1]

On the other hand, Mill actually adopts a physiological explanation when the incompleteness of purely psychological analysis is really brought home to him—as in the case of those phenomena which Hamilton and others had explained by the hypothesis of "unconscious mental" modifications; and he sometimes affirms the dependence of all exact psychology upon physiology.[2] Even when he does not do this, he seems to entertain a view of the functions of psychology which applies rather to such a physiological development of it as Hartley had suggested than to the mere description of mental states and changes. A psychology fitted to be the basis of ethology and of social science, and to dis-

[1] Pp. 36 ff., 39 note 1.   P. 39 note 1.

cover the laws according to which human nature and society develop, must be an analysis of mental life, and must neglect no means by which changes in its object can be connected with unconditional relations.

Hartley's Associationism and his doctrine of Vibrations combine with the tradition of English ethics and with the point of view of economic science to influence Mill's conception of the logic of ethics. It is largely under Hartley's guidance that he comes to regard conduct and character as capable of being inductively studied, and of being explained in terms of causality; and this view of conduct corroborates the theory that the same method of investigation is proper to the discovery not only of the causes and tendencies of conduct, but also of the principle which should determine our moral judgment of it.

ESSAY II

ETHICS AND PSYCHOLOGY

ESSAY II

ETHICS AND PSYCHOLOGY

It has been suggested that Mill's interest in psychology, and especially in Hartley's development of it, is in some degree responsible for the application of inductive method to ethics which his determinism is meant to assert and vindicate. But Mill's psychological way of conceiving conduct has even more definite and characteristic effects on his theory of morality.

Mill does not, indeed, profess to bring forward "proof," in the ordinary sense of the word, in support of his hedonistic theory of the moral end; but neither does he hold himself excused from giving grounds for his belief that the "greatest happiness of the greatest number" is the principle of moral judgment;[1] and one of the main considerations which he urges in favour of this theory is the doctrine that happiness or pleasure is the only object of desire.[2]

The hedonistic account of morality—the conclusion that the moral quality of actions depends upon their

[1] Pp. 86, 87, 146.   [2] Pp. 146 ff.

tendency to give pleasure—can, indeed, be argued for on other grounds than this; and the validity of an argument from the theory that men always desire their own pleasure to the duty of promoting the general happiness is more than questionable. But it is still true that Mill, as well as other writers, has made hedonism a consequence of this view of desire. It is this which determines for him the nature of those effects in relation to which conduct is judged: because pleasure is the object of all desire, the effects in virtue of which actions are good are their pleasure-giving effects.[1] The hedonistic account of desire plays, in this way, an important part in Mill's ethical theory. It not only gives point to his determinism, by making desire, which is the source of conduct, an effect of the order in which circumstances may have thrown pleasures in the individual's way; it is also a ground on which he defends his main ethical doctrine. It is, therefore, interesting to remark that this theory of motives forms part of a way of regarding morality which is connected with Mill's philosophical attitude as a whole.

The account of desire which Mill presents has, indeed, no claim to novelty. The idea that it is always determined by the anticipation of pleasure, and that this is a complete account of it, was not only explicitly announced, but was really operative in the theories of his more remote as well as of his immediate predecessors: it formed part of his inheritance from that de-

[1] Pp. 146 ff.

velopment of ethical theory, the results of which were more directly transmitted to him by Bentham. But its influence on English thought, and especially Mill's acceptance of it, must be explained, in part at all events, by its intimate connection with other philosophical theories.

Mill himself, although his official conception of morality depends for him on the acceptance of this doctrine, wavers in his adherence to it;[1] and his hesitation suggests that his belief in it is due not so much to the direct pressure of facts as to its connection with a general theory by which he does not find it easy to abide consistently. The doctrine is, in truth, one of the most significant results of his psychological account of experience; for if the attempt to explain experience resolves itself, as it generally does with Mill, into a statement of the way in which mental changes take place, and if subjective states are thus regarded as the whole object of knowledge, the hedonistic theory of motives is the most natural explanation of them that can be given. If we know nothing except our own minds and the changes which take place in them, it is easy to conclude that these changes form the object of all desire; for desire takes its character from the ideas that determine it, and we can desire only what we can think. Now if the objects of desire are conceived merely as mental states, they are apt to lose their individual character, and to retain only that relation to the satisfaction of the personal subject which is their

[1] Pp. 23 and note 1, 147 ff.

common quality ; and, when desires are considered only in this context, their chief characteristic is undoubtedly the contrast between the pain of their presence and the pleasure of their removal or satisfaction. The theory that desire is always for pleasure is the only account of it which can be given if the method of explanation that is adopted abstracts from every relation of desire except its existence as a fact in the mental history of an individual; and it is thus the natural sequel to that view of knowledge which Mill usually takes.[1]

The psychological idea of explanation is one to which Mill is invariably prone. It is at once his weakness and his strength to consider everything in relation to the life and growth of individual minds: his strength, because thought is our only clue to reality; his weakness, because he conceives thought inadequately as a mere private succession of mental changes, brought about by the operation of a real world which is external to them, and with whose existence they have, in themselves, no necessary connection.

This is a view of thought which Mill owes to his place in the development of English speculation. The philosophical system which was developed by Locke, Berkeley, and Hume, and which largely determined Mill's conception of knowledge, not only tended progressively to reduce the whole of known reality to changes of individual minds: it also conveyed a view of the knowing mind and of knowledge itself, by which

[1] System of Logic, pp. 39 ff.

Mill's idea of explanation is affected in the most significant way.

The reduction of the known qualities of things to changes in the "ideas" of a thinking or knowing subject had been made by Locke, and applied by Berkeley and Hume to an increasing range of objects; and this was not merely a revised idea of what constitutes the real existence of the world we know. It contained an even more striking change in the conception of knowledge. For if knowledge be limited to the changes of the knowing consciousness itself, as Hume almost consistently argued, then experience can only be explained by a reduction of that consciousness to the lowest terms in which it can be expressed. Reality, on this theory, is explained when we are able to say of what elements the knowing process is built up; for it is simply a combination of ideas, and to know what these ideas are is to explain it. In this way introspective psychology became a philosophical system in the very period of its creation: and the discovery and development of the psychological point of view impressed upon English philosophy an idea of explanation which determined the general character of Mill's speculative outlook. The habit of identifying reality with ideas, which he learned from his English predecessors, led him to conceive the problem of philosophy as solved by the mere discovery of the elements out of which the conscious process is compounded. He explicitly announces and actually makes use of this idea of explanation.

It makes him regard logic as "a part or branch of psychology"; and it is responsible for important elements in his account of morality. He makes ethics psychological because he forgets the abstract character of the view of personal life to which psychology is committed.

The foundation of Mill's psychological treatment of ethics is his idea of "ethology"—the science of character. He regards it as a branch or application of psychology; and his way of conceiving both the actual nature and the ideal relations of conduct is largely governed by this view.[1]

This idea of the method of ethology is partly due to Mill's anxiety to raise it—and with it ethics and sociology—to the level of deductive science.[1] Mill's advocacy of inductive method, and his criticism of syllogistic argument, are apt to be thought of as the whole of his logical system; but the necessity of deductive corroboration of every law is an essential element in his theory of science. No general truth, that is to say, attains for him the highest degree of certainty until it is shown to be not merely a generalisation inductively based on particulars, but also the deductive consequence of a truth or law of a higher degree of generality.[1] In the case of ethology this scientific character can only be attained by making it "a system of corollaries from psychology."[2] The generalisations which result from ordinary experience of human nature and human affairs are merely Empirical Laws:[3] that is

---

[1] Pp. 70 ff.   [2] P. 74.   [3] Pp. 54 ff.

to say, they are true only within certain limits, and are not "the ultimate laws of human action," or "the principles of human nature."[1] "The really scientific truths," Mill tells us, "are not those empirical laws, but the causal laws which explain them";[2] and these "causal laws" which are the "universal laws of the Formation of Character"[3] cannot be ascertained by direct observation and experiment, but must be arrived at by deduction from the general laws of mind.[4] Psychology, therefore, which discovers the simple laws of mind by observation, is the only and sufficient basis of a scientific ethology.[5] Mill admits that we can only know empirically the details of individual character and conduct; and he is careful to point out that ethology must verify by specific experience the conclusions which are deduced from psychological principles.[6] But he does not hesitate to suppose that character and conduct are fully and adequately apprehended by psychology, from its own point of view. He does not doubt that psychological laws are potentially the complete truth of that concrete reality which is called character, and of the conduct which its activities constitute.

It is not necessary to describe here the difficulties which beset the attempt to make psychology do duty for a theory of knowledge, and the discovery of which on the one hand by Reid, and on the other hand in Kant's more critical examination of experience, has

[1] P. 55. [2] P. 56. [3] P. 60.
[4] Pp. 62 ff. [5] Pp. 70 ff. [6] P. 77.

had a decisive influence upon the method of philosophy. Knowledge in any worthy or real sense is made impossible by that "individualism" which finds in it only a series of conscious states produced by an unknown reality. But the difficulties of the psychological account of experience culminate in the attempt to apply it to volition.

The question which we have to consider—and it is a question which raises large issues for Mill's theory of ethical methods and principles—is whether the account of voluntary action which is or can be given by psychology is complete; or, if it is not, to what extent its incompleteness interferes with its claim to be the basis of ethical theory.

Mill himself consistently regards psychology as a science of observed facts—a statement of the way in which mental events follow one another. Its subject is "the uniformities of succession, the laws, whether ultimate or derivative, according to which one mental state succeeds another, is caused by another, or at least is caused to follow another."[1] Psychology, that is to say, is a science merely of mental phenomena: it is an attempt to infer, from the observed facts of mental life, what laws govern the connection of these facts with one another; and Mill never abandons his statement that "the Mind is only known to itself phenomenally, as the series of its feelings or consciousnesses."[2] The science, then, whose aim it is to investigate the connections of the known facts of mind,

[1] P. 40.   [2] P. 34 note 1.

is limited in its subject-matter to these "feelings or consciousnesses." These are its sphere: the laws, in the discovery of which its work consists, are the ways in which these facts behave. It can take account of no explanations, except such as are to be found in these phenomena. Mill does, indeed, permit himself to fill up, by assuming the physiological relations of mental states, the gaps which cannot be denied in the continuity of the mental process.[1] But he never consents to put forward as psychological explanations hypotheses (such as that of "unconscious mental modifications") by which an artificial and apparent or nominal completeness can be given to psychology, at the expense of its character as a science of observed facts. Even when he is most aware of the discontinuous character of the facts which psychology observes, and of their failure to give a complete or satisfying explanation of what the mind is, he perceives the impossibility of completing the psychological explanation by introducing into it such foreign elements as the idea of an unconscious mental process or of a self which is not an object of knowledge.

This view which Mill takes of the province and method of psychology is essentially just. The very words in which the hypothesis of "unconscious mental modifications" is stated, convict it of irrelevancy. Consciousness is the characteristic of that "mind" which psychology investigates; and the "unconscious" is, in its very nature, alien to psychology. The suggestion

[1] P. 39 note 1.

offered is that the mental process runs underground, as it were, yet all the while retains its mental character; and this theory connects itself with a conception of mind of which psychology, as an observational science, can take no heed. It bears no relation to the idea of a mind as a series of phenomena of consciousness: it implies, rather, that notion of intelligence which makes it depend upon the presence and support of a self, or organising unity, within which all thought is carried on. It need not be denied that this is the ultimate presupposition of thought; and Mill himself perceives the dependence of knowledge upon this organic or internal unity of intelligence;[1] but he is none the less justified in refusing to make the "self" an element in his psychological account of mind. Hume's discovery that the "self" can never be "caught" and made an object, does not indeed prove that it cannot be known, but only that we cannot know it in an isolation in which it really does not exist. But this experience—that the self is not to be found as one among the facts of mental life—is fatal to the attempt to make it a term of psychological explanation. Just because the unity of the self is neither an observed state of mind nor a mental element curiously hid from knowledge, but is the great characteristic of mental life or an aspect of its whole being — just on this account it cannot be called in as a *deus ex machina* to explain those mental events for which no plainer cause can be found. The "self"

[1] Pp. 206-208.

does not exist and is not known in that abstraction from objective reality in which psychology views the mental process. It is known only in the synthesis of objective experiences; and psychology, which abstracts from the objective aspect of intelligence, and considers it only as a series of subjective events, is thus, by its very nature, debarred from taking account of the self.

The limit which this conception of its method sets upon the province of psychological science is one which Mill himself does not fail to recognise. It is characteristic of his inquisitive and candid spirit, that he makes no secret of the incompleteness of his psychological account of mind. "If we speak," he says, "of the mind as a series of feelings, we are obliged to complete the statement by calling it a series of feelings which is aware of itself as past and future: and we are reduced to the alternative of believing that the mind or ego is something different from any series of feelings, or possibilities of them, or of accepting the paradox that something, which *ex hypothesi* is but a series of feelings, can be aware of itself as a series."[1] He perceives that the organic unity and continuity which characterise experience, and without which there would not be knowledge, depend upon the relation of experience to a single knowing subject which is not a mere series of conscious states; and, if he entertains a conception of human activity which does no justice to this important admission, it should yet be remembered that

[1] P. 206.

his interest in the idea of "moral freedom," and his attempt to reconcile it with his determinism, betray a certain sense of the inadequacy of his official theory of conduct.[1] He is not wholly unaware of the unreality of the account of voluntary action that is arrived at by the external or mechanical way of explaining it which he sometimes adopts.

The problem of explaining volition is one which offers serious difficulties to a psychological method like that of Mill. Their relation to the "self" is no merely accidental quality of voluntary acts. It belongs to their nature, and apart from it they would not be what they are in our experience; for the mode of existence which we call personal takes its character from its relation to self-consciousness; and whatever concrete or "material" elements it may contain are part of it only in so far as they become functions or qualities of a self-conscious subject. Such a subject is no mere separate existence, whose occasional interference renders personal action uncertain or accidental, and which may be alternately the passive creature and the incalculable governor of the medium of action and experience which is known as character. The "self" which is here spoken of is simply the characteristic or determining principle of personal life; and its necessity means only that no function of that life can be truly understood when it is conceived in abstraction from self-consciousness. But this self-related unity, which we call personality, is not merely a

[1] Pp. 11-22.

factor or element in volition: it is the very being and stuff of voluntary acts; and they are not external effects which it produces, but its very self in its relation to the call and stress of circumstance. The volitions, then, in which personal life expresses itself, are not truly described as the "product" of character and circumstances; for personal life and the circumstances in which it is found are not co-ordinate factors in bringing about the voluntary act. Circumstances, no doubt, exert upon conduct an influence which is not confined to its external qualities, but which affects profoundly its most hidden springs and its most inward meaning; yet their relation to conduct is not really the same in kind as that of the personal life in which it arises. They affect it, but they are not elements in it; and their relation to it is always external. Very different is the relation of the individual personality to its actions. They do not come from it and pass into an independent existence. They never are at all except as they belong to it. They are its "functions," in that true sense of the word which expresses the fact that they are simply changes in its condition: they are the changes to which, in relation to circumstances, its inner nature determines it, and by which it alters its character without losing its internal unity and identity or changing into some other part of the order of events.

Voluntary actions are thus not mere external effects of personal life, but changes or developments of it, in which it exists, and which have no reality apart from it. It follows that they involve, at every stage, the subject-object relation which is characteristic of human experience, and that they cannot be fully explained by a theory which deliberately abstracts from this relation. They are not adequately accounted for by a mere statement of the appearance which they present to the observation of the mental process which psychology undertakes; for they can only be truly understood when they are considered in that relation to the self-hood or unity of consciousness which psychology expressly neglects. It is thus not possible for a science of ethology which is derived in the way that Mill suggests from psychology, as he rightly conceives it, to be an adequate or complete theory of human conduct.

It would, indeed, be an ill-considered and futile project to attempt to explain conduct, without taking into account the facts which psychology investigates. It is the function of psychology, in however limited a way we understand it, to give a description and an analysis of certain phenomena which volition exhibits. In the same way physics and physiology describe qualities of volition, aspects of it which are as real, if not so relevant, as that with which psychology deals; and no account of volition can be accepted as finally true which contradicts any of the facts that are adduced by these descriptions. Man is a mechanism, and he is an organism, and he is a conscious being. It is not open to us to give an account of his activity which is inconsistent with any of these aspects of his nature; for the facts of his nature, as the special sciences reveal it, are what we ought to explain.

If the results of physics and physiology must be considered in the explanation of conduct, this is still more definitely the case with the purely human science of psychology. If we may require of such explanation that it shall not be inconsistent with the mechanical and organic properties of its subject-matter, it is certainly not less necessary that it should agree with the phenomena of consciousness and the laws which can be found in them; and psychology is an analysis of these phenomena: its aim is to gain a clear idea of the way in which thought and action occur as mental facts. It needs no argument to show that a science of conduct, like every other science whose subject-matter is mental, must always presuppose such an idea.

On the other hand, this analytical character, which belongs to the method and problem of psychology, defines the limits of its use in the explanation of conduct. Its aim is to furnish, with or without the aid of physiology, a complete analysis of mental phenomena —to find the elements of the conscious process; but analysis can never, in the nature of the case, be a complete explanation. An analysis is an account of the elements of which a phenomenon is built up. Its aim is to interpret the complex whole in terms of the simpler parts of which it can be shown to consist, and in this way to express reality in its lowest terms, or to explain each individual fact or event by describing the way in which its component elements behave. It resolves concrete experiences into the more general laws upon which they depend.

It is impossible to ignore the necessity for a complete explanation of this way of investigating the facts of experience; for the worth of explanations depends, in the first instance, upon a clear and definite idea of the fact to be explained. On the other hand, this resolution of things into their lowest terms is not itself an explanation of them; or, to put the fact otherwise, to know things in this way — to know their parts or elements — is not really to understand them.

The fact that this analytical knowledge of reality exhibits it only "in disconnection, dull and spiritless," does not mean simply that the idea of things which is gained in this way fails to satisfy demands which feeling and imagination make upon experience. It means also that such knowledge fails to satisfy the demand of thought itself. That rational impulse to seek a complete explanation of things, which is the ground of knowledge, is not arrested by the mere discovery and description of the way in which they take place. The reason for their being what they are is the one truth in which inquiry can rest. The truth of things—their real meaning—is their relation to the system of reality; so that they are only understood when this relation is made plain and intelligible; and no statement, however minute, of the simpler elements which compose them can ever lead to this which is the goal of knowledge.

But although analysis can never discover the relation of its objects to the system which explains them, the impossibility of understanding things apart from their relation to a complete system of reality appears even in the issue of an analytical account of them. There can be no analysis of anything—no statement of its actual nature and constitution—which does not unfold its relation to other things. Nothing exists really in isolation; and no description of the elements of which any concrete fact is made up—no real analysis of a complex individual—can fail to be an account of the way in which it is related to other facts. Everything that can be said to describe the structure of the individual fact must inevitably connect it with other objects of experience. It is only in relation that we know things; and the analysis of their nature is always an investigation of the way in which they are connected with one another.

Now this interconnection of things, which all analysis serves to discover, shows the incompleteness of the method of analysis itself; for the relation of things to one another means their common membership in an objective system: that facts derive their character from their relation to each other implies that they are determined in their own nature by the system to which they belong. If things did not form a single system, there could be no real or objective connection between them, and relation would be the "fiction" which it has sometimes been called; for things are only related to one another in so far as they are determined by a common principle, and to be determined in this way is to form a system. The account of things which analysis yields is thus of necessity framed in such a way as to imply its own inadequacy; for it is an account of relations, and these involve the determination of things by a system, which the analytical study of them neglects.

Since the existence and character of individual things depend upon their place in a system, or their determination by a principle—since they are only known and only exist as elements in a whole—it is obvious that no explanation which ignores this aspect of them can be completely true. The meaning of things—in knowing which we understand them—is thus not ascertained by mere examination of their parts. It is only revealed in the relations in which the objects of our knowledge appear to us; and it can only be studied by an inquiry into the conditions upon which those relations ultimately depend. Only in knowing these do we understand the objects which we experience. The only true explanation of things is the principle by which their relations are determined—the system to which they belong.

This necessity for an interpretation of experiences different from mere analysis of them into their simplest elements, or description of the manner in which they come into existence, is not confined to those experiences in which we learn the nature of physical objects. If these stand in need of explanation which is not afforded even by the most complete account of the elements that compose them, it is not less necessary to seek such explanation of the experiences which form the ground of moral judgment; for the conduct and character which are judged to be morally good or bad do not exist in isolation from the world of things and persons: in every change which they undergo, and every quality which they exhibit, they are inseparable from the order of nature and society; and no account of them can be complete which deliberately regards them in an artificial abstraction from the world by which their nature is determined. But the moral quality of actions is specially dependent upon this relation which they bear to a whole or system of which no complete account is given in the mere analysis of mental states. In the first place, actions are right and wrong only in their relation to the unity of mental life: it is their membership in a system of which self-consciousness is the determining principle that gives them their moral quality. In the second place, the moral quality of self-conscious actions depends upon the relation of the individual agent to a system wider than his personal life. Regarded merely as states or changes of the individual, actions have no moral character: they are morally good or bad only because the individual belongs to a community, and his acts are thus connected with an order beyond the changes of his private mind.

Mill does more than merely suggest such views of morality. He makes a real effort to consider its connection with personal life as a whole and with social relations. But we have seen that such elements in his account of it are hardly consistent with his intention of founding ethics upon a science of ethology derived as a system of corollaries from the psychological conception of character — from the view of conduct which makes it a mere series of mental events. The real nature of personal life is indeed the basis of morality; and ethical science can never wisely set before itself the task of making "bricks without straw" by trying to conceive man's moral end in abstraction from the character in which alone it can be realised. But, just because a true idea of personal life must be the foundation of ethical science — because man's duty depends upon what he really is—it is futile to derive a view of morality from that incomplete account of conduct which psychology gives. We have seen not only that psychology treats in a way which is essentially inadequate the voluntary actions that are the proper subject of moral judgments, but also that the aspects of conduct which psychology neglects are essential to its moral significance. Since psychology is analytic, and abstracts from the relation of mental states to the self and to the outer world, its account of conduct cannot be made the basis of ethical theory; for morality exists only because voluntary actions are self-conscious and personal, and because self-conscious persons are in vital relation to a system of reality which imparts significance to their behaviour. Psychology has no more claim to be the basis of ethics than it has to be a complete theory of volition. Its application to ethics is of the same negative kind as its validity in the explanation of conduct: while a true ethical theory must not contradict the psychological account of action, that account cannot lead to positive conclusions as to the right and wrong of conduct, because it omits to consider relations of action apart from which it cannot be understood, and upon which its moral quality depends. In allowing his theory of morality to be determined by a psychological conception of conduct, Mill creates for himself difficulties which prevent him from giving a consistent account of the moral life.

ESSAY III

ETHICS AND MORALITY

ESSAY III

ETHICS AND MORALITY

WE have found it impossible to appreciate Mill's ethical opinions without considering the influence which was exerted on them by his idea of the method of studying moral subjects; and we have seen that his notion of what conduct is and should be is partly due to his attempt to derive ethics from psychology. We must also examine the relation between his theory of morality and the moral consciousness itself.

The word morality is used in such various senses that it is apt to be an illusory term in discussions. Sometimes, for example, it means a kind or type of conduct, while at other times it is used to indicate a way in which conduct is judged; and, within each of these main senses, its meaning varies with the view which is taken of moral good and evil. But the true and natural meaning of the word—the meaning from which the other is derived—is the second which has been suggested. Morality is the system of beliefs in accordance with which actions are judged to be right or wrong; and the morality of an act is its relation to the judgments which make up this system, or to the principle which these judgments express.

There are various ways in which morality may be subjected to scientific examination. We may, for example, study the process by which any system of moral judgments has come into existence and acquired the character which it exhibits; or we may analyse these judgments to find out how they take place, and of what simpler mental elements they consist; or we may examine the grounds of morality, and try to discover the principle by which its judgments are determined, and which they apply to conduct.

These ways of studying morality all come within the scope of ethical science, as it is generally understood: they deal with the same facts, and differ as they are designed to answer various questions about them. But, while morality is the subject-matter of all these inquiries, so that each of them must in some sense account for it, the last kind of study which has been named—that which investigates the grounds of morality, and which is properly called moral philosophy — stands in closer relations with the moral consciousness itself than any other method of approaching the subject. While other explanations of the moral judgment must account for its existence as a fact, and the mode in which it originates or takes place, they may explain it by showing its connection with facts essentially different from itself; and they do not directly consider the question of its validity. It is otherwise with the attempt to declare the grounds of moral experience. This account of morality cannot explain it in terms of that which is essentially alien to it. The principle which is held to determine moral judgment, and be its basis or reason, must be shown to be actually present and at work in it; and must explain not merely the process by which moral experience comes into being, but also the reasonableness of the judgments of which that experience consists. It is to this ultimate problem of ethics that Mill's work is mainly directed: he investigates the moral judgment in order to discover the principle by which it is determined; and it is therefore important to consider how far his ethical theory is influenced by moral experience, and how far his explanation of the moral judgment is true to the character which that judgment bears.[1]

These are questions which cannot be neglected; for in what purports to be an interpretation of moral experience we are not at liberty to set aside the moral consciousness or to consider it from a point of view external to itself; and the truth and value of ethical theories depend upon the degree in which they maintain contact with the moral life. Theories of morality are only true in so far as they explain it by a principle which can be shown to determine particular moral judgments and to be a reasonable ground for making them; and the speculative interest of ethical science — its significance for our idea of the reality which philosophy seeks to interpret — depends upon

[1] Pp. 79 ff.

this relation to morality. The aim of philosophy is to interpret experience—to conceive it as informed by principle, and corresponding to the nature of reason itself. Ethical science—in the sense in which Mill's interpretation of moral judgment belongs to it—is the attempt to realise this speculative ideal in the conception formed of moral experience. It is the search for a principle by which that experience can be explained; and only in so far as it ascertains such a principle does it make any contribution to our power to understand the world. In an attempt to explain the reality which surrounds us, we cannot rightly ignore the experience or expression of the human mind which is called morality. A philosophy which failed to account for this would remain partial or incomplete: it could not be the true explanation of existence. Ethical science is therefore necessary to philosophy; but it is so only because it considers facts which philosophy cannot neglect, because it interprets demands which human beings make upon the world and upon themselves. If it omits to do this, it loses speculative worth. Its conclusions may be true enough, when they are not mistaken for the explanation which they fail to be; but since they do not show what moral experience means, they give no clue to the effect which its existence ought to have on our idea of the universe. It is thus necessary to ascertain what contribution Mill makes to a true conception of actual morality, and how far and in what direction he is influenced by his appreciation of moral experience, in order that we may estimate the truth and the speculative value of his ethics.

While there is reason to think that Mill's derivation of ethics from psychology is apt to lead to an inadequate conception of morality, this must not be taken to mean that he himself is unaware of the true significance of virtue.

Virtue has, indeed, been recognised by almost all hedonistic writers, and specially by Mill's predecessors in the development of English Utilitarianism, as an essential means to happiness — as being more necessary to wellbeing than any other single condition.[1] But it is the very principle of consistent Hedonism to define virtue by its tendency to produce happiness, and in this way to make it subordinate to an end external to itself. It indicates a higher estimate of the worth of good conduct that Mill promotes it to the honourable, though rather ill-defined, position of being not simply an external cause but a "part" or "ingredient" of the happiness which he considers to be the true end of human actions.[2] He realises that it is, in point of fact, of no second-rate importance. In feeling, at all events, if not in theory, he makes virtue the supreme element in the good which realises the end of human conduct; and even his explicit theory tends to subordinate the other elements in happiness to qualities of personal life and conduct.[3]

Mill's interest in these personal qualities—the place which he gives to good character in his conception

[1] Pp. 92, 93, 99.   [2] Pp. 99, 150 ff.   [3] P. 154 note 1.

of human wellbeing—appears in the kind of working criterion which he adopts in his political and practical writings. It is the effect of economic factors upon character that he considers when he draws practical conclusions from his investigation of the laws of political economy; and whether he discusses the value of liberty in thought and action, or the usefulness of popular institutions, or the conditions which ought to regulate marriage and the position of woman in the family and the state, we find him always at the same point of view. He does indeed weigh the probable effect on the general happiness of the alternatives which he compares. But in his estimate of what constitutes happiness he ascribes to virtue a supreme position among the human interests; and his conclusions are invariably determined not by such a calculation of pleasures and pains as might be the legitimate outcome of a Hedonism like that of Bentham, but by his view of the way in which the characters of individual persons are likely to be affected.[1] The extent to which Mill's ethical reflection is influenced by his interest in morality appears still more clearly in his assertion of a difference of kind among pleasures. He finds it to be "quite compatible with the principle of utility to recognise the fact that some *kinds* of pleasure are more desirable and more valuable than others";[2] and his ethical theory owes its importance partly to this discrimination of pleasures. The distinction between pleasures is not, in his opinion, merely quantitative.

[1] Pp. 154 note 1, 182-184, 193 note 1.   [2] Pp. 93 ff.

They differ also in quality; and those are to be preferred which are connected with the exercise of "higher faculties," even if they are less intense than the pleasures of the animal nature.[1] This assertion that pleasures vary in quality as well as in quantity is a new element in English hedonism. There is, indeed, as Mill says, " no known Epicurean theory of life which does not assign to the pleasures of the intellect, of the feelings and imagination, and of the moral sentiments, a much higher value as pleasures than to those of mere sensation";[2] but this inevitable sense of the spiritual character of human interests plays no such part in the official theory of other hedonists as it does in that of Mill. Bentham, for example, had recognised no differences between pleasures which could not be explained as differences of amount or degree. The whole use of his hedonistic account of morality consisted in the ground which it gave for a calculation of the effects of action in terms of hypothetical pleasure-units. It is obvious that such calculation ceases to have any meaning when other aspects of pleasures are considered more important than their mere amount; and Bentham expressly reckoned all pleasures as alike except in their quantity. Mill's contention that pleasures differ in kind as well as in amount—that they cannot be valued or preferred without considering the way in which they arise—indicates a new conception of the moral life; and the kind of distinction which he makes shows the ethical trend of his theory even more clearly than the fact

[1] Pp. 93 ff.   [2] P. 92.

of the distinction itself. The worth of pleasures depends, according to Mill, on the kind of function that gives rise to them. The judgment of those who are equally capable of various kinds of pleasure is in favour of "the manner of existence which employs their higher faculties";[1] and Mill makes this judgment of those who are capable of the higher pleasures a final criterion of the relative worth of enjoyments. The relation to different faculties, which is here employed to distinguish pleasures, is an aspect of them to which orthodox or consistent hedonism could hardly give this supreme position; for to distinguish pleasures in this way is to admit the reality of a difference between them, which is not simply a greater or less degree of pleasantness, and to make this difference—the "higher" or "lower" character of the capacities which are satisfied—determine the value of every gratification. But this is to make qualities of personal life the decisive element in human good. Further, the significance of this way of distinguishing pleasures is confirmed by the argument which Mill uses to enforce the paramount importance of the "higher" pleasures. In making the judgment of the persons who are capable of these pleasures the final court of appeal, he develops out of the question which he explicitly argues,—what is really the most pleasant feeling,—another question, namely, the question of what is really preferable—what ought to be chosen. For even the wisest people can hardly be allowed to contradict "the fool, the dunce, or the rascal" in his state-

[1] P. 94.

ment of what he *actually* likes. Pleasures and preferences are of such curious growth, they blend so strangely the wisdom of experience and the folly of inherited craving, they express so many elements of health and disease, so many tendencies to life and death, that no state of knowledge between omniscience and imbecility could excuse the impertinence of pretending to know any one's likings better than he knows them himself. The wise and the good know what ought to be liked; they know what desires connect themselves with breadth and vigour of life, and in what preferences lurk the seeds of death and loss. That is the privilege of wisdom and goodness. But to admit it is to say that there is more in good and evil than the feeling of pleasure or pain — that pleasures exist in relation to systems of life and conduct, and are made good or evil by these. When he makes the judgment of those who are capable of higher pleasures decide what pleasures are really worth having, Mill discusses the question not what men do like, but what they should like, and gives to qualities of personal character a practical significance which is not warranted by the logic of Hedonism.[1]

Mill's avowal of a qualitative difference among pleasures, and the ground on which that difference is asserted, show that he perceives more clearly than his Utilitarian masters the complete solidarity of human life; his recognition of the social character of morality

[1] P. 94 note 1.

marks a similar advance upon their conception of the way in which individuals are related to human society. It was the influence of Bentham, no doubt, which first gave to Mill's ethical opinions their political cast; for Bentham's ethics were ancillary to his politics, and made morality a mere branch of statecraft. But Bentham's assertion of the social or political nature of morality was made in a very one-sided and imperfect way. He was satisfied to show how various "sanctions" or external influences could be applied so as to direct the conduct of individuals towards the general happiness; and he was so little of a moralist that it does not seem to have occurred to him that more than this was required to constitute morality. He never explained, therefore, how morality might, for the individual agent, acquire or possess a social character; because he did not perceive that society itself is a moral institution, and realises its end only in bringing about the moral good of its members.

Mill's idea of the way in which morality is social does more complete justice to the moral and philanthropic seriousness of Utilitarian ethics. He is not satisfied to show how society, by its laws or its opinions, can mould outward conduct to the production of a balance of pleasure. He makes the moral needs of men the foundation of society itself.[1] He sees the necessity of social institutions in the fact that human life cannot be made perfect in isolation; and he is thus led to ascribe to society moral functions far more subtle

[1] P. 154 note 1.

and more powerful than Bentham had conceived. He attributes to its influence all the excellences of human life — its moralities, its charities, its courtesies, the moral faiths and the ideals of a common good, by which man is elevated above the dominion of brute passion. He finds in social intercourse, with its educative restraint and its never-failing demands upon character, the very school of virtue; and he justifies and criticises society itself and every social institution in relation to the development of personal goodness. It is thus possible for him to regard society as at once the parent, and, in a sense, the product of moral intention—of a disinterested desire for virtue and the good of others, which Bentham had not even admitted to be possible.[1]

It would be no easy task to give a full account of the influences under which the moral seriousness of Mill's character led him to formulate this all but complete reconstruction of the Utilitarian account of morality. There can be little doubt, however, that his interest in the ethical and religious system of Comte, and in the communistic scheme of St Simon, combined with other influences to convince him of the possibility of disinterested and unselfish action. He found the conception of "economic" motives which he inherited to be an inadequate account of the facts; and he was led to modify his disbelief in the possibility of desiring anything which did not present itself under the guise of a personal pleasure. Under these influ-

[1] Pp. 137-145.

ences he became aware of the complexity of human motives and of the degree in which they express not merely the untutored demands of primordial craving, but the effects of social circumstance. But unquestionably Mill's appreciation of this aspect of human nature was chiefly brought about through a tendency in literature which began to affect English thought while he was still young. His criticism of Bentham — which expressed his direct and active interest in morality — took its special form under the influence of Coleridge and Wordsworth, and, at second-hand, of German Idealism.

Coleridge himself had been, in earlier life, a sympathetic student of the "Hartleian Metaphysic," by which Mill was so profoundly influenced; but he became one of the most active critics of the view of human life to which Hartley had given systematic expression; and his literary activity was carried on, and his real power, exerted under the constant and overwhelming influence of metaphysical idealism, and especially of the systems of Kant and Schelling.

The ruling idea of Coleridge's philosophy is the Kantian distinction of understanding and reason. The understanding, with him, is a private human faculty, by which man explores certain limited regions of fact, and which depends even for its narrow enlightenment upon a higher aspect of intelligence — upon reason, which is not confined to the minds of individual men, and which is primarily not human, but spiritual and universal. While the understanding is a discursive faculty, and must always refer to some other faculty as its ultimate authority, the decisions of reason appeal to reason itself as the ground and substance of their truth. Accordingly, while understanding is merely reflective, reason is a direct contemplation of truth; and its relation to reality is nearer to that of sense than of understanding. In this distinction of reason from understanding Coleridge found a possibility of escape from the purely analytical way of conceiving reality with the results of which he was familiar in Hartley's psychology. He was content to admit the truth of the conclusions reached by understanding in its own sphere, so long as the limits of that sphere and the existence of truth and reality beyond it were not denied. This limitation of the understanding left the way open for moral and religious faith; and these received a real and positive character from Coleridge's conception of reality as a spiritual system. He maintained the object of reason —the object of completed knowledge—to be spiritual; since every advance in our knowledge of reality leads us to conceive it less as a material and more as a spiritual order—as the expression of laws or principles rather than of unintelligent force; and this spiritual conception of reality derived a further moral interest from Coleridge's idea of the constitution of reason or spirit. In his view reason is fundamentally practical: will and activity are its determining elements; and thus the world—which is spiritual and rational—may be regarded as ultimately moral. The "spiritual philosophy" of reality which Coleridge learned from Schelling leads to a conception of the world which makes it the natural home of man's moral life, and which gives to the experiences of religion and morality more than a merely subjective importance. The insight of imagination and conscience becomes as true as the results which understanding yields in its own sphere. This belief that morality is the very nature of things, and not an accidental or superficial element in reality, enables Coleridge to represent man as a free agent, whose conduct has a significance determined not by the outward consequences of his acts, but by the degree in which they express rationally determined motives.

This view of man and his moral interests, together with the emotional and imaginative idea of Nature which he learned from Wordsworth, exerted no slight or insignificant influence upon Mill. His sense of the worth of personal life was deepened in such a way as to give a new meaning and importance to his utilitarian interest in virtuous character. He was specially led to seek for a unity of personal and social interests, and to conceive morality to be a realisation at once of individual and general good. He thus came to attach increasing importance to the idea of moral freedom, and to give a less precise and rigorous meaning to his hedonistic account of motives.

It would, of course, be idle to call this change in Mill's attitude an approach to Idealism. It must be remembered that even the "spiritual philosophy" of

Coleridge and his disciples is in no true sense idealistic. It is a philosophy which accepts certain of the more positive conclusions of German Idealism, simply in order to make them the basis of a "spiritual" conception of man and his moral relations. But of the characteristic methods, or of the complete result, of Idealism, this philosophy knows almost nothing. Idealism is primarily a logic: it is an account of reality which shows it to be a rational or systematic unity, and to be determined by principles that satisfy the demands of rational self-consciousness. What Coleridge offers is something very different from this. He propounds an imaginative and religious reflection upon life; but it is a reflection which is merely warranted or sanctioned in a very general way by a limitation of the sphere of reasoned knowledge and an assertion of the necessity for teleological and ethical explanation, and which is never shown either to depend upon a single and necessary principle or to explain and illuminate experience. He proposes an addition to experience, constructed out of ethical data; but of experience itself he gives no explanation. This partial and ambiguous character of Coleridge's attempt to express the spiritual nature of morality appears also in the modifications of Utilitarianism which Mill effects. Under the influence of Coleridge's philosophy Mill was confirmed in regarding virtue as the supreme human interest; and he was led to define it, not simply by its tendency to produce certain consequences, but also as a quality of personal life. But he did not consider how far removed such ideas are from the presuppositions on which he continued to base his ethical theory. That every man desires his own pleasure, and nothing else, is no ground for believing that every man ought to produce the greatest possible amount of happiness for others; and virtue, when it is defined as conduct which is influenced by sympathy and by interest in society to the production of a common good, has no direct connection with a character which is conceived to be limited in its interests and motives to the sphere of private pains and pleasures. Mill modified his conception of human character and conduct; but he never learned to think of them in a way which was really consistent with his own ethical position. His conception of virtue is one which cannot be made intelligible except by supposing that human character and the human interests are organic to a personal consciousness capable of recognising itself as related to other persons, and thus becoming a member of a community. His actual theory of human motives—that they are all incidental to desire for pleasant feeling—implies the widely different view that personal life is merely a series of impressions, and the individual consciousness is without any bond of relation to the real world, or to other persons.

The fact is, that Mill's advance upon the Utilitarianism of his predecessors was not brought about by an idealistic revision of their metaphysical conceptions. He did indeed modify his idea of man's relation to the sense world and to society, but he did so chiefly in obedience to ethical interests; and his enlarged idea of moral good depends mainly upon the fact that he recognises the worth for ethical science of moral experience itself. In doing so, he gives its true effect to his own conception of the method of ethics. For the idea that ethics is an inductive science finds its best expression not in the attempt to derive moral conclusions from the partial conceptions of conduct which psychology affords, but in a study of moral judgments and feelings, fitted to discover the standard which the moral consciousness makes use of and the results which moral experience yields.

With the adoption of this method hedonism is, of course, not inconsistent; for hedonism, like almost every ethical theory, describes a real characteristic of morality. Its central truth is that the good act satisfies desire; and this is certainly a quality of morally good actions; for if moral goodness be a state of intention and will—if it be a condition of personal life—the moral end can only be realised when it is accepted by the will of the agent; and this means that the moral end must be an object of desire, for it cannot be willed without being desired. The realisation of the moral end is thus a satisfaction of desire, and a source of happiness to the agent whose conduct is good. Nor again is such Hedonism as Mill's inconsistent with a genuine recognition of the distinctive character of the moral judgment. To make the production of happiness the moral criterion does not confuse the judgment of morality with that of mere expediency, when it is understood, as it is by Mill, that the act itself, and not merely the outward effect of it, is judged; and Mill's development of hedonism imports into it a sense of social obligation which is derived rather from moral experience than from the psychological basis of his theory.

It is thus more characteristic of Mill's Utilitarianism than of any preceding hedonistic system of ethics to consider the facts of moral experience directly, and to make them the basis of ethical theory. He never loses that sense of an objective and obligatory end for human conduct which is the essential element in the moral judgment of actions; and if it must be admitted that to call it "utility" or "the greatest happiness of the greatest number" is an inadequate and misleading account of this end, it should be remembered that the kind of utility in which Mill finds the criterion of conduct is that which affects man as a moral agent. It is a satisfaction of desires which depend upon moral interests. It is a common good which every man enjoys along with others. It is the good of a rational being; and the forms of its realisation are revealed in an experience determined by the idea of it.

ANALYSIS

ON THE LOGIC OF THE MORAL SCIENCES

(SYSTEM OF LOGIC, BOOK VI.)

CHAPTER I

INTRODUCTORY REMARKS

§ 1. Theories of Scientific Method can only be developed by studying the way in which investigations have actually been conducted; and this truth, which is exemplified by the history of other sciences, awaits confirmation in the case of those which relate to man himself; for, while a considerable body of truths is already established concerning man's physical constitution, the laws of Mind, and especially of society, are so little known that it is even questioned whether they are capable of becoming subjects of science; and, if agreement as to these subjects is to be obtained, this can only be done by deliberately applying the methods which have been successfully employed in investigating simpler phenomena. To facilitate this is the object of the present discussion.

§ 2. Abstract logical discussion can only make a slight and vague contribution to this task, the completion of which requires the actual construction of the sciences of Ethics and Politics. All that can be done here is to examine the relation of logical methods to various branches of moral inquiry, and to consider whether moral sciences exist, or can exist, and how far and how they can be developed. At the threshold of this inquiry we are met by an objection, which, if not removed, would be fatal to the attempt to treat human conduct as a subject of science. It is often denied that human actions are subject to invariable laws, or that constancy of causation obtains among them; and this subject must be deliberately considered.

CHAPTER II

OF LIBERTY AND NECESSITY

§ 1. The question whether the law of causality applies as strictly to human actions as to other phenomena is the controverted question of the Freedom of the Will. The affirmative opinion is called the doctrine of Necessity—as asserting human volitions and actions to be necessary and inevitable. The negative maintains that the will is determined, not, like other phenomena, by antecedents, but by itself—that volitions have no causes which they uniformly obey. The metaphysical theory of free will was invented because the alternative of admitting actions to be necessary was thought inconsistent with instinctive consciousness as well as humiliating and degrading; and the doctrine of necessity, as sometimes misconceived by its supporters, is open to these imputations.

§ 2. Correctly conceived, the doctrine of necessity means that from the motives present to an individual's mind and his character and disposition, his action might be unerringly inferred; and this simply states a universal conviction based on experience; for hesitation in predicting conduct arises merely from uncertainty as to the circumstances or character of the agent. Nor does this doctrine conflict with our feeling of freedom; for freedom is not felt to be inconsistent with the possibility of predicting actions; and it is not the doctrine that actions are consequents of antecedent states which is contradicted by consciousness, or felt to be degrading. But the doctrine is always conceived to involve more than this; for causation is not generally believed or felt to be merely certain and unconditional sequence; and even if the reason repudiates, the imagination retains the feeling of some more intimate connection, of some peculiar tie or mysterious constraint exercised by the antecedent over the consequent. Now this it is which, considered as applying to the human will, conflicts with our consciousness and revolts our feelings. But such mysterious compulsion forms no element in the causal relation: it would be more correct to say that matter is not bound by necessity, than that mind is so. This mistake cannot surprise us in free-will metaphysicians, who generally reject Hume's and Brown's analysis of Cause and Effect; but it is more astonishing that Necessitarians should forget that analysis, which they generally accept. Necessitarians do not habitually feel that the Necessity which they recognise in actions is but uniformity of order and capability of being predicted. They feel as if their theory meant more than this, and sometimes suffer, through this mistake, the depressing consequences which their opponents impute to the Necessitarian doctrine.

§ 3. This error is chiefly an effect of the associations of the inappropriate word Necessity; for that word implies irresistibleness; its ordinary use means the operation of causes that cannot be counteracted; and its application to the causes of human action creates a feeling that these are uncontrollable. But this is a mere illusion; for actions are never ruled by one motive so absolutely that no other has any influence. The causes of action are not uncontrollable, and the word necessity is therefore not applicable. Its use tends to make Necessitarians fatalistic in their feelings, though the doctrine of Necessity is remote from fatalism. Fatalism means that it is useless to struggle against what is going to happen; and a Necessitarian is apt to regard his own actions in this way, and to suppose that, since his character is formed *for* him, and not *by* him, therefore his wishing it different is useless, and cannot alter it. This is a grand error. He has a certain power to alter his character; for, though formed for him, it may be partly formed *by* him as an intermediate agent. His character is formed by circumstances; but among these his desire to alter it is influential. We cannot directly will to be different, but we can change our circumstances. We are as capable of making our own character, *if we will*, as others are of making it for us. The answer, that the wish to form our own character is a product of circumstances, confuses the view that we have no power to alter character with the truth that we shall not use our power unless we desire to use it. These are very different statements. Only the person who wishes to alter his character can be depressed by thinking himself unable to do so; and what is practically important is, that we should not be prevented from forming this desire by thinking the attainment impracticable. The feeling of ability to modify our character, *if we wish*, is itself the feeling of moral freedom. This feeling is of course partly dependent on past success in forming our characters; and none but a person of confirmed virtue is completely free.

The use of the term Necessity is misleading and practically unfortunate; and the free-will doctrine has kept in view that power of the mind to form character, which the word Necessity puts out of sight. It has thus given to its adherents a practical feeling nearer to the truth than has generally existed in the minds of Necessitarians. It has fostered a stronger spirit of self-culture.

§ 4. One fact still requires to be noticed. When the will is said to be determined by motives, a motive does not mean always, or solely, the anticipation of a pleasure or of a pain. Without inquiring how far pleasure is the original aim of all actions, we may be sure that actions themselves are ultimately desired for their own sake; and even if the pleasure of the action be the motive to perform it, the action is eventually performed without any reference to its pleasurableness. Actions are still desired and performed, when they have ceased to be pleasant. This is exemplified both in habits of hurtful excess and in moral heroism.

Habits of willing are called purposes; and these, as well as desires, are causes of volitions. A confirmed character consists in the existence of purposes independent of feelings of pain or pleasure; and when character is confirmed, action is not always determined by passive susceptibilities.

CHAPTER III

THAT THERE IS, OR MAY BE, A SCIENCE OF HUMAN NATURE

§ 1. The common notion that human beings are not a subject of science depends upon confusions which should be cleared up. Any facts which follow one another according to constant laws may be scientifically known. This is true even where—as in the case of meteorology — accurate prediction of phenomena has not yet become possible. Meteorology is, from the inaccessibility of its facts, a very imperfect science; but sciences may fall short of perfection, and yet be more highly developed than this. It may be possible to explain the general character of a phenomenon, but not its minor variations, so as to render prediction possible, but only approximately accurate. The theory of the tides is in this position. General laws may be laid down respecting them; predictions may be founded on these laws; and the result will in the main, though often not with complete accuracy, correspond to the predictions. This is what is or ought to be meant, by those who speak of sciences which are not *exact* sciences. Astronomy was once a science, without being an exact science; and tidology is still in this position. We can lay down general propositions which will be true in the main, and on which, with allowance for the degree of this probable inaccuracy, we may safely ground our expectations and our conduct.

§ 2. The science of human nature is of this description. It may be as much a science as tidology is, or as astronomy was when its calculations had only mastered the main phenomena, but not the perturbations. It would be perfect if it enabled us to foretell the thoughts, feelings, and actions of an individual with complete accuracy. This is made impossible not only by our ignorance of the circumstances in which an individual will be placed; but also by the complexity of the influences by which character is formed, and the importance of character as a factor in determining impressions and actions: because the data are not all given we can neither make positive predictions nor lay down universal propositions. But, since many of the most important effects depend much more upon circumstances and qualities common to mankind than upon individual idiosyncrasies, statements can be made which are generally true with regard to these; and whenever it is sufficient to know how a majority will act, these general propositions are equivalent to universal ones. For the purposes of political and social science this *is* sufficient; since what is probable when asserted of individual human beings indiscriminately selected is certain when affirmed of the character and collective conduct of masses.

It is no disparagement, therefore, to the science of Human Nature that its predictions are only approximately true; but the scientific character of the study depends upon a deductive derivation of its empirical laws from the laws of nature from which they result. The science of human nature exists in proportion as the approximate truths which compose a practical knowledge of mankind can be exhibited as corollaries from the universal laws of human nature on which they rest.

CHAPTER IV

OF THE LAWS OF MIND

§ 1. What the Mind is, need not be considered here. We shall understand by the laws of mind those of mental phenomena, of the various feelings or states of consciousness of sentient beings. These are Thoughts, Emotions, Volitions, and Sensations; for sensations themselves are mental, although their conditions may be physical. The phenomena of mind are the feelings of our nature; and the laws of mind are the laws according to which those feelings generate one another.

§ 2. States of mind are produced by other states of mind or by states of body. In the first case, the law concerned is a law of Mind, in the second, a law of Body. Sensations are physically conditioned, and their laws belong to physiology. The question remains how far this is the case with other mental states. Many physiologists derive all mental changes from organic conditions. On this theory, there are no original laws of Mind: mental science becomes, as Comte urges, a mere branch of physiology. It cannot, however, be denied that uniformities among mental phenomena can be discovered by observation and experiment; nor can it be proved that every mental state depends immediately on physical antecedents. Our knowledge of nervous processes is not sufficient to admit of our deriving mental states from them. Mental phenomena must be studied directly; and there is a distinct and separate science of Mind. This science is related to physiology; for laws of Mind may be results of laws of animal life, and the influence of physiological facts is an important subject in psychology; but psychology cannot be confined to physiological data.

§ 3. The subject of Psychology is the laws of mental change. The following are examples of these laws. First, whenever any state of consciousness has once been excited in us, no matter by what cause, an inferior degree of the same state of consciousness, a state of consciousness resembling the former but inferior in intensity, is capable of being reproduced in us, without the presence of any such cause as excited it at first. Secondly, these ideas, or secondary mental states, are excited by our impressions, or by other ideas, according to the laws of Association. Similar ideas, and ideas frequently experienced simultaneously, or successively, excite one another; and intensity in either or both of the impressions has the same effect as frequency of conjunction. These laws have been ascertained by experimental inquiry. But it may also be asked how far these laws explain actual phenomena. Some philosophers, such as Hartley and James Mill, think that all mental contents are generated from simple sensations; and they have made out a great part, but not the whole, of their case. They have shown that ideas may originate from others which are different from them; but they have not demonstrated precisely that all complex contents originate in this way; and even if the derivation of complex from simple phenomena were completely established, it would not be possible to dispense with specific observation of the more complex facts.

§ 4. The influence of bodily upon mental states must be examined carefully, especially in relation to the differences of individual minds. These differences are probably connected in the closest way with differences of bodily structure; but it does not follow that organic differences always influence mental phenomena directly and immediately. The influence often takes place through the effect of organic states on other psychological elements; and the general laws of mind themselves account for more mental peculiarities than is generally supposed. The investigation of the psychology of individual peculiarities, which has been neglected under the influence of German metaphysics, and also of Comte, shows that differences in education and in outward circumstances are capable of affording an adequate explanation of by far the greatest portion of character; and the remainder may be in great part accounted for by physical differences in the sensations produced in different individuals by the same external or internal cause. Some mental facts, however, do not admit of these explanations. Such are animal instincts and the portion of human nature which corresponds to them. These cannot be explained psychologically, and are probably directly connected with cerebral conditions. The rapid advance of cerebral physiology makes it probable that whatever connection exists between cerebral conditions and individual peculiarities will soon be found out. The tendency of recent discoveries is to show that the phrenological theory of the connection is false.

CHAPTER V

OF ETHOLOGY, OR THE SCIENCE OF THE FORMATION OF CHARACTER

§ 1. The laws of mind compose the universal or abstract portion of the philosophy of human nature; and the truths of common experience are its Empirical Laws. An Empirical Law is a uniformity which holds true within, but which may not exist beyond the limits of our knowledge, since it does not depend on direct causal relation: it is a law whose truth is not absolute, but depends on more general conditions. Observations collected from common experience of human affairs are of this nature: they are not principles of human nature, but results of these principles in special circumstances; and the really scientific truths are not these empirical laws, but the causal laws which explain them. Empirical laws have no function in science but that of verifying the conclusions of theory, especially when they are only approximate generalisations.

§ 2. This is not a peculiarity of moral sciences. It is only in the simplest sciences that empirical laws are ever exactly true; and this approximate character of empirical generalisations does not warrant an inference against the universality or simplicity of the ultimate laws. Mental capacities are modified by so many circumstances that only approximate generalisations can be expected regarding them; but although there is scarcely any mode of feeling or conduct common to all mankind, yet all modes of feeling and conduct have causes which produce them. Mankind have not one universal character; but there exist universal laws of the Formation of Character; and these are the basis of the science of human nature.

§ 3. When we inquire which is the best way of ascertaining the laws of the formation of character, we find that the Deductive Method is best fitted for the investigation of this as of all very complex phenomena. Laws of Nature must be ascertained either deductively or observationally. But it is impossible to make accurate observations on the development of character either with or without the aid of experiment, since in both cases many important circumstances are inaccessible to our knowledge. Accurate judgments may be arrived at by connecting such observations as we are able to make with more general laws by which the particular facts may be interpreted.

§ 4. Since we cannot obtain accurate propositions as to the formation of character from observation and experiment alone, we must use the method of investigating not only the complex facts, but the simpler elements of which they are compounded, and considering how far these explain the approximate generalisations arrived at by observing the complex phenomena. The laws of the formation of character are derivative laws, resulting from the general laws of mind; and by investigating the effect of circumstances on character according to these general laws, a science is formed to which the name Ethology may be given. This science corresponds to the art of education—of the formation of character, whether collective or individual. It is the Exact Science of Human Nature; and its truths are not empirical, but real laws. Its propositions, however, must remain hypothetical.

§ 5. While psychology is mainly observational, ethology is thus wholly deductive. The one ascertains simple laws of Mind, while the other traces their operation in complex circumstances. Ethology stands to psychology in a relation similar to that in which the various branches of Natural Philosophy stand to mechanics: its principles are the middle principles, which stand between empirical laws and the highest generalisations. Bacon has rightly observed that the *axiomata media* of every science constitute its principal value; but he is wrong in maintaining that induction must always proceed from the lowest to the middle principles, and from these to the highest, so that new principles can never be discovered by deduction. In his day deductive sciences did not exist; but in such sciences as mechanics, astronomy, optics, &c., some of the highest generalisations were among the earliest results; and less general truths were derived from these. Bacon's achievement was not the abolition of the deductive method, which is that actually followed by science, but the institution of rigorous methods of induction and verification. The order of discovery of truths of various degrees of generality cannot be absolutely fixed; but in every science which has become a science of causes, the most general truths should be investigated first, although a knowledge of the empirical laws is an essential preliminary to verification. The science of the formation of character is a science of causes; the simplest and most general laws of causation should, therefore, first be ascertained, and the middle principles deduced from them. Ethology, the deductive science, is a system of corollaries from psychology, the experimental science.

§ 6. Of these, the earlier alone has been, as yet, really conceived or studied as a science; while the other, ethology, is still to be created. Its creation, however, has at length become practicable; for empirical laws have been formed in abundance to verify ethological deductions, and the laws of human nature are sufficiently understood to allow such deductions to be made from them. A science of ethology founded on psychology is, therefore, possible, though little has yet been done towards forming it. Its progress will depend upon, first, deduction of the ethological consequences of particular circumstances, and, second, increased study by competent observers of the various types of human nature. For the experimental part of this process the materials are continually accumulating; and the great problem of ethology is to deduce the requisite middle principles from the general laws of psychology. When ethology is furnished with these, practical education will be the mere transformation of those principles into a parallel system of precepts, and adaptation of these to circumstances.

Verification *à posteriori* must proceed *pari passu* with deduction *à priori*. Inferences must be tested by specific experience. The conclusions of theory cannot be trusted unless confirmed by observation; nor those of observation unless affiliated to theory by deducing them from laws of human nature. The accordance of these two kinds of evidence separately taken is the only sufficient ground for the principles of any science so complex and concrete as ethology.

UTILITARIANISM

CHAPTER I

GENERAL REMARKS

It is remarkable how little progress has been made in the controversy respecting the criterion of right and wrong. From the dawn of philosophy, the question of the foundation of morality has been the main problem of speculative thought; yet this question seems to be no nearer settlement than it has ever been. Similar uncertainty exists respecting the first principles of all sciences, without damage to their conclusions; for the doctrines of a science do not generally depend upon its first principles. These are really the last results of metaphysical analysis. But though in science particular truths precede the general theory, the contrary might be expected to be the case in a practical art, such as morals or legislation; for actions must take their character from the end which they subserve; and a test of right and wrong should be the means, and not a consequence, of ascertaining what is right and wrong.

The difficulty is not avoided by the theory of a sense which informs us of right and wrong; for all serious upholders of this theory make the moral faculty a source only of general principles of moral judgment. The intuitive and the inductive schools of ethics agree that the morality of actions is a matter not of perception but of application of a law to an individual case. They recognise, also, the same moral laws, but differ as to the source of their authority. On one theory moral principles are evident *à priori*; on the other, right and wrong are known by experience; but both hold that morality must be deduced from principles. Intuitionists, however, while holding that there is a science of morals, seldom attempt to determine its principles, and still more rarely try to reduce these to one first principle. They assume ordinary moral precepts as of *à priori* authority. But to support their pretensions there should be a single fundamental moral principle.

Whatever steadiness or consistency moral beliefs have attained has been mainly due to the tacit influence of a standard not recognised. The effect of conduct on happiness has influenced moral feelings and judgments, and is universally admitted to be an element in the moral quality of actions. Utilitarian arguments are indispensable to all *à priori* moralists who argue at all, as we see in the case of Kant, who really appeals to experience of the consequence of actions.

It is evident that such proof as the Utilitarian theory is susceptible of cannot be proof in the ordinary sense of the term; for questions of ultimate ends are not amenable to direct proof. Proof that anything is good consists in showing its relation to something admitted to be good without proof; and this is impossible in the case of things good in themselves. Yet the acceptance of an ultimate end is not arbitrary. In a larger meaning of the word proof, this question is as amenable to it as any other; for the subject is within the cognisance of the rational faculty. Considerations may be presented capable of determining the intellect to give or to withhold its assent to the doctrine; and this is equivalent to proof.

The discussion of the nature and value of this proof must be preceded by an attempt to explain and illustrate the utilitarian doctrine.

CHAPTER II

WHAT UTILITARIANISM IS

It is only necessary to point out the mistake of criticising Utilitarianism as an advocacy of utility in the restricted sense in which it is opposed to pleasure. Utility always means, for utilitarians, pleasure and exemption from pain. Utilitarianism is the theory that actions are right in proportion as they tend to promote happiness, wrong as they tend to produce the reverse of happiness. Pleasure and freedom from pain are, on this theory, the only things desirable as ends; and desirable things are desirable either because they are pleasant or because they are means to pleasure.

Such a theory of life excites in many minds inveterate dislike. It appears to them to be mean and grovelling—worthy only of swine. Epicureans answer to this that it is not they but their accusers who represent human nature in a degrading light, since the accusation supposes human beings to be capable of no pleasures except those of which swine are capable. Human beings have faculties more elevated than the animal appetites, and, when once made conscious of them, do not regard anything as happiness which does not include their gratification; and there is no known Epicurean theory of life which does not assign to the pleasures of the intellect, of the feelings and imagination, and of the moral sentiments, a much higher value as pleasures than to those of mere sensation. Utilitarians have generally made more of the circumstantial advantages than of the intrinsic superiority of mental pleasures. Yet it is quite compatible with the principle of utility to recognise the fact that some *kinds* of pleasure are more desirable and more valuable than others; and this difference of quality in pleasures means that the more desirable of two pleasures is that which is preferred by all or almost all who have experience of both. Now it is an unquestionable fact that those who are equally acquainted with, and equally capable of appreciating and enjoying, both, do give a most marked preference to the manner of existence which employs their higher faculties. In spite of his liability to greater unhappiness, a being of higher faculties can never really wish to sink to a lower grade of existence. This unwillingness to sink in the scale of existence may be called pride, love of liberty, love of power or excitement, or, most appropriately, a sense of dignity. To suppose that the superior being is not happier than the inferior, is to confound happiness and content. Low capacities of enjoyment are most likely to be satisfied; and high endowments make all happiness appear imperfect; but the highly endowed being will not envy the being who is unconscious of imperfection. It is better to be a human being dissatisfied than a pig satisfied; better to be Socrates dissatisfied than a fool satisfied. And if the fool or the pig is of a different opinion, it is because they only know their own side of the question. The other party to the comparison knows both sides.

It may be objected that persons capable of higher pleasures sometimes postpone them to lower. But men often pursue what they know to be worse. The deterioration, which sometimes comes with advancing years, really arises from a growing incapacity for the higher pleasures, rather than from a voluntary preference of the lower. It may be doubted whether any one equally susceptible to both has ever preferred lower to higher pleasures.

From this verdict of competent judges there can be no appeal. The judgment of those who know both must decide between pleasures, or modes of existence; and this applies to the quantity as well as to the quality of pleasures.

Important as this doctrine of a difference of kind among pleasures is, it is not indispensable to Utilitarianism; for moral excellence is essential to the general happiness, whether the happiness of the individual depends on it or no.

Thus, the ultimate end is pleasure and freedom from pain—the test of pleasure being the preference of experienced persons. Happiness is also the standard of morality; and morality consists in rules for human conduct, by observing which the greatest happiness of mankind might be secured, along with as much happiness as possible for the whole sentient creation.

It is objected to this that happiness cannot be the rational purpose of human life and action, because it is unattainable, and because it is not a right of human beings, and can be done without by them.

If happiness be unattainable it cannot be the moral end; though the mitigation of pain must still be desirable. But the assertion that human life cannot be happy is an exaggeration. If happiness means a continuity of highly pleasurable excitement, it is evidently impossible; for states of exalted pleasure are short and occasional. This is quite well known to those who regard happiness as the end of life; and they mean by happiness, not a life of rapture, but moments of it in an existence of few pains and many pleasures, predominantly active, and founded on moderate expectations. Such a life has always seemed worthy of the name of happiness; and such a life is enjoyed by many even now, and only hindered by bad education, and bad social arrangements.

It may be doubted whether human beings, if taught to consider happiness as the end of life, would be satisfied with such a moderate share of it. But many men have been satisfied with less. Satisfaction consists mainly of tranquillity and excitement; and these exist in natural alliance, each making the other desirable. When people who are tolerably fortunate in their outward lot do not find in life sufficient enjoyment to make it valuable, the cause generally is, caring for nobody but themselves; and next to selfishness, the principal cause which makes life unsatisfactory is want of mental cultivation. Now, there is no reason why sufficient culture should not be the inheritance of every one born in a civilised country; nor is egotism a necessity for human beings. Every one may have a happy existence, unless prevented by being deprived of liberty, or subjected to great physical or mental suffering. The main stress of the problem is in conflict with removable evils, such as poverty, disease, and vicissitudes of fortune; for all the great sources of human suffering are largely conquerable by human care; and the contest with them is itself a source of noble enjoyment.

It is certainly possible to do without happiness, since this is done both voluntarily and involuntarily. But the resignation of one's own happiness must be for some end. It is not its own end; and the true purpose which warrants renunciation of one's own happiness is that of securing greater happiness for others. So long as the world is imperfect, readiness to sacrifice one's own happiness is the highest virtue which can be found in man; and the conscious ability to do without happiness gives the best prospect of realising such happiness as is attainable; for nothing except this can raise a person above the chances of life. The morality of self-devotion belongs to Utilitarians by as good a right as to Stoics or Transcendentalists; for Utilitarianism approves the self-renunciation which consists in devotion to the happiness of others.

The Utilitarian standard is the happiness not of the agent, but of all concerned. To do as one would be done by, and to love one's neighbour as oneself, constitute the ideal perfection of utilitarian morality. Utility enjoins that laws and social arrangements should reconcile the interest of every individual with that of the whole, and that education and opinion should establish an association in each man's mind between his own happiness and that of the whole, especially between his own happiness and such conduct as regard for the general happiness prescribes, so that an impulse to promote the general good may be a habitual motive to action.

Some objectors to Utilitarianism, again, find fault with its standard as being too high for humanity, since it requires that men shall always act to promote social interests. But this is to confound the rule of action with the motive to it. Ethics investigates the test of right action, but does not require that a feeling of duty should be the sole motive of all action. Utilitarianism especially insists that motives affect only the worth of the agent, and not the morality of actions. It does not imply that people should fix their minds upon so wide a generality as the world, or society at large. Those alone, the influence of whose actions extends to society in general, need concern themselves habitually about so large an object. The exception, in the case of abstinences for the sake of maintaining a rule useful to society, is one which is common to all ethical systems.

It is often affirmed that Utilitarianism renders men cold and unsympathising. If this means that utilitarians do not let their estimate of actions be affected by the character of the persons performing them, it is an objection to the very idea of a standard of morality. Otherwise there is nothing in utilitarianism inconsistent with the fact that other things interest us in persons besides the rightness and wrongness of their actions; although utilitarians refuse to consider any mental disposition as good, of which the predominant tendency is to produce bad conduct. This reproach is not one which a conscientious utilitarian need be anxious to repel. It may be admitted that utilitarians who have cultivated their moral feelings, but not their sympathies nor their artistic perceptions, do fall into the mistake of considering the morality of actions to the exclusion of other beauties of character. If there is to be an error, it is better that it should be on that side. Utilitarians differ in strictness, and in moral opinions; but such differences are not peculiar to Utilitarianism, and it supplies a real way of deciding them.

Utilitarianism is often inveighed against as a *godless* doctrine. The question of its being so depends upon our idea of the Deity. If God desires the happiness of his creatures, utility is the most religious of ethical theories. If it be meant that Utilitarianism does not recognise the revealed will of God as the supreme law of morals, a Utilitarian, who believes in the perfect goodness and wisdom of God, must believe that God's revelation of morals will fulfil the requirements of utility; and others besides Utilitarians regard Christianity as fitted rather to change the spirit of mankind than to formulate moral precepts. In any case we need a doctrine of ethics to interpret the will of God; and whatever aid religion can afford is as open to the Utilitarian moralist as to any other.

Utility is often stigmatised as an immoral doctrine, by calling it Expediency, and contrasting it with Principle. The expedient as opposed to the right, however, generally means the private interest of the agent himself, or else a temporary and lower expediency. The expedient, in this sense, is not useful, but hurtful—as in the case of lying, which may be temporarily useful, but is ultimately injurious. The validity of the rule of veracity, and the exceptions to it, are both matters of utility.

Again, Utilitarianism is sometimes objected to on the ground that there is not time, previous to action, for calculating and weighing the effects of any line of conduct on the general happiness. But there has been ample time — namely, the whole past duration of the human species — in which mankind have been learning the tendencies of actions by experience, on which all prudence and morality depend. It is not necessary to reason out moral questions from the beginning on every occasion. The work has been done by education and opinion. The moral beliefs which have been acquired by experience are the rules of morality. They are not divine or perfect; and mankind have still much to learn as to the effects of actions on the general happiness; but this does not mean that every individual action is to be tested directly by the first principle. The acknowledgment of a first principle is not inconsistent with the admission of secondary ones; and whatever fundamental principle we adopt, we require subordinate principles to apply it by; but it is absurd to speak as if such secondary principles were unattainable, or as if no general conclusions could be drawn from the experience of human life.

Other stock arguments against Utilitarianism lay to its charge the common infirmities of human nature. We are told that Utilitarians will be apt to make exceptions from moral rules in their own favour. But any doctrine which recognises conflicting considerations in morals is open to the same objection; and the existence of such difficulties is the fault not of ethical theories, but of the complexity of human affairs. One is not less qualified to deal with them from possessing an ultimate standard of reference; and Utilitarianism offers such a standard to decide between conflicting obligations; although it is only in cases where secondary principles are in conflict, that it is necessary to refer to first principles at all.

CHAPTER III

OF THE ULTIMATE SANCTION OF THE PRINCIPLE OF UTILITY

It may be asked in regard to any moral standard, What is its sanction? whence does it derive its binding force? Moral philosophy must answer this question, which arises whenever one is called on to *adopt* any standard. Customary morality is taken to be *in itself* obligatory; and is apt to seem more certain than the grounds on which it is made to rest in theory. According to the utilitarian view of the moral sense, this difficulty must remain until moral influences have taken the same hold of the moral principle as of some of its consequences. The difficulty is not in any case peculiar to utilitarianism, but applies to every attempt to analyse morality.

The principle of utility either has, or there is no reason why it might not have, all the sanctions which belong to any other system of morals. These sanctions are either external or internal. Evidently the external sanctions—hope of favour or fear of displeasure from God or man — may attach themselves to utilitarian morality as completely and as powerfully as to any other; indeed, those of them which refer to our fellow-creatures are sure to do so, in proportion to the amount of general intelligence; while with regard to the religious motive, belief in the goodness of God leads to the conclusion that, if general happiness be the criterion of morality, it is also what God approves.

The internal sanction of duty, whatever our standard of duty may be, is one and the same—a feeling in our own mind; a pain, more or less intense, attendant on violation of duty, which in properly cultivated moral natures rises, in the more serious cases, into shrinking from it as an impossibility. This feeling is the essence of conscience; though it is generally incrusted with collateral associations, derived from sympathy, love, fear, religious feeling, recollections, self-esteem, desire of esteem, and self-abasement. This complication gives to the idea of obligation its mystical character; but its binding force consists in the existence of a mass of feeling which supports our standard of right. This is what essentially constitutes conscience. The conscientious feelings of mankind are thus the sanction of the utilitarian as of every other standard. This sanction has, of course, no binding efficacy on those who do not possess the feelings. This difficulty applies to every moral principle; but the feelings are a fact in human nature, and no reason has been shown why they should not be cultivated in connection with the utilitarian as intensely as with any other rule of morals.

It is believed that one who sees in moral obligation a transcendent fact is likely to obey it better than one who believes it to be entirely subjective; but the binding force is subjective feeling. All belief operates on conduct only through feeling: the sanction is always in the mind. What is meant, therefore, is that the sanction will not exist *in* the mind unless believed to have its root out of the mind. But the facts show that strong conscientious feeling has very little connection with belief in an external source of moral obligation.

It is not necessary, for the present purpose, to decide whether the feeling of duty is innate or implanted; for it is agreed that intuitive perception must be of principles and not of details. If there be anything innate, it may be regard for the pleasures and pains of others; so that intuitive ethics would coincide with utilitarian. As it is, intuitive moralists hold that a large *portion* of morality turns upon consideration for the interests of our fellow-creatures; and thus utilitarian morality already has whatever efficacy the internal sanction may derive from belief in its transcendent origin. On the other hand, if moral feelings are acquired, they are none the less natural. They are not indeed natural in the sense of being universal; but they are a natural outgrowth from our nature, and capable of cultivation and development. Moral feeling can be cultivated in almost any direction, good or bad, and may be made to support the principle of utility.

Artificial moral associations, however, are dissolved by analysis; and if there were not a natural basis of sentiment for utilitarian morality, the association of moral feeling with utility might be analysed away. But there *is* this basis of powerful natural sentiment; and this is the strength of utilitarian morality. Its firm foundation is that of the social feelings of mankind,—the growing desire to be in unity with our fellow-creatures. The social state is at once so natural, so necessary, and so habitual to man that, except in some unusual circumstances or by an effort of voluntary abstraction, he never conceives himself otherwise than as a member of a body; and what is necessary to society thus becomes part of every individual's idea of his surroundings and destiny. Now the great condition of society between equals is that the interests of all should be consulted; and disregard of others thus becomes inconceivable. The development of society leads each individual to identify his feelings more and more with the good of others; and this feeling of unity is nourished by sympathy and education, and supported by the external sanctions. Taught and directed like a religion, it might become an adequate sanction for utilitarian morality, as Comte's '*Système de Politique Positive*' shows. The influence of social feeling might become so great as even to interfere unduly with human freedom and individuality.

This feeling need not wait for the influences which would make its obligation generally felt. Already it has become impossible, for those in whom social feeling is at all developed, to regard others as mere rivals. Every man's idea of himself as a social being makes unity with others one of his natural wants. Even when he differs from them he still needs to be conscious of an ultimate unity of his aims and theirs. To those who have it, this feeling appears natural—not a superstition, or external law, but an attribute which it would not be well for them to be without. This is the ultimate sanction of the greatest happiness morality. This makes any well-developed mind co-operate with the external sanctions. It is a powerful internal binding force in proportion to the sensitiveness and thoughtfulness of the character.

CHAPTER IV

OF WHAT SORT OF PROOF THE PRINCIPLE OF UTILITY IS SUSCEPTIBLE

To be incapable of proof by reasoning is common to all first principles; but first premises of knowledge may be tested by an appeal to the senses or to consciousness. Can one do this in relation to practical ends?

Questions about ends are questions what things are desirable; and the utilitarian doctrine is that happiness alone is desirable as an end. The proof that an object is visible or a sound audible is that people see or hear it; and the sole evidence that anything is desirable is that people do actually desire it. No reason can be given why the general happiness is desirable, except that each person desires his own happiness; and this is the only proof which can be required of the fact that each person's happiness is a good to him, and the general happiness a good to the aggregate of all persons. Happiness is thus *one* of the criteria of morality. But to show that it is the sole criterion, we must show that only happiness is desired. People seem actually to desire other things, such as virtue; and Utilitarianism maintains that virtue is and should be desired disinterestedly for itself. Whatever account they give of virtue, Utilitarian moralists make it the principal means to the ultimate end, and recognise that it may be itself a good to the individual, and that it should be desired for its own sake. Virtue may become part of the end—not a means to happiness, but a part of happiness. Virtue is not the only thing which is originally desired as a means and comes to be desired for itself. This is the case also with money, honour, and fame; and life would be a poor thing if there were not this provision of nature by which things originally indifferent become sources of pleasure. Virtue, according to the utilitarian conception, is a good of this description. There was no original desire for it, but only for its effects. But it may come to be felt as a good in itself, by association; and, since its coming to be desired is a benefit to society, the utilitarian standard, while it approves other desires only in moderation, enjoins and requires the cultivation of the love of virtue up to the greatest strength possible, as being above all things important to the general happiness.

Thus nothing is really desired except happiness—other things being desired as means to happiness or part of happiness. When virtue is desired for its own sake it is desired as a pleasure.

But if only happiness can be desired, happiness is the sole end and criterion of conduct and of morality; and self-observation and observation of others show that only happiness is desired — that desiring a thing and finding it pleasant are two parts of the same phenomenon, two modes of naming the same fact. To desire anything except in proportion as the idea of it is pleasant is a physical and metaphysical impossibility.

It will be objected to this, not that desire can be directed to anything except pleasure, but that will is different from desire, and that purposes are carried out without any thought of the pleasures connected with them. Will, the active phenomenon, certainly is a different thing from desire, the state of passive sensibility, and may become so detached from it that instead of willing because we desire, we desire because we will.

This is an instance of the power of habit, which acts unconsciously, or else consciously either in opposition to, or in fulfilment of, deliberate preference. But will, in the beginning, is entirely produced from desire. The will to be virtuous can be awakened or strengthened only by increasing the desire for virtue, through the association of right action with pleasure. Will is the child of desire, and passes out of the dominion of its parent only to come under that of habit. That which is habitual is not necessarily good; and the only reason for making the purpose of virtue independent of pleasure and pain is the constancy which it gains in this way. Both in feeling and conduct, habit is the only thing which imparts certainty; and this constitutes the importance of habitual virtue. This state of will is only a means to good; and it remains true that nothing is a good to human beings except pleasure and the means to it. But, if this be true, the principle of utility is proved.

CHAPTER V

ON THE CONNECTION BETWEEN JUSTICE AND UTILITY

One of the strongest obstacles to Utilitarianism has been drawn from the idea of Justice. The powerful sentiment and apparently clear perception recalled by that word have seemed to point to an absoluteness in

Justice by which it is opposed to Expediency. In the case of this, as of other moral sentiments, there is no necessary connection between its origin and its binding force: that a feeling is natural does not make it authoritative. Instinct is not infallible; and justice may be instinctive, yet need to be controlled and enlightened; but the naturalness and the authority of a feeling are apt to be identified with one another. A feeling not otherwise explained is often regarded as a revelation of some objective reality. The present question is whether the reality, to which the feeling of justice corresponds, is one which needs any such special revelation,—whether the justice of an action is distinct from, or a combination of, some of its other qualities. We should first ask whether the feeling itself is *sui generis* or derivative, since, while the dictates of justice admittedly coincide with a part of the field of general Expediency, the special character of the feeling of Justice prevents people from regarding it as only a branch of utility We have to ascertain the distinguishing character of justice—the quality which is common to all unjust acts, and distinguishes them from other wrong acts. Then we shall be able to judge whether this quality accounts for the feeling in question.

The actions judged in this way must first be surveyed in the concrete. First, it is unjust to deprive any one of liberty, property, or anything which belongs to him by law. Here injustice means violation of *legal rights*. But, secondly, these legal rights may be such as *ought* not to belong to the man. The law may be bad; and in this case opinions differ as to the justice of infringing it. But the badness or injustice of the law means that it infringes some one's rights; and in this case injustice means infringement of a person's *moral right*. Thirdly, it is just that each person should obtain that which he *deserves*. This is the clearest popular conception of justice. The question arises what constitutes desert; and it is generally answered in the sense that a person deserves good from those to whom he has done good, and evil from those to whom he has done evil. Fourthly, it is unjust to *break faith* with any one — to violate engagements, or disappoint expectations which we have raised; but this, like the other obligations of justice, is not absolute. Fifthly, it is unjust to be *partial*, or to show favour improperly; but impartiality is rather a means to other duties than itself a duty. It is obligatory where rights are concerned, on account of the general obligation to give every one his rights. In other cases impartiality means being solely influenced by desert, or by consideration for the public interest. In general, it means being influenced only by the considerations which should influence the particular case in hand. Nearly allied to impartiality is *equality*, which is sometimes thought to be the essence of justice. But in this, still more than in other cases, the notion of justice varies in different persons, according to their notion of utility: the justice of equality is always limited by expediency.

Among so many applications of the term Justice, it

is not easy to seize the mental link which holds them together. In most languages the etymology of the word which corresponds to Just points to an origin connected either with positive law or with custom. *Justum* is *jussum* — what has been ordered. Δίκαιον comes from δίκη, a suit at law. *Recht* is synonymous with law; while its original meaning pointed to physical straightness, as *wrong* and its Latin equivalent meant tortuous. The courts of justice are the courts of law. The primitive element in the idea of justice is conformity to law; and this was the whole idea among the Hebrews. The Greeks and Romans saw the possibility of unjust laws, and regarded as unjust the violations only of those laws which *ought* to exist. But, while the idea of law is prominent in the notion of justice, mankind apply the notion to things not regulated by law— *e.g.*, to the details of private life. In such cases legal interference is thought inconvenient; but the idea of legal constraint is still the generating idea of the notion of justice. Yet all this does not distinguish justice from moral obligations in general. The idea of penal sanction enters into that of all wrong; this indeed distinguishes morality from expediency: duty is a thing which may be *exacted* from a person, as one exacts a debt. Other things we wish people to do, yet do not consider them bound to do. The character, however, is still to be sought which distinguishes justice from other branches of morality. The distinction coincides with that drawn between perfect obligation, which entails a right, and imperfect obligation, which does not. This is the specific difference between justice and generosity —one can be claimed as a moral right, while the other cannot. If the distinction be not grounded on this, it cannot be made at all.

Such being the elements of the idea of justice, is the feeling which accompanies it attached to it by a special dispensation of nature, or may it have grown out of the idea itself? The sentiment itself does not arise from an idea of expediency; yet, whatever is moral in it does. The two essential ingredients in it are, the desire to punish a person who has done harm, and the belief that there is an individual to whom harm has been done. Now the desire to punish a person who has done harm to any one is a spontaneous outgrowth from two natural and instinctive sentiments— the impulse of self-defence and the feeling of sympathy. Resentment and retaliation are natural—whether instinctive or intelligent: every animal tries to hurt those who have hurt itself or its young. Human beings only differ from animals in two respects. First, they can sympathise with all human, and even with all sentient, beings. Secondly, their more developed intelligence gives a wider range to all their sentiments. A human being can thus resent and resist conduct which threatens the society of which he forms a part. The sentiment of justice, so far as the desire to punish is concerned, is thus the natural feeling of retaliation applied to injuries which affect us only through or with society. This sentiment, in itself, has nothing moral in it; what is moral is the exclusive subordination of it to the social sympathies. It is no objection to this doctrine that, when we feel the sentiment of justice outraged, we think only of the individual case. It is common, though not commendable, to feel resentment only because we have suffered pain; but moral resentment is the conscious assertion of a beneficial rule. A man who does not feel this is not consciously just. This is admitted by anti-utilitarian moralists, such as Kant. Thus, the idea of justice supposes a rule of conduct and a sentiment which sanctions the rule. The rule must be common to mankind and intended for their good. The sentiment is a desire that punishment may be suffered by those who infringe the rule. There is involved also the idea of a definite person who suffers by the infringement. The sentiment of justice is the animal desire to retaliate, widened by enlarged sympathy and intelligent self-interest to include all persons. From the latter elements, the feeling derives its morality; from the former, its peculiar impressiveness, and energy of self-assertion. The two elements of a hurt to an individual and a demand for punishment include all that we mean when we speak of violation of a right. To have a right is to have something which society ought to defend one in the possession of; and it ought to do so simply on grounds of general utility. The apparent inadequacy of this ground is due to the animal thirst for retaliation, which forms an element in the sentiment of justice, and which derives its intensity and its justification from the importance of the utility involved—the interest of security. This most indispensable of all necessaries, after physical nutriment, cannot be had, unless the machinery for providing it is kept unintermittedly in active play. Hence, the feelings which are associated with this notion are more intense than in the case of any other utility. The claim for security comes to appear absolute, incommensurable with other considerations, right and not merely expedient. It becomes a moral necessity.

We are often told that Utility is an uncertain standard, while Justice is self-evident and stable; but there is as much discussion about what is just as about what is useful to society. Nations and individuals differ about it; and every one's idea of it is made up of various, and sometimes conflicting, elements. Some think punishment is just for the sake of the person punished, others that it is only just to prevent evil to others. Mr Owen thinks it unjust to punish at all. None of these opinions can be refuted, on the question of justice; and various expedients have been devised, in order to escape from the consequences of each of them. Again, as to the amount of punishment, the simple *lex talionis* really satisfies the primitive sentiment of justice better than any other penal rule; and by mere reflection on the sentiment no well-grounded rule can be framed. In the same way, in an industrial association, should talent or skill give a title to superior remuneration? The idea of justice seems to lead to conflicting answers; and social utility is the only ground for a decision between them. In the matter of taxation, again, the idea of justice leads to confusions, from which there is no escape except in utilitarianism.

Yet, apart from the pretensions of any theory which sets up an imaginary standard of justice not grounded on utility, the justice which is grounded on utility is the chief part, and incomparably the most sacred and binding part, of all morality. It concerns the essentials of human wellbeing more nearly, and is more binding, than any other rule. The notion of a right residing in an individual, which is of the essence of justice, testifies to this more binding obligation. The moral rules which forbid mankind to hurt one another, or interfere with one another's freedom, are more vital to human wellbeing than any special maxims of expediency, and they are the main elements in determining the social feelings of mankind. It is their observance which alone preserves peace among human beings; and they are the precepts which mankind have the strongest and the most direct inducements for impressing upon one another. Observance of these is the test of fitness for the fellowship of human beings; and these primarily compose the obligations of justice.

The same motives which command these primary moralities enjoin the punishment of their violation; and thus retribution is associated with the sentiment, and included in the idea, of justice. Good for good is also one of the dictates of justice; and this also is really connected with abstinence from injury, since disappointment of a natural expectation is an injury of a real kind. The principle of giving to each what he deserves is included in the idea of justice, as we have defined it, and is a proper object of that intensity of sentiment which places the Just, in human estimation, above the simply Expedient.

Most of the current maxims of justice give effect to the principles now spoken of, and prevent them from being perverted. Impartiality has this significance; but it also rests on a still deeper foundation. It is involved in the very meaning of utility, or the greatest-happiness principle, which implies that all have an equal claim to all the means of happiness. Like other maxims, this is limited by ideas of social expediency; but whenever it is deemed applicable, it is held to be the dictate of justice; and the range of its application grows steadily wider.

Justice is thus a name for certain moral requirements, which, regarded collectively, stand higher in the scale of utility, and are therefore of more paramount obligation than any others. But particular cases may occur in which some other social duty is so important as to overrule any one of the general maxims of justice. These are usually explained by saying, not that the obligation of justice is overruled, but that justice has a different significance.

The considerations now adduced resolve the only real difficulty in the utilitarian theory of morals. If the sentiment of justice has been sufficiently accounted for on utilitarian principles, the idea of justice is no longer a difficulty. Justice remains the appropriate name for certain important and imperative social utilities, guarded by a sentiment which is distinguished by the definiteness of its commands, and by the stern character of its sanctions.

FROM THE ETHICAL WRITINGS OF
JOHN STUART MILL

I. ON THE LOGIC OF THE MORAL SCIENCES

(SYSTEM OF LOGIC, BOOK VI)

CHAPTER I

INTRODUCTORY REMARKS

§ 1. PRINCIPLES of Evidence and Theories of Method are not to be constructed *à priori*. The laws of our rational faculty, like those of every other natural agency, are only learnt by seeing the agent at work. The earlier achievements of science were made without the conscious observance of any Scientific Method; and we should never have known by what process truth is to be ascertained if we had not previously ascertained many truths. But it was only the easier problems which could be thus resolved : natural sagacity, when it tried its strength against the more difficult ones, either failed altogether, or if it succeeded here and there in obtaining a solution, had no sure means of convincing others that its solution was correct. In scientific investigation, as in all other works of human skill, the way of obtaining the end is seen as it were instinctively by superior minds in some comparatively simple case, and is then, by judicious generalisation, adapted to the variety of complex cases. We learn to do a thing in difficult circumstances by attending to the manner in which we have spontaneously done the same thing in easier ones.

This truth is exemplified by the history of the various branches of knowledge which have successively, in the ascending order of their complication, assumed the character of sciences; and will doubtless receive fresh confirmation from those of which the final scientific constitution is yet to come, and which are still abandoned to the uncertainties of vague and popular discussion. Although several other sciences have emerged from this state at a comparatively recent date, none now remain in it except those which relate to man himself, the most complex and most difficult subject of study on which the human mind can be engaged.

Concerning the physical nature of man as an organised being,— though there is still much uncertainty and much controversy, which can only be terminated by the general acknowledgment and employment of stricter rules of induction than are commonly recognised,—there is, however, a considerable body of truths which all who have attended to the subject consider to be fully established; nor is there now any radical imperfection in the method observed in this department of science by its most distinguished modern teachers. But the laws of Mind, and, in even a greater degree, those of Society, are so far from having attained a similar state of even partial recognition, that it is still a controversy whether they are capable of becoming subjects of science in the strict sense of the term; and among those who are agreed on this point there reigns the most irreconcilable diversity on almost every other. Here, therefore, if anywhere, the principles laid down in the preceding Books may be expected to be useful.

If, on matters so much the most important with which human intellect can occupy itself, a more general agreement is ever to exist among thinkers; if what has been pronounced "the proper study of mankind" is not destined to remain the only subject which Philosophy cannot succeed in rescuing from Empiricism; the same process through which the laws of many simpler phenomena have by general acknowledgment been placed beyond dispute must be consciously and deliberately applied to those more difficult inquiries. If there are some subjects on which the results obtained have finally received the unanimous assent of all who have attended to the proof, and others on which mankind have not yet been equally successful; on which the most sagacious minds have occupied themselves from the earliest date, and have never succeeded in establishing any considerable body of truths, so as to be beyond denial or doubt; it is by generalising the methods successfully followed in the former inquiries, and adapting them to the latter, that we may hope to remove this blot on the face of science.[1] The remaining chapters are an endeavour to facilitate this most desirable object.

§ 2. In attempting this, I am not unmindful how little can be done towards it in a mere treatise on Logic, or how vague and unsatisfactory all precepts of Method must necessarily appear when not practically exemplified in the establishment of a body of doctrine. Doubtless, the most effectual mode of showing how the sciences of Ethics and Politics may be constructed would be to construct them: a task which, it needs scarcely be said, I am not about to undertake. But even if there were no other examples, the memorable one of Bacon would be sufficient to demonstrate that it is sometimes both possible and useful to point out the way, though without being oneself prepared to adventure far into it. And if more were to be attempted, this at least is not a proper place for the attempt.

In substance, whatever can be done in a work like this for the Logic of the Moral Sciences, has been or ought to have been accomplished in the five preceding Books; to which the present can be only a kind of

---

[1] Compare with this Mill's statement in his Essay on De Tocqueville's 'Democracy in America,' 'Dissertations and Discussions,' vol. ii. p. 4: "The value of his work is less in the conclusions, than in the mode of arriving at them. He has applied to the greatest question in the art and science of government, those principles and methods of philosophising to which mankind are indebted for all the advances made by modern times in the other branches of the study of nature."

supplement or appendix, since the methods of investigation applicable to moral and social science must have been already described, if I have succeeded in enumerating and characterising those of science in general. It remains, however, to examine which of those methods are more especially suited to the various branches of moral inquiry; under what peculiar faculties or difficulties they are there employed; how far the unsatisfactory state of those inquiries is owing to a wrong choice of methods, how far to want of skill in the application of right ones; and what degree of ultimate success may be attained or hoped for by a better choice and more careful employment of logical processes appropriate to the case. In other words, whether moral sciences exist or can exist; to what degree of perfection they are susceptible of being carried; and by what selection or adaptation of the methods brought to view in the previous part of this work that degree of perfection is attainable.

At the threshold of this inquiry we are met by an objection which, if not removed, would be fatal to the attempt to treat human conduct as a subject of science. Are the actions of human beings, like all other natural events, subject to invariable laws? Does that constancy of causation, which is the foundation of every scientific theory of successive phenomena, really obtain among them?[1] This is often denied; and for the sake

---

[1] Mill's interest in this question connects itself with his view of the nature and presuppositions of Induction. Cf. 'System of Logic,' p. 208: "The problem of Inductive Logic may be summed

of systematic completeness, if not from any very urgent practical necessity, the question should receive a deliberate answer in this place. We shall devote to the subject a chapter apart.

up in two questions: How to ascertain the laws of nature; and how, after having ascertained them, to follow them into their results."

'System of Logic,' p. 247: "To ascertain, therefore, what are the laws of causation which exist in nature, to determine the effect of every cause, and the causes of all effects, is the main business of Induction; and to point out how this is done is the chief object of Inductive Logic."

'Unsettled Questions of Political Economy,' p. 149: "These causes (in politics) are laws of human nature and external circumstances capable of exciting the human will to action. The desires of man, and the nature of the conduct to which they prompt him, are within the reach of our observation."

Vide also Appendix A.

CHAPTER II

OF LIBERTY AND NECESSITY

§ 1. The question whether the law of causality applies in the same strict sense to human actions as to other phenomena, is the celebrated controversy concerning the freedom of the will, which, from at least as far back as the time of Pelagius, has divided both the philosophical and the religious world. The affirmative opinion is commonly called the doctrine of Necessity, as asserting human volitions and actions to be necessary and inevitable. The negative maintains that the will is not determined, like other phenomena, by antecedents, but determines itself; that our volitions are not, properly speaking, the effects of causes, or at least have no causes which they uniformly and implicitly obey.

I have already made it sufficiently apparent that the former of these opinions is that which I consider the true one; but the misleading terms in which it is often expressed, and the indistinct manner in which it is usually apprehended, have both obstructed its reception, and perverted its influence when received. The metaphysical theory of free-will, as held by philosophers (for the practical feeling of it, common in a greater or less degree to all mankind, is in no way inconsistent with the contrary theory), was invented because the supposed alternative of admitting human actions to be *necessary* was deemed inconsistent with every one's instinctive consciousness, as well as humiliating to the pride, and even degrading to the moral nature, of man. Nor do I deny that the doctrine, as sometimes held, is open to these imputations; for the misapprehension in which I shall be able to show that they originate, unfortunately, is not confined to the opponents of the doctrine, but is participated in by many, perhaps we might say by most, of its supporters.

§ 2. Correctly conceived, the doctrine called Philosophical Necessity is simply this: that, given the motives which are present to an individual's mind, and given likewise the character and disposition of the individual, the manner in which he will act might be unerringly inferred; that if we knew the person thoroughly, and knew all the inducements which are acting upon him, we could foretell his conduct with as much certainty as we can predict any physical event.[1] This proposition I take to be a mere interpretation of universal

---

[1] 'Examination of Hamilton,' p. 576: "Now the so-called Necessitarians demand the application of the same rule of judgment (cause and effect) to our volitions. They maintain that there is the same evidence for it. They affirm, as a truth of experience, that volitions do, in point of fact, follow determinate moral antecedents with the same uniformity, and (when we have

experience, a statement in words of what every one is internally convinced of. No one who believed that he knew thoroughly the circumstances of any case, and the characters of the different persons concerned, would hesitate to foretell how all of them would act. Whatever degree of doubt he may in fact feel arises from the uncertainty whether he really knows the circumstances or the character of some one or other of the persons with the degree of accuracy required; but by no means from thinking that if he did know these things, there could be any uncertainty what the conduct would be. Nor does this full assurance conflict in the smallest degree with what is called our feeling of freedom. We do not feel ourselves the less free because those to whom we are intimately known are well assured how we shall will to act in a particular case. We often, on the contrary, regard the doubt what our conduct will be as a mark of ignorance of our character, and sometimes even resent it as an imputation. The religious metaphysicians who have asserted the freedom of the will have always maintained it to be consistent with divine foreknowledge of our actions; and if with divine,

sufficient knowledge of the circumstances) with the same certainty, as physical effects follow their physical causes."

Ib., p. 578: "A volition is a moral effect which follows the corresponding moral causes as certainly and invariably as physical effects follow their physical causes."

Ib., p. 603: "If necessity means more than this abstract possibility of being foreseen; if it means any mysterious compulsion, apart from simple invariability of sequence, I deny it as strenuously as any one in the case of human volitions, but I deny it just as much of all other phenomena."

then with any other foreknowledge. We may be free, and yet another may have reason to be perfectly certain what use we shall make of our freedom. It is not, therefore, the doctrine that our volitions and actions are invariable consequents of our antecedent states of mind that is either contradicted by our consciousness or felt to be degrading.

But the doctrine of causation, when considered as obtaining between our volitions and their antecedents, is almost universally conceived as involving more than this. Many do not believe, and very few practically feel, that there is nothing in causation but invariable, certain, and unconditional sequence. There are few to whom mere constancy of succession appears a sufficiently stringent bond of union for so peculiar a relation as that of Cause and Effect. Even if the reason repudiates, the imagination retains the feeling of some more intimate connection, of some peculiar tie or mysterious constraint exercised by the antecedent over the consequent. Now this it is which, considered as applying to the human will, conflicts with our consciousness and revolts our feelings. We are certain that, in the case of our volitions, there is not this mysterious constraint. We know that we are not compelled, as by a magical spell, to obey any particular motive. We feel that if we wished to prove that we have the power of resisting the motive, we could do so (that wish being, it needs scarcely be observed, a *new antecedent*); and it would be humiliating to our pride, and (what is of more importance) paralysing to our desire of excellence, if we thought otherwise. But neither is any such mysterious compulsion now supposed, by the best philosophical authorities, to be exercised by any other cause over its effect. Those who think that causes draw their effects after them by a mystical tie are right in believing that the relation between volitions and their antecedents is of another nature. But they should go further, and admit that this is also true of all other effects and their antecedents. If such a tie is considered to be involved in the word Necessity, the doctrine is not true of human actions; but neither is it then true of inanimate objects. It would be more correct to say that matter is not bound by necessity than that mind is so.[1]

That the free-will metaphysicians, being mostly of the school which rejects Hume's and Brown's analysis of Cause and Effect, should miss their way for want of the light which that analysis affords, cannot surprise us. The wonder is that the Necessitarians, who usually admit that philosophical theory, should in practice equally lose sight of it. The very same misconception of the doctrine called Philosophical Necessity which prevents the opposite party from recognising its truth, I believe to exist more or less obscurely in the minds of most Necessitarians, however they may in words disavow it. I am much mistaken if they habitually feel that the necessity which they recognise in actions is but uniformity of order, and capability of being predicted. They have a feeling as if there were at

[1] *Vide* Appendix A.

bottom a stronger tie between the volitions and their causes: as if, when they asserted that the will is governed by the balance of motives, they meant something more cogent than if they had only said that whoever knew the motives, and our habitual susceptibilities to them, could predict how we should will to act. They commit, in opposition to their own scientific system, the very same mistake which their adversaries commit in obedience to theirs; and in consequence do really in some instances suffer those depressing consequences which their opponents erroneously impute to the doctrine itself.

§ 3. I am inclined to think that this error is almost wholly an effect of the associations with a word, and that it would be prevented by forbearing to employ, for the expression of the simple fact of causation, so extremely inappropriate a term as Necessity. That word, in its other acceptations, involves much more than mere uniformity of sequence: it implies irresistibleness. Applied to the will, it only means that the given cause will be followed by the effect, subject to all possibilities of counteraction by other causes; but in common use it stands for the operation of those causes exclusively, which are supposed too powerful to be counteracted at all. When we say that all human actions take place of necessity, we only mean that they will certainly happen if nothing prevents: when we say that dying of want, to those who cannot get food, is a necessity, we mean that it will certainly happen, whatever may be done to prevent it. The application of the same term to the agencies on which human actions depend as is used to express those agencies of nature which are really uncontrollable, cannot fail, when habitual, to create a feeling of uncontrollableness in the former also. This, however, is a mere illusion. There are physical sequences which we call necessary, as death for want of food or air; there are others which, though as much cases of causation as the former, are not said to be necessary, as death from poison, which an antidote, or the use of the stomach-pump, will sometimes avert. It is apt to be forgotten by people's feelings, even if remembered by their understandings, that human actions are in this last predicament: they are never (except in some cases of mania) ruled by any one motive with such absolute sway that there is no room for the influence of any other. The causes, therefore, on which action depends are never uncontrollable, and any given effect is only necessary provided that the causes tending to produce it are not controlled. That whatever happens could not have happened otherwise unless something had taken place which was capable of preventing it, no one surely needs hesitate to admit. But to call this by the name necessity is to use the term in a sense so different from its primitive and familiar meaning, from that which it bears in the common occasions of life, as to amount almost to a play upon words. The associations derived from the ordinary sense of the term will adhere to it in spite of all we can do; and though the doctrine of Necessity, as stated by most who hold it, is very remote from fatalism, it is probable that most Necessitarians are Fatalists, more or less, in their feelings.

A Fatalist believes, or half believes (for nobody is a consistent Fatalist), not only that whatever is about to happen will be the infallible result of the causes which produce it (which is the true Necessitarian doctrine), but, moreover, that there is no use in struggling against it; that it will happen however we may strive to prevent it. Now, a Necessitarian, believing that our actions follow from our characters, and that our characters follow from our organisation, our education, and our circumstances, is apt to be, with more or less of consciousness on his part, a Fatalist as to his own actions, and to believe that his nature is such, or that his education and circumstances have so moulded his character, that nothing can now prevent him from feeling and acting in a particular way, or at least that no effort of his own can hinder it. In the words of the sect which in our own day has most perseveringly inculcated and most perversely misunderstood this great doctrine, his character is formed *for* him, and not *by* him; therefore his wishing that it had been formed differently is of no use,— he has no power to alter it. But this is a grand error. He has, to a certain extent, a power to alter his character. Its being, in the ultimate resort, formed for him, is not inconsistent with its being, in part, formed *by* him as one of the intermediate agents. His character is formed by his circumstances (including among these his particular organisation), but his own desire to mould it in a particular way is one of those circumstances, and by no means one of the least influential. We cannot, indeed, directly will to be different from what we are; but neither did those who are supposed to have formed our characters directly will that we should be what we are. Their will had no direct power except over their own actions. They made us what they did make us by willing, not the end, but the requisite means; and we, when our habits are not too inveterate, can, by similarly willing the requisite means, make ourselves different. If they could place us under the influence of certain circumstances, we in like manner can place ourselves under the influence of other circumstances. We are exactly as capable of making our own character, *if we will*, as others are of making it for us.[1]

[1] 'Examination of Hamilton,' p. 377: "I can indeed influence my own volitions, but only as other people can influence my volitions, by the employment of appropriate means. Direct power over my volitions I am conscious of none."

Ib., p. 601: "The true doctrine of the Causation of human actions maintains, in opposition to both, that not only our conduct but our character is in part amenable to our will; that we can, by employing the proper means, improve our character; and that if our character is such that while it remains what it is it necessitates us to do wrong, it will be just to apply motives which will necessitate us to strive for its improvement, and so emancipate ourselves from the other necessity."

'Essays on Religion,' p. 17: "Every alteration of circumstances alters more or less the laws of nature under which we

Yes (answers the Owenite), but these words, "if we will," surrender the whole point, since the will to alter our own character is given us, not by any efforts of ours, but by circumstances which we cannot help: it comes to us either from external causes or not at all. Most true: if the Owenite stops here, he is in a position from which nothing can expel him. Our character is formed by us as well as for us: but the wish which induces us to attempt to form it is formed for us; and how? Not, in general, by our organisation, nor wholly by our education, but by our experience — experience of the painful consequences of the character we previously had, or by some strong feeling of admiration or aspiration accidentally aroused.[1] But to think that we have

act; and by every choice which we make, either of ends or of means, we place ourselves to a greater or less extent under one set of laws of nature instead of another."

Cf., however, 'Liberty,' p. 34: "The human faculties of perception, judgment, discriminative feeling, mental activity, and even moral preference, are exercised only in making a choice. . . . The mental and moral, like the muscular, powers are improved only by being used."

[1] This account of the relation of character to circumstances connects itself with Mill's theory of the development of knowledge, 'System of Logic,' p. 425: "It is not a law of our intellect that, in comparing things with each other and taking note of their agreement, we merely recognise as realised in the outward world something that we already had in our minds. The conception originally found its way to us as the result of such a comparison."

Ib., p. 427: "The conceptions, then, which we employ for the colligation and methodisation of facts do not develop themselves from within, but are impressed upon the mind from without; they are never obtained otherwise than by way of comparison and abstraction, and in the most important and the most numerous cases are evolved by abstraction from the very phenomena which it is their office to colligate."

Ib., p. 428: "The conception is

ON THE LOGIC OF THE MORAL SCIENCES 19

no power of altering our character, and to think that we shall not use our power unless we desire to use it, are very different things, and have a very different effect on the mind.[1] A person who does not wish

not furnished *by* the mind until it has been furnished *to* the mind; and the facts which supply it are sometimes extraneous facts, but more often the very facts which we are attempting to arrange by it."

Cf. also 'System of Logic,' p. 157: "I cannot but wonder that so much stress should be laid upon the circumstance of inconceivableness, when there is such ample experience to show that our capacity or incapacity of conceiving a thing has very little to do with the possibility of the thing in itself; but is in truth very much an affair of accident, and depends upon the past history and habits of our own minds."

Ib.: "When we have often seen and thought of two things together, and have never in any one instance either seen or thought of them separately, there is by the primary law of association an increasing difficulty, which may in the end become insuperable, of conceiving the two things apart."

Cf. 'Examination of Hamilton,' pp. 181 ff. and 328.

Cf. 'Essays on Religion,' p. 7: "In the sense of the word Nature which has just been defined, and which is the true scientific sense, Art is as much Nature as anything else; and everything which is artificial is natural—Art has no independent power of its own: Art is but the employment of the powers of Nature for an end. Phenomena produced by human agency, no less than those which as far as we are concerned are spontaneous, depend on the properties of the elementary forces, or of the elementary substances and their compounds."

Ib., p. 8: "Even the volition which designs, the intelligence which contrives, and the muscular force which executes these movements, are themselves powers of nature."

Ib., p. 16: "To bid people conform to the laws of nature when they have no power but what the laws of nature give them—when it is a physical impossibility for them to do the smallest thing otherwise than through some law of nature—is an absurdity."

Ib., p. 64: "In the first of these senses ('the entire system of things') the doctrine that man ought to follow nature is unmeaning, since man has no power to do anything else than follow nature; all his actions are done through, and in obedience to, some one or many of nature's physical or mental laws."

[1] Cf. 'Examination of Hamilton,' p. 582: "I ask my con-

to alter his character cannot be the person who is supposed to feel discouraged or paralysed by thinking himself unable to do it. The depressing effect of the Fatalist doctrine can only be felt where there *is* a wish to do what that doctrine represents as impossible. It is of no consequence what we think forms our character, when we have no desire of our own about forming it; but it is of great consequence that we should not be prevented from forming such a desire by thinking the attainment impracticable, and that if we have the desire we should know that the work is not so irrevocably done as to be incapable of being altered.

And, indeed, if we examine closely, we shall find that this feeling of our being able to modify our own character *if we wish*, is itself the feeling of moral freedom which we are conscious of. A person feels morally free who feels that his habits or his temptations are not his masters, but he theirs: who even in yielding to them knows that he could resist; that were he desirous of altogether throwing them off, there would not be required for that purpose a stronger

sciousness what I do feel, and I find, indeed, that I feel (or am convinced) that I could, and even should, have chosen the other course if I had preferred it— that is, if I had liked it better —but not that I could have chosen one course while I preferred the other."

Ib., p. 585: "The difference between a bad and a good man is not that the latter acts in opposition to his strongest desires; it is that his desire to do right, and his aversion to doing wrong, are strong enough to overcome, and in the case of perfect virtue to silence, any other desire or aversion which may conflict with them."

Cf. also Appendix C.

desire than he knows himself to be capable of feeling. It is of course necessary, to render our consciousness of freedom complete, that we should have succeeded in making our character all we have hitherto attempted to make it; for if we have wished and not attained, we have, to that extent, not power over our own character —we are not free.[1] Or at least, we must feel that our wish, if not strong enough to alter our character, is strong enough to conquer our character when the two are brought into conflict in any particular case of conduct. And hence it is said with truth, that none but a person of confirmed virtue is completely free.

The application of so improper a term as Necessity to the doctrine of cause and effect in the matter of human character seems to me one of the most signal instances in philosophy of the abuse of terms, and its practical consequences one of the most striking examples of the power of language over our associations. The subject will never be generally understood until that

---

[1] 'Examination of Hamilton,' p. 580: "We never know that we are able to do a thing, except from having done it, or something equal and similar to it. We should not know that we were capable of action at all, if we had never acted. Having acted, we know as far as that experience reaches, how we are able to act; and this knowledge, when it has become familiar, is often confounded with, and called by the name of, consciousness. But it does not derive any increase of authority from being misnamed; its truth is not supreme over, but depends on, experience. If our so-called consciousness of what we are able to do is not borne out by experience, it is a delusion. It has no title to credence but as an interpretation of experience, and if it is a false interpretation, it must give way."

objectionable term is dropped. The free-will doctrine, by keeping in view precisely that portion of the truth which the word Necessity puts out of sight, namely, the power of the mind to co-operate in the formation of its own character, has given to its adherents a practical feeling much nearer to the truth than has generally (I believe) existed in the minds of Necessitarians. The latter may have had a stronger sense of the importance of what human beings can do to shape the characters of one another; but the free-will doctrine has, I believe, fostered in its supporters a much stronger spirit of self-culture.[1]

---

[1] Mill gives an account of facts in his personal history, which underlie these conclusions, 'Autobiography,' p. 169: "I pondered painfully on the subject till gradually I saw light through it. I perceived that the word Necessity, as a name for the doctrine of Cause and Effect applied to human action, carried with it a misleading association; and that this association was the operative force in the depressing and paralysing influence which I had experienced. I saw that though our character is formed by circumstances, our own desires can do much to shape these circumstances; and that what is really inspiriting and ennobling in the doctrine of free will, is the conviction that we have real power over the formation of our own character, that our will, by influencing some of our circumstances, can modify our future habits or capabilities of willing. All this was entirely consistent with the doctrine of circumstances, or rather, was that doctrine itself, properly understood. From that time I drew, in my own mind, a clear distinction between the doctrine of circumstances, and Fatalism, discarding altogether the misleading word Necessity. The theory, which I now for the first time rightly apprehended, ceased altogether to be discouraging, and besides the relief to my spirits, I no longer suffered under the burden, so heavy to one who aims at being a reformer in opinions, of thinking one doctrine true, and the contrary doctrine morally beneficial."

Cf. 'Examination of Hamilton,' p. 595: "I am entitled to postulate the reality, and the knowledge and feeling, of moral distinc-

§ 4. There is still one fact which requires to be noticed (in addition to the existence of a power of self-formation) before the doctrine of the causation of human actions can be freed from the confusion and misapprehensions which surround it in many minds. When the will is said to be determined by motives, a motive does not mean always, or solely, the anticipation of a pleasure or of a pain.[1] I shall not here inquire whether it be true that, in the commencement, all our voluntary actions are mere means consciously employed to obtain some pleasure or avoid some pain. It is at least certain that we gradually, through the influence of association, come to desire the means without thinking of the end: the action itself becomes an object of desire, and is performed without reference to any motive beyond itself. Thus far, it may still be objected, that the action having through association become pleasurable, we are, as much as before, moved to act by the anticipation of a pleasure, namely, the pleasure of the action itself. But granting this, the matter does not end here. As we proceed in the formation of habits, and become accustomed to will

---

tions. These, it is both evident metaphysically and notorious historically, are independent of any theory concerning the will."

[1] Contrast with this the following statement ('Examination of Hamilton,' p. 605): "Those who say that the will follows the strongest motive, do not mean the motive which is strongest in relation to the will, or, in other words, that the will follows what it does follow. They mean the motive which is strongest in relation to pain and pleasure; since a motive being a desire or aversion, is proportional to the pleasantness, as conceived by us, of the thing desired, or the painfulness of the thing shunned."

a particular act or a particular course of conduct because it is pleasurable, we at last continue to will it without any reference to its being pleasurable. Although, from some change in us or in our circumstances, we have ceased to find any pleasure in the action, or perhaps to anticipate any pleasure as the consequence of it, we still continue to desire the action, and consequently to do it. In this manner it is that habits of hurtful excess continue to be practised although they have ceased to be pleasurable; and in this manner also it is that the habit of willing to persevere in the course which he has chosen does not desert the moral hero, even when the reward, however real, which he doubtless receives from the consciousness of well-doing, is anything but an equivalent for the sufferings he undergoes or the wishes which he may have to renounce.

A habit of willing is commonly called a purpose; and among the causes of our volitions, and of the actions which flow from them, must be reckoned not only likings and aversions, but also purposes. It is only when our purposes have become independent of the feelings of pain or pleasure from which they originally took their rise that we are said to have a confirmed character. "A character," says Novalis, "is a completely fashioned will;" and the will, once so fashioned, may be steady and constant, when the passive susceptibilities of pleasure and pain are greatly weakened or materially changed.

With the corrections and explanations now given,

the doctrine of the causation of our volitions by motives, and of motives by the desirable objects offered to us, combined with our particular susceptibilities of desire, may be considered, I hope, as sufficiently established for the purposes of this treatise.*

* Some arguments and explanations, supplementary to those in the text, will be found in 'An Examination of Sir William Hamilton's Philosophy,' chap. xxvi.

CHAPTER III

THAT THERE IS, OR MAY BE, A SCIENCE OF HUMAN NATURE

§ 1. IT is a common notion, or at least it is implied in many common modes of speech, that the thoughts, feelings, and actions of sentient beings are not a subject of science, in the same strict sense in which this is true of the objects of outward nature. This notion seems to involve some confusion of ideas, which it is necessary to begin by clearing up.

Any facts are fitted, in themselves, to be a subject of science, which follow one another according to constant laws; although those laws may not have been discovered, nor even be discoverable by our existing resources. Take, for instance, the most familiar class of meteorological phenomena, those of rain and sunshine. Scientific inquiry has not yet succeeded in ascertaining the order of antecedence and consequence among these phenomena, so as to be able, at least in our regions of the earth, to predict them with certainty, or even with any high degree of probability. Yet no one doubts that the phenomena depend on laws, and that these must be derivative laws resulting from known ultimate laws—those of heat, electricity, vaporisation, and elastic fluids. Nor can it be doubted that if we were acquainted with all the antecedent circumstances, we could, even from those more general laws, predict (saving difficulties of calculation) the state of the weather at any future time. Meteorology, therefore, not only has in itself every natural requisite for being, but actually is, a science; though, from the difficulty of observing the facts on which the phenomena depend (a difficulty inherent in the peculiar nature of those phenomena), the science is extremely imperfect; and were it perfect, might probably be of little avail in practice, since the data requisite for applying its principles to particular instances would rarely be procurable.

A case may be conceived of an intermediate character between the perfection of science and this its extreme imperfection. It may happen that the greater causes, those on which the principal part of the phenomena depends, are within the reach of observation and measurement; so that if no other causes intervened, a complete explanation could be given not only of the phenomenon in general, but of all the variations and modifications which it admits of. But inasmuch as other, perhaps many other, causes, separately insignificant in their effects, co-operate or conflict in many or in all cases with those greater causes, the effect, accordingly, presents more or less of aberration from what would be produced by the greater causes alone. Now if these minor causes are not so constantly accessible, or not accessible at all to accurate observation, the principal mass of the effect may still, as before, be accounted for, and even predicted; but there will be variations and modifications which we shall not be competent to explain thoroughly, and our predictions will not be fulfilled accurately, but only approximately.

It is thus, for example, with the theory of the tides. No one doubts that Tidology (as Dr Whewell proposes to call it) is really a science. As much of the phenomena as depends on the attraction of the sun and moon is completely understood, and may in any, even unknown, part of the earth's surface be foretold with certainty; and the far greater part of the phenomena depends on those causes. But circumstances of a local or casual nature, such as the configuration of the bottom of the ocean, the degree of confinement from shores, the direction of the wind, &c., influence in many or in all places the height and time of the tide; and a portion of these circumstances being either not accurately knowable, not precisely measurable, or not capable of being certainly foreseen, the tide in known places commonly varies from the calculated result of general principles by some difference that we cannot explain, and in unknown ones may vary from it by a difference that we are not able to foresee or conjecture. Nevertheless, not only is it certain that these variations depend on causes, and follow their causes by laws of unerring uniformity; not only, therefore, is tidology a science, like meteorology, but it is what, hitherto at least, meteorology is not, a science largely available in practice. General laws may be laid down respecting the tides; predictions may be founded on those laws, and the result will in the main, though often not with complete accuracy, correspond to the predictions.

And this is what is, or ought to be, meant by those who speak of sciences which are not *exact* sciences. Astronomy was once a science, without being an exact science. It could not become exact until not only the general course of the planetary motions, but the perturbations also, were accounted for, and referred to their causes. It has become an exact science, because its phenomena have been brought under laws comprehending the whole of the causes by which the phenomena are influenced, whether in a great or only in a trifling degree, whether in all or only in some cases, and assigning to each of those causes the share of effect which really belongs to it. But in the theory of the tides, the only laws as yet accurately ascertained are those of the causes which affect the phenomenon in all cases, and in a considerable degree; while others which affect it in some cases only, or, if in all, only in a slight degree, have not been sufficiently ascertained and studied to enable us to lay down their laws, still less to deduce the completed law of the phenomenon, by compounding the effects of the greater with those of the minor causes. Tidology, therefore, is not yet an exact science; not from any inherent incapacity of being so, but from the difficulty of ascertaining with complete precision the real derivative uniformities. By combining, however, the exact laws of the greater causes, and of such of the minor ones as are sufficiently known, with such empirical laws or such approximate generalisations respecting the miscellaneous variations as can be obtained by specific observation, we can lay down general propositions which will be true in the main, and on which, with allowance for the degree of their probable inaccuracy, we may safely ground our expectations and our conduct.

§ 2. The science of human nature is of this description. It falls far short of the standard of exactness now realised in Astronomy; but there is no reason that it should not be as much a science as Tidology is, or as Astronomy was when its calculations had only mastered the main phenomena, but not the perturbations.

The phenomena with which this science is conversant being the thoughts, feelings, and actions of human beings, it would have attained the ideal perfection of a science if it enabled us to foretell how an individual would think, feel, or act throughout life, with the same certainty with which astronomy enables us to predict the places and the occultations of the heavenly bodies. It needs scarcely be stated that nothing approaching to this can be done. The actions of individuals could not be predicted with scientific accuracy, were it only because we cannot foresee the whole of the circumstances in which those individuals will be placed. But further, even in any given combination of (present) circumstances, no assertion, which is both precise and universally true, can be made respecting the manner in which human beings will think, feel, or act. This is not, however, because every person's modes of thinking, feeling, and acting do not depend on causes; nor can we doubt that if, in the case of any individual, our data could be complete, we even now know enough of the ultimate laws by which mental phenomena are determined to enable us in many cases to predict, with tolerable certainty, what, in the greater number of supposable combinations of circumstances, his conduct or sentiments would be. But the impressions and actions of human beings are not solely the result of their present circumstances, but the joint result of those circumstances and of the characters of the individuals; and the agencies which determine human character are so numerous and diversified (nothing which has happened to the person throughout life being without its portion of influence), that in the aggregate they are never in any two cases exactly similar. Hence, even if our science of human nature were theoretically perfect, that is, if we could calculate any character as we can calculate the orbit of any planet, *from given data;* still, as the data are never all given, nor ever precisely alike in different cases, we could neither make positive predictions nor lay down universal propositions.

Inasmuch, however, as many of those effects which it is of most importance to render amenable to human foresight and control are determined, like the tides, in an incomparably greater degree by general causes, than by all partial causes taken together; depending in the main on those circumstances and qualities which are common to all mankind, or at least to large bodies of them, and only on a small degree on the idiosyncrasies of organisation or the peculiar history of individuals; it is evidently possible, with regard to all such effects, to make predictions which will *almost* always be verified, and general propositions which are almost always true. And whenever it is sufficient to know how the great majority of the human race, or of some nation or class of persons, will think, feel, and act, these propositions are equivalent to universal ones. For the purposes of political and social science this *is* sufficient. As we formerly remarked, an approximate generalisation is, in social inquiries, for most practical purposes equivalent to an exact one; that which is only probable when asserted of individual human beings indiscriminately selected, being certain when affirmed of the character and collective conduct of masses.[1]

---

[1] 'System of Logic,' p. 394: "There is a case in which approximate propositions, even without our taking note of the conditions under which they are not true of individual cases, are yet, for the purposes of science, universal ones — namely, in the inquiries which relate to the properties not of individuals, but of multitudes. The principal of these is the science of politics, or of human society. This science is principally concerned with the actions not of solitary individuals, but of masses; with the fortunes not of single persons, but of communities. For the statesman, therefore, it is generally enough to know that *most* persons act or are acted upon in a particular way, since his speculations and his practical arrangements refer almost exclusively to cases in which the whole community, or some large portion of it, is acted upon at once, and in which, therefore, what is done or felt by *most* persons determines the result produced by or upon the body at large. He can get on well enough with approximate generalisations on human nature, since what is true approximately of all individuals is true absolutely of all masses. And even when the

It is no disparagement, therefore, to the science of Human Nature that those of its general propositions which descend sufficiently into detail to serve as a foundation for predicting phenomena in the concrete are for the most part only approximately true. But in order to give a genuinely scientific character to the study, it is indispensable that these approximate generalisations, which in themselves would amount only to the lowest kind of empirical laws, should be connected deductively with the laws of nature from which they result—should be resolved into the properties of the causes on which the phenomena depend. In other words, the science of Human Nature may be said to exist in proportion as the approximate truths which compose a practical knowledge of mankind can be exhibited as corollaries from the universal laws of human nature on which they rest, whereby the proper limits of those approximate truths would be shown, and we should be enabled to deduce others for any new state of circumstances, in anticipation of specific experience.

The proposition now stated is the text on which the two succeeding chapters will furnish the comment.

operations of individual men have a part to play in his deductions, as when he is reasoning of kings, or other single rulers, still, as he is providing for indefinite duration, involving an indefinite succession of such individuals, he must in general both reason and act as if what is true of most persons were true of all."

Ib., p. 395: "There are reasons enough why the moral sciences must remain inferior to at least the more perfect of the physical: why the laws of their more complicated phenomena cannot be so completely deciphered, nor the phenomena predicted with the same degree of assurance. But though we cannot attain to so many truths, there is no reason that those we can attain should deserve less reliance, or have less of a scientific character."

CHAPTER IV

OF THE LAWS OF MIND

§ 1. WHAT the Mind is, as well as what Matter is, or any other question respecting Things in themselves, as distinguished from their sensible manifestations, it would be foreign to the purposes of this treatise to consider. Here, as throughout our inquiry, we shall keep clear of all speculations respecting the mind's own nature, and shall understand by the laws of mind those of mental phenomena—of the various feelings or states of consciousness of sentient beings.[1] These, according

---

[1] 'System of Logic,' p. 41: "There is something I call Myself, or, by another form of expression, my mind, which I consider as distinct from these sensations, thoughts, &c.; a something which I conceive to be not the thoughts, but the being that has the thoughts, and which I can conceive as existing for ever in a state of quiescence, without any thoughts at all. But what this being is, although it is myself, I have no knowledge other than the series of its states of consciousness. As bodies manifest themselves to me only through the sensations of which I regard them as the causes, so the thinking principle, or mind, in my own nature, makes itself known to me only by the feelings of which it is conscious. I know nothing about myself, save my capacities of feeling or being conscious (including, of course, thinking and willing): and were I to learn anything new concerning my own nature, I cannot with my present faculties conceive this new information to be

to the classification we have uniformly followed, consist of Thoughts, Emotions, Volitions, and Sensations—the last being as truly states of Mind as the three former. It is usual, indeed, to speak of sensations as states of body, not of mind. But this is the common confusion of giving one and the same name to a phenomenon and to the proximate cause or conditions of the phenomenon. The immediate antecedent of a sensation is a state of body, but the sensation itself is a state of mind. If the word mind means anything, it means that which feels. Whatever opinion we hold respecting the fundamental identity or diversity of matter and mind, in any case the distinction between mental and physical facts, between the internal and the external world, will always remain as a matter of classification; and in that classification, sensations, like all other feelings, must be ranked as mental phenomena. The mechanism of their

anything else than that I have some additional capacities, as yet unknown to me, of feeling, thinking, or willing.

"Thus, then, as body is the unsentient cause to which we are naturally prompted to refer a certain portion of our feelings, so mind may be described as the sentient *subject* (in the scholastic sense of the term) of all feelings; that which has or feels them. But of the nature of either body or mind, further than the feelings which the former excites, and which the latter experiences, we do not, according to the best existing doctrine, know anything."

'Examination of Hamilton,' p. 263: "I . . . affirm (being here in entire accordance with Sir W. Hamilton) that whatever be the nature of the real existence we are compelled to acknowledge in Mind, the Mind is only known to itself phenomenally, as the series of its feelings or consciousness. . . . The feelings or consciousness which belong or have belonged to it, and its possibilities of having more, are the only facts there are to be asserted of Self—the only positive attributes, except permanence, which we can ascribe to it."

Cf. also Appendix B.

production, both in the body itself and in what is called outward nature, is all that can with any propriety be classed as physical.

The phenomena of mind, then, are the various feelings of our nature, both those improperly called physical and those peculiarly designated as mental; and by the laws of mind I mean the laws according to which those feelings generate one another.

§ 2. All states of mind are immediately caused either by other states of mind or by states of body. When a state of mind is produced by a state of mind, I call the law concerned in the case a law of Mind. When a state of mind is produced directly by a state of body, the law is a law of Body, and belongs to physical science.

With regard to those states of mind which are called sensations, all are agreed that these have for their immediate antecedents states of body. Every sensation has for its proximate cause some affection of the portion of our frame called the nervous system, whether this affection originate in the action of some external object, or in some pathological condition of the nervous organisation itself. The laws of this portion of our nature—the varieties of our sensations and the physical conditions on which they proximately depend—manifestly belong to the province of Physiology.

Whether the remainder of our mental states are similarly dependent on physical conditions, is one of the *vexatæ questiones* in the science of human nature. It is still disputed whether our thoughts, emotions, and volitions are generated through the intervention of material mechanism; whether we have organs of thought and of emotion in the same sense in which we have organs of sensation. Many eminent physiologists hold the affirmative. These contend that a thought (for example) is as much the result of nervous agency as a sensation; that some particular state of our nervous system, in particular of that central portion of it called the brain, invariably precedes, and is presupposed by, every state of our consciousness. According to this theory, one state of mind is never really produced by another; all are produced by states of body. When one thought seems to call up another by association, it is not really a thought which recalls a thought; the association did not exist between the two thoughts, but between the two states of the brain or nerves which preceded the thoughts: one of those states recalls the other, each being attended, in its passage, by the particular state of consciousness which is consequent on it. On this theory the uniformities of succession among states of mind would be mere derivative uniformities, resulting from the laws of succession of the bodily states which cause them. There would be no original mental laws, no Laws of Mind in the sense in which I use the term, at all; and mental science would be a mere branch, though the highest and most recondite branch, of the science of Physiology. M. Comte, accordingly, claims the scientific cognisance of moral and intellectual phenomena exclusively for physiologists; and not only denies to Psychology, or

Mental Philosophy properly so called, the character of a science, but places it, in the chimerical nature of its objects and pretensions, almost on a par with astrology.

But, after all has been said which can be said, it remains incontestable that there exist uniformities of succession among states of mind, and that these can be ascertained by observation and experiment. Further, that every mental state has a nervous state for its immediate antecedent and proximate cause, though extremely probable, cannot hitherto be said to be proved, in the conclusive manner in which this can be proved of sensations; and even were it certain, yet every one must admit that we are wholly ignorant of the characteristics of these nervous states; we know not, and at present have no means of knowing, in what respect one of them differs from another; and our only mode of studying their successions or co-existences must be by observing the successions and co-existences of the mental states of which they are supposed to be the generators or causes. The successions, therefore, which obtain among mental phenomena do not admit of being deduced from the physiological laws of our nervous organisation; and all real knowledge of them must continue, for a long time at least, if not always, to be sought in the direct study, by observation and experiment, of the mental successions themselves. Since, therefore, the order of our mental phenomena must be studied in those phenomena, and not inferred from the laws of any phenomena more general, there is a distinct and separate Science of Mind.

The relations, indeed, of that science to the science of physiology must never be overlooked or undervalued. It must by no means be forgotten that the laws of mind may be derivative laws resulting from laws of animal life, and that their truth therefore may ultimately depend on physical conditions; and the influence of physiological states or physiological changes in altering or counteracting the mental successions is one of the most important departments of psychological study. But, on the other hand, to reject the resource of psychological analysis, and construct the theory of the mind solely on such data as physiology at present affords, seems to me as great an error in principle, and an even more serious one in practice. Imperfect as is the science of mind, I do not scruple to affirm that it is in a considerably more advanced state than the portion of physiology which corresponds to it; and to discard the former for the latter appears to me an infringement of the true canons of inductive philosophy, which must produce, and which does produce, erroneous conclusions in some very important departments of the science of human nature.[1]

[1] 'Auguste Comte and Positivism,' p. 66: "Without, then, rejecting any aid which study of the brain and nerves can afford to psychology (and it has afforded, and will yet afford, much), we may affirm that M. Comte has done nothing for the constitution of the positive method of mental science. . . . This great mistake (the denial of Psychology) is not a mere hiatus in M. Comte's system, but the parent of serious errors in his attempt to create a Social Science."

Cf., however, Mill's assertion of the physiological character of the mental continuity, 'Examination of Hamilton,' p. 355: "I am myself inclined to agree with Sir W. Hamilton, and to admit his unconscious mental modifica-

§ 3. The subject, then, of Psychology is the uniformities of succession, the laws, whether ultimate or derivative, according to which one mental state succeeds another—is caused by, or at least is caused to follow, another. Of these laws, some are general, others more special. The following are examples of the most general laws.

First, Whenever any state of consciousness has once been excited in us, no matter by what cause, an inferior degree of the same state of consciousness, a state

tions, in the only shape in which I can attach any very distinct meaning to them — namely, unconscious modifications of the nerves. . . . It may well be believed that the apparently suppressed links in a chain of association—those which Sir W. Hamilton considers as latent—really are so; that they are not even momentarily felt; the chain of causation being continued only physically, by one organic state of the nerves succeeding another so rapidly that the state of mental consciousness appropriate to each is not produced."

Ib., p. 357: "The elementary feelings may then be said to be latently present, or to be present but not in consciousness. The truth, however, is, that the feelings themselves are not present consciously or latently, but that the nervous modifications which are their usual antecedents have been present, while the consequents have been frustrated, and another consequent has been produced instead."

'Dissertations and Discussions,' vol. iii. p. 109: "But if it be materialism to endeavour to ascertain the material conditions of our mental operations, all theories of the mind which have any pretension to comprehensiveness must be materialistic."

Cf. also the following statement: 'Essays on Religion,' p. 147: "The will does not, any more than other causes, create Force. Granting that it originates motion, it has no means of doing so but by converting into that particular manifestation a portion of Force which already existed in other forms. It is known that the source from which this portion of Force is derived is chiefly or entirely the Force evolved in the processes of chemical composition and decomposition which constitute the body of nutrition: the force so liberated becomes a fund upon which every

of consciousness resembling the former, but inferior in intensity, is capable of being reproduced in us, without the presence of any such cause as excited it at first. Thus, if we have once seen or touched an object, we can afterwards think of the object though it be absent from our sight or from our touch. If we have been joyful or grieved at some event, we can think of or remember our past joy or grief, though no new event of a happy or painful nature has taken place. When a poet has put together a mental picture of an imaginary object, a Castle of Indolence, a

muscular and even every merely nervous action, as of the brain in thought, is a draft. It is in this sense only that, according to the best lights of science, volition is an originating cause."

Ib., p. 198: "The evidence is wellnigh complete that all thought and feeling has some action of the bodily organism for its immediate antecedent or accompaniment; that the specific variations, and especially the different degrees of complication of the nervous and cerebral organisation, correspond to differences in the development of the mental faculties; and though we have no evidence, except negative, that the mental consciousness ceases for ever when the functions of the brain are at an end, we do know that diseases of the brain disturb the mental functions, and that decay or weakness of the brain enfeebles them. We have therefore sufficient evidence that cerebral action is, if not the cause, at least, in our present state of existence, a condition *sine quâ non* of mental operations; and that assuming the mind to be a distinct substance, its separation from the body would not be, as some have vainly flattered themselves, a liberation from trammels and restoration to freedom, but would simply put a stop to its functions and remand it to unconsciousness, unless and until some other set of conditions supervenes, capable of recalling it into activity, but of the existence of which experience does not give us the smallest indication."

Ib., p. 199: "The relation of thought to a material brain is no metaphysical necessity, but simply a constant coexistence within the limits of observation."

Cf. also Appendix C.

Una, or a Hamlet, he can afterwards think of the ideal object he has created without any fresh act of intellectual combination. This law is expressed by saying, in the language of Hume, that every mental *impression* has its *idea*.

Secondly, These ideas, or secondary mental states, are excited by our impressions, or by other ideas, according to certain laws which are called Laws of Association. Of these laws the first is, that similar ideas tend to excite one another. The second is, that when two impressions have been frequently experienced (or even thought of), either simultaneously or in immediate succession, then whenever one of these impressions, or the idea of it, recurs, it tends to excite the idea of the other. The third law is, that greater intensity in either or both of the impressions is equivalent, in rendering them excitable by one another, to a greater frequency of conjunction. These are the laws of ideas, on which I shall not enlarge in this place, but refer the reader to works professedly psychological—in particular, to Mr James Mill's 'Analysis of the Phenomena of the Human Mind,' where the principal laws of association, along with many of their applications, are copiously exemplified, and with a masterly hand.*

* When this chapter was written, Professor Bain had not yet published even the first part ("The Senses and the Intellect") of his profound Treatise on the Mind. In this the laws of association have been more comprehensively stated and more largely exemplified than by any previous writer ; and the work, having been completed by the publication of "The Emotions and the Will," may now be referred to as incomparably the most complete analytical exposition of the mental phenomena, on the basis of a legitimate induction, which has yet been

These simple or elementary Laws of Mind have been ascertained by the ordinary methods of experimental inquiry; nor could they have been ascertained in any other manner. But a certain number of elementary laws having thus been obtained, it is a fair subject of scientific inquiry how far those laws can be made to go in explaining the actual phenomena. It is obvious that complex laws of thought and feeling not only may, but must, be generated from these simple laws. And it is to be remarked that the case is not always one of Composition of Causes: the effect of concurring causes is not always precisely the sum of the effects of those causes when separate, nor even always an effect of the same kind with them. Reverting to the distinction which occupies so prominent a place in the theory of induction, the laws of the phenomena of mind are sometimes analogous to mechanical, but sometimes also to chemical, laws. When many impressions or ideas are operating in the mind together, there sometimes takes place a process of a similar kind to chemical combination. When impressions have been so often experienced in conjunction that each of them calls up readily and instantaneously the ideas of the whole group, those ideas sometimes melt and coalesce into one another, and appear not several ideas, but one, in

produced. More recently still, Mr Bain has joined with me in appending to a new edition of the 'Analysis' notes intended to bring up the analytic science of Mind to its latest improvements.

Many striking applications of the laws of association to the explanation of complex mental phenomena are also to be found in Mr Herbert Spencer's 'Principles of Psychology.'

the same manner as, when the seven prismatic colours are presented to the eye in rapid succession, the sensation produced is that of white. But as in this last case it is correct to say that the seven colours when they rapidly follow one another *generate* white, but not that they actually *are* white; so it appears to me that the Complex Idea, formed by the blending together of several simpler ones, should, when it really appears simple (that is, when the separate elements are not consciously distinguishable in it), be said to *result from*, or *be generated by*, the simple ideas, not to *consist* of them. Our idea of an orange really *consists* of the simple ideas of a certain colour, a certain form, a certain taste and smell, &c., because we can, by interrogating our consciousness, perceive all these elements in the idea. But we cannot perceive, in so apparently simple a feeling as our perception of the shape of an object by the eye, all that multitude of ideas derived from other senses, without which it is well ascertained that no such visual perception would ever have had existence; nor, in our idea of Extension, can we discover those elementary ideas of resistance derived from our muscular frame in which it has been conclusively shown that the idea originates. These, therefore, are cases of mental chemistry, in which it is proper to say that the simple ideas generate rather than that they compose the complex ones.

With respect to all the other constituents of the mind, its beliefs, its abstruser conceptions, its sentiments, emotions, and volitions, there are some (among whom are Hartley and the author of the 'Analysis') who think that the whole of these are generated from simple ideas of sensation by a chemistry similar to that which we have just exemplified.[1] These philosophers have made out a great part of their case, but I am not satisfied that they have established the whole of it. They have shown that there is such a thing as mental chemistry; that the heterogeneous nature of a feeling A, considered in relation to B and C, is no conclusive argument against its being generated from B and C. Having proved this, they proceed to show that where A is found B and C were or may have been present; and why, therefore, they ask, should not A have been generated from B and C? But even if this evidence were carried to the highest degree of completeness which it admits of; if it were shown (which hitherto it has not, in all cases, been) that cer-

---

[1] Cf. 'Autobiography,' p. 68: "Hartley's explanation, incomplete as in many points it is, of the more complex mental phenomena by the law of association commended itself to me at once as a real analysis, and made me feel by contrast the insufficiency of the merely verbal generalisations of Condillac, and even of the instructive gropings and feelings about for psychological explanations, of Locke."

Ib., p. 108: "In psychology his [James Mill's] fundamental doctrine was the formation of all human character by circumstances, through the universal Principle of Association, and the consequent unlimited possibility of improving the moral and intellectual condition of mankind by education."

'Dissertations and Discussions,' vol. iii. p. 108: "The most complete and scientific form of the *à posteriori* psychology is that which considers the law of association as the governing principle, by means of which the more complex and recondite mental phenomena shape themselves, or are shaped out of the simpler mental elements."

tain groups of associated ideas not only might have been but actually were present whenever the more recondite mental feeling was experienced, this would amount only to the Method of Agreement, and could not prove causation until confirmed by the more conclusive evidence of the Method of Difference. If the question be whether Belief is a mere case of close association of ideas, it would be necessary to examine experimentally if it be true that any ideas whatever, provided they are associated with the required degree of closeness, give rise to belief. If the inquiry be into the origin of moral feelings, the feeling, for example, of moral reprobation, it is necessary to compare all the varieties of actions or states of mind which are ever morally disapproved, and see whether in all these cases it can be shown, or reasonably surmised, that the action or state of mind had become connected by association, in the disapproving mind, with some particular class of hateful or disgusting ideas; and the method employed is, thus far, that of Agreement. But this is not enough. Supposing this proved, we must try further by the Method of Difference whether this particular kind of hateful or disgusting ideas, when it becomes associated with an action previously indifferent, will render that action a subject of moral disapproval. If this question can be answered in the affirmative, it is shown to be a law of the human mind that an association of that particular description is the generating cause of moral reprobation. That all this is the case has been rendered extremely probable, but the experiments have not been tried with the degree of precision necessary for a complete and absolutely conclusive induction.*

It is further to be remembered, that even if all which this theory of mental phenomena contends for could be proved, we should not be the more enabled to resolve the laws of the more complex feelings into those of the simpler ones. The generation of one class of mental phenomena from another, whenever it can be made out, is a highly interesting fact in psychological chemistry; but it no more supersedes the necessity of an experimental study of the generated phenomenon, than a knowledge of the properties of oxygen and sulphur enables us to deduce those of sulphuric acid without specific observation and experiment. Whatever, therefore, may be the final issue of the attempt to account for the origin of our judgments, our desires, or our volitions, from simpler mental phenomena, it is not the less imperative to ascertain the sequences of the complex phenomena themselves by special study in conformity to the canons of Induction. Thus, in respect to Belief, psychologists will always have to inquire what beliefs we have by direct consciousness, and according to what laws one belief produces another; what are the laws in virtue of which one thing is re-

* In the case of the moral sentiments, the place of direct experiment is to a considerable extent supplied by historical experience, and we are able to trace with a tolerable approach to certainty the particular associations by which those sentiments are engendered. This has been attempted, so far as respects the sentiment of justice, in a little work by the present author, entitled 'Utilitarianism.'

cognised by the mind, either rightly or erroneously, an evidence of another thing. In regard to Desire, they will have to examine what objects we desire naturally, and by what causes we are made to desire things originally indifferent, or even disagreeable, to us; and so forth. It may be remarked that the general laws of association prevail among these more intricate states of mind, in the same manner as among the simpler ones. A desire, an emotion, an idea of the higher order of abstraction, even our judgments and volitions when they have become habitual, are called up by association, according to precisely the same laws as our simple ideas.

§ 4. In the course of these inquiries it will be natural and necessary to examine how far the production of one state of mind by another is influenced by any assignable state of body. The commonest observation shows that different minds are susceptible in very different degrees to the action of the same psychological causes. The idea, for example, of a given desirable object will excite in different minds very different degrees of intensity of desire. The same subject of meditation presented to different minds will excite in them very unequal degrees of intellectual action. These differences of mental susceptibility in different individuals may be, first, original and ultimate facts, or, secondly, they may be consequences of the previous mental history of those individuals, or, thirdly, and lastly, they may depend on varieties of physical organisation. That the previous mental history of the individuals must have some share in producing or in modifying the whole of their mental character is an inevitable consequence of the laws of mind; but that differences of bodily structure also co-operate is the opinion of all physiologists, confirmed by common experience. It is to be regretted that hitherto this experience, being accepted in the gross without due analysis, has been made the groundwork of empirical generalisations most detrimental to the progress of real knowledge.

It is certain that the natural differences which really exist in the mental predispositions or susceptibilities of different persons, are often not unconnected with diversities in their organic constitution. But it does not therefore follow that these organic differences must in all cases influence the mental phenomena directly and immediately. They often affect them through the medium of their psychological causes. For example, the idea of some particular pleasure may excite in different persons, even independently of habit or education, very different strengths of desire, and this may be the effect of their different degrees or kinds of nervous susceptibility; but these organic differences, we must remember, will render the pleasurable sensation itself more intense in one of these persons than in the other; so that the idea of the pleasure will also be an intenser feeling, and will, by the operation of mere mental laws, excite an intenser desire, without its being necessary to suppose that the desire itself is directly influenced by the physical peculiarity. As in this, so in many cases, such differences in the kind or in the intensity of the physical sensations as must necessarily result from differences of bodily organisation will of themselves account for many differences, not only in the degree, but even in the kind, of the other mental phenomena. So true is this, that even different *qualities* of mind, different types of mental character, will naturally be produced by mere differences of intensity in the sensations generally ; as is well pointed out in the able essay on Dr Priestley by Mr Martineau, mentioned in a former chaper :—

"The sensations which form the elements of all knowledge are received either simultaneously or successively ; when several are received simultaneously, as the smell, the taste, the colour, the form, &c., of a fruit, their association together constitutes our idea of an *object ;* when received successively, their association makes up the idea of an *event.* Anything, then, which favours the associations of synchronous ideas will tend to produce a knowledge of objects, a perception of qualities ; while anything which favours association in the successive order will tend to produce a knowledge of events, of the order of occurrences, and of the connection of cause and effect : in other words, in the one case a perceptive mind, with a discriminate feeling of the pleasurable and painful properties of things, a sense of the grand and the beautiful will be the result ; in the other, a mind attentive to the movements and phenomena, a ratiocinative and philosophic intellect.

Now it is an acknowledged principle that all sensations experienced during the presence of any vivid impression become strongly associated with it and with each other, and does it not follow that the synchronous feelings of a sensitive constitution (*i.e.*, the one which has vivid impressions) will be more intimately blended than in a differently formed mind ? If this suggestion has any foundation in truth, it leads to an inference not unimportant,—that when nature has endowed an individual with great original susceptibility, he will probably be distinguished by fondness for natural history, a relish for the beautiful and great, and moral enthusiasm ; where there is but a mediocrity of sensibility, a love of science, of abstract truth, with a deficiency of taste and of fervour, is likely to be the result."

We see from this example that when the general laws of mind are more accurately known, and, above all, more skilfully applied to the detailed explanation of mental peculiarities, they will account for many more of those peculiarities than is ordinarily supposed. Unfortunately the reaction of the last and present generation against the philosophy of the eighteenth century has produced a very general neglect of this great department of analytical inquiry, of which, consequently, the recent progress has been by no means proportional to its early promise. The majority of those who speculate on human nature prefer dogmatically to assume that the mental differences which they perceive, or think they perceive, among human beings are ultimate facts, incapable of being either explained or altered, rather than take the trouble of fitting themselves, by the requisite processes of thought, for referring those mental differences to the outward causes by which they are for the most part produced, and on the removal of which they would cease to exist. The German school of metaphysical speculation, which has not yet lost its temporary predominance in European thought, has had this among many other injurious influences; and at the opposite extreme of the psychological scale, no writer, either of early or of recent date, is chargeable in a higher degree with this aberration from the true scientific spirit than M. Comte.

It is certain that, in human beings at least, differences in education and in outward circumstances are capable of affording an adequate explanation of by far the greatest portion of character, and that the remainder may be in great part accounted for by physical differences in the sensations produced in different individuals by the same external or internal cause. There are, however, some mental facts which do not seem to admit of these modes of explanation. Such, to take the strongest case, are the various instincts of animals, and the portion of human nature which corresponds to those instincts. No mode has been suggested, even by way of hypothesis, in which these can receive any satisfactory, or even plausible, explanation from psychological causes alone; and there is great reason to think that they have as positive, and even as direct and immediate, a connection with physical conditions of the brain and nerves as any of our mere sensations have. A supposition which (it is perhaps not superfluous to add) in no way conflicts with the indisputable fact that these instincts may be modified to any extent, or entirely conquered, in human beings, and to no inconsiderable extent even in some of the domesticated animals, by other mental influences, and by education.

Whether organic causes exercise a direct influence over any other classes of mental phenomena is hitherto as far from being ascertained as is the precise nature of the organic conditions even in the case of instincts. The physiology, however, of the brain and nervous system is in a state of such rapid advance, and is continually bringing forth such new and interesting results, that if there be really a connection between mental peculiarities and any varieties cognisable by our senses in the structure of the cerebral and nervous apparatus, the nature of that connection is now in a fair way of being found out. The latest discoveries in cerebral physiology appear to have proved that any such connection which may exist is of a radically different character from that contended for by Gall and his followers, and that whatever may hereafter be found to be the true theory of the subject, phrenology at least is untenable.

CHAPTER V

OF ETHOLOGY, OR THE SCIENCE OF THE FORMATION OF CHARACTER

§ 1. THE laws of mind, as characterised in the preceding chapter, compose the universal or abstract portion of the philosophy of human nature; and all the truths of common experience, constituting a practical knowledge of mankind, must, to the extent to which they are truths, be results or consequences of these. Such familiar maxims, when collected *à posteriori* from observation of life, occupy among the truths of the science the place of what, in our analysis of Induction, have so often been spoken of under the title of Empirical Laws.

An Empirical Law (it will be remembered) is an uniformity, whether of succession or of co-existence, which holds true in all instances within our limits of observation, but is not of a nature to afford any assurance that it would hold beyond those limits, either because the consequent is not really the effect of the antecedent, but forms part along with it of a chain of effects, flowing from prior causes not yet ascertained, or because there is ground to believe that the sequence (though a case of causation) is resolvable into simpler sequences, and, depending therefore on a concurrence of several natural agencies, is exposed to an unknown multitude of possibilities of counteraction. In other words, an empirical law is a generalisation, of which, not content with finding it true, we are obliged to ask why is it true? knowing that its truth is not absolute, but dependent on some more general conditions, and that it can only be relied on in so far as there is ground of assurance that those conditions are realised.

Now, the observations concerning human affairs collected from common experience are precisely of this nature. Even if they were universally and exactly true within the bounds of experience, which they never are, still they are not the ultimate laws of human action; they are not the principles of human nature, but results of those principles under the circumstances in which mankind have happened to be placed. When the Psalmist "said in his haste that all men are liars," he enunciated what in some ages and countries is borne out by ample experience; but it is not a law of man's nature to lie, though it is one of the consequences of the laws of human nature that lying is nearly universal when certain external circumstances exist universally, especially circumstances productive of habitual distrust and fear. When the character of the old is asserted to be cautious, and of the young impetuous, this, again, is but an empirical law; for it is not because of their youth that the young are impetuous, nor because of their age that the old are cautious. It is chiefly, if not wholly, because the old, during their many years of life, have generally had much experience of its various evils, and having suffered or seen others suffer much from incautious exposure to them, have acquired associations favourable to circumspection; while the young, as well from the absence of similar experience as from the greater strength of the inclinations which urge them to enterprise, engage themselves in it more readily. Here, then, is the *explanation* of the empirical law; here are the conditions which ultimately determine whether the law holds good or not. If an old man has not been oftener than most young men in contact with danger and difficulty, he will be equally incautious: if a youth has not stronger inclinations than an old man, he probably will be as little enterprising. The empirical law derives whatever truth it has from the causal laws of which it is a consequence. If we know those laws, we know what are the limits to the derivative law; while, if we have not yet accounted for the empirical law — if it rests only on observation — there is no safety in applying it far beyond the limits of time, place, and circumstance in which the observations were made.

The really scientific truths, then, are not these empirical laws, but the causal laws which explain them. The empirical laws of those phenomena which depend on known causes, and of which a general theory can therefore be constructed, have, whatever may be their value in practice, no other function in science than that of verifying the conclusions of theory. Still more must this be the case when most of the empirical laws amount, even within the limits of observation, only to approximate generalisations.

§ 2. This, however, is not, so much as is sometimes supposed, a peculiarity of the sciences called moral. It is only in the simplest branches of science that empirical laws are ever exactly true, and not always in those. Astronomy, for example, is the simplest of all the sciences which explain, in the concrete, the actual course of natural events. The causes or forces on which astronomical phenomena depend are fewer in number than those which determine any other of the great phenomena of nature. Accordingly, as each effect results from the conflict of but few causes, a great degree of regularity and uniformity might be expected to exist among the effects; and such is really the case: they have a fixed order, and return in cycles. But propositions which should express with absolute correctness all the successive positions of a planet until the cycle is completed would be of almost unmanageable complexity, and could be obtained from theory alone. The generalisations which can be collected on the subject from direct observation, even such as Kepler's law, are mere approximations: the planets, owing to their perturbations by one another, do not move in exact ellipses. Thus even in astronomy perfect exactness in the mere empirical laws is not to be looked for; much less, then, in more complex subjects of inquiry.

The same example shows how little can be inferred against the universality, or even the simplicity, of the ultimate laws, from the impossibility of establishing any but approximate empirical laws of the effects. The laws of causation according to which a class of phenomena are produced may be very few and simple, and yet the effects themselves may be so various and complicated that it shall be impossible to trace any regularity whatever completely through them. For the phenomena in question may be of an eminently modifiable character; insomuch that innumerable circumstances are capable of influencing the effect, although they may all do it according to a very small number of laws. Suppose that all which passes in the mind of man is determined by a few simple laws: still, if those laws be such that there is not one of the facts surrounding a human being, or of the events which happen to him, that does not influence in some mode or degree his subsequent mental history, and if the circumstances of different human beings are extremely different, it will be no wonder if very few propositions can be made respecting the details of their conduct or feelings which will be true of all mankind.

Now, without deciding whether the ultimate laws of our mental nature are few or many, it is at least certain that they are of the above description. It is certain that our mental states, and our mental capacities and susceptibilities, are modified, either for a time or permanently, by everything which happens to us in life. Considering, therefore, how much these modifying causes differ in the case of any two individuals, it would be unreasonable to expect that the empirical laws of the human mind, the generalisations which can be made respecting the feelings or actions of mankind without reference to the causes that determine them, should be anything but approximate generalisations. They are the common wisdom of common life, and as such are invaluable; especially as they are mostly to be applied to cases not very dissimilar to those from which they were collected. But when maxims of this sort, collected from Englishmen, come to be applied to Frenchmen, or when those collected from the present day are applied to past or future generations, they are apt to be very much at fault. Unless we have resolved the empirical law into the laws of the causes on which it depends, and ascertained that those causes extend to the case which we have in view, there can be no reliance placed in our inferences. For every individual is surrounded by circumstances different from those of every other individual; every nation or generation of mankind from every other nation or generation; and none of these differences are without their influence in forming a different type of character. There is, indeed, also a certain general resemblance; but peculiarities of circumstances are continually constituting exceptions even to the propositions which are true in the great majority of cases.

Although, however, there is scarcely any mode of feeling or conduct which is, in the absolute sense, common to all mankind; and though the generalisations which assert that any given variety of conduct or feeling will be found universally (however nearly they may approximate to truth within given limits of observation), will be considered as scientific propositions by no one who is at all familiar with scientific investigation; yet all modes of feeling and conduct met with among mankind have causes which produce them; and in the propositions which assign those causes will be found the explanation of the empirical laws, and the limiting principle of our reliance on them. Human beings do not all feel and act alike in the same circumstances; but it is possible to determine what makes one person, in a given position, feel or act in one way, another in another; how any given mode of feeling and conduct, compatible with the general laws (physical and mental) of human nature, has been, or may be, formed. In other words, mankind have not one universal character, but there exist universal laws of the Formation of Character. And since it is by these laws, combined with the facts of each particular case, that the whole of the phenomena of human action and feeling are produced, it is on these that every rational attempt to construct the science of human nature in the concrete and for practical purposes must proceed.[1]

§ 3. The laws, then, of the formation of character being the principal object of scientific inquiry into human nature, it remains to determine the method of investigation best fitted for ascertaining them. And the logical principles according to which this question is to be decided must be those which preside over every other attempt to investigate the laws of very complex phenomena. For it is evident that both the character of any human being, and the aggregate of the circumstances by which that character has been formed, are facts of a high order of complexity. Now to such cases we have seen that the Deductive Method, setting out from general laws, and verifying their consequences by specific experience, is alone applicable. The grounds of this great logical doctrine have formerly been stated,[2] and its truth

---

[1] 'Subjection of Women,' p. 122: "Nor is it possible that this should be known, so long as the psychological laws of the formation of character have been so little studied even in a general way, and in the particular case (*i.e.*, natural equality in mental capacity of the sexes) never scientifically applied at all; so long as the most obvious external causes of difference of character are habitually disregarded—left unnoticed by the observer, and looked down upon with a kind of supercilious contempt by the prevalent schools both of natural history and of mental philosophy: who, whether they look for the source of what mainly distinguishes human beings from one another in the world of matter or in that of spirit, agree in running down those who prefer to explain these differences by the different relations of human beings to society and life."

[2] 'System of Logic,' book iii., chaps. x., xi., xii.

will derive additional support from a brief examination of the specialities of the present case.

There are only two modes in which laws of nature can be ascertained—deductively and experimentally, including under the denomination of experimental inquiry, observation as well as artificial experiment. Are the laws of the formation of character susceptible of a satisfactory investigation by the method of experimentation? Evidently not; because, even if we suppose unlimited power of varying the experiment (which is abstractedly possible, though no one but an Oriental despot has that power, or, if he had, would probably be disposed to exercise it), a still more essential condition is wanting — the power of performing any of the experiments with scientific accuracy.

The instances requisite for the prosecution of a directly experimental inquiry into the formation of character would be a number of human beings to bring up and educate from infancy to mature age; and to perform any one of these experiments with scientific propriety, it would be necessary to know and record every sensation or impression received by the young pupil from a period long before it could speak, including its own notions respecting the sources of all those sensations and impressions. It is not only impossible to do this completely, but even to do so much of it as should constitute a tolerable approximation. One apparently trivial circumstance which eluded our vigilance might let in a train of impressions and associations sufficient to vitiate the experiment as an authentic exhibition of the effects flowing from given causes. No one who has sufficiently reflected on education is ignorant of this truth; and whoever has not, will find it most instructively illustrated in the writings of Rousseau and Helvetius on that great subject.

Under this impossibility of studying the laws of the formation of character by experiments purposely contrived to elucidate them there remains the resource of simple observation. But if it be impossible to ascertain the influencing circumstances with any approach to completeness even when we have the shaping of them ourselves, much more impossible is it when the cases are further removed from our observation, and altogether out of our control.[1] Consider the difficulty of the very first step—of ascertaining what actually is the character of the individual in each particular case that we examine. There is hardly any person living, concerning some essential part of whose character there are not differences of opinion even among his intimate acquaintances; and a single action, or conduct continued only for a short time, goes a very

[1] 'Subjection of Women,' p. 125 : "The first point, the origin of the differences actually observed, is the one most accessible to speculation ; and I shall attempt to approach it by the only path by which it can be reached ; by tracing the mental consequences of external influences. We cannot isolate a human being from the circumstances of his condition, so as to ascertain experimentally what he would have been by nature ; but we can consider what he is, and what his circumstances have been, and whether the one would have been capable of producing the other."

little way towards ascertaining it. We can only make our observations in a rough way and *en masse*, not attempting to ascertain completely in any given instance what character has been formed, and still less by what causes; but only observing in what state of previous circumstances it is found that certain marked mental qualities or deficiencies *oftenest* exist. These conclusions, besides that they are mere approximate generalisations, deserve no reliance, even as such, unless the instances are sufficiently numerous to eliminate not only chance, but every assignable circumstance in which a number of the cases examined may happen to have resembled one another. So numerous and various, too, are the circumstances which form individual character, that the consequence of any particular combination is hardly ever some definite and strongly marked character, always found where that combination exists, and not otherwise. What is obtained, even after the most extensive and accurate observation, is merely a comparative result; as, for example, that in a given number of Frenchmen, taken indiscriminately, there will be found more persons of a particular mental tendency, and fewer of the contrary tendency, than among an equal number of Italians or English, similarly taken; or thus: of a hundred Frenchmen and an equal number of Englishmen, fairly selected, and arranged according to the degree in which they possess a particular mental characteristic, each number 1, 2, 3, &c., of the one series will be found to possess more of that characteristic than the corresponding number of the other. Since, therefore, the comparison is not one of kinds, but of ratios and degrees; and since in proportion as the differences are slight, it requires a greater number of instances to eliminate chance; it cannot often happen to any one to know a sufficient number of cases with the accuracy requisite for making the sort of comparison last mentioned—less than which, however, would not constitute a real induction. Accordingly, there is hardly one current opinion respecting the characters of nations, classes, or descriptions of persons, which is universally acknowledged as indisputable.*

And finally, if we could even obtain by way of ex-

---

* The most favourable cases for making such approximate generalisations are what may be termed collective instances, where we are fortunately enabled to see the whole class respecting which we are inquiring in action at once, and, from the qualities displayed by the collective body, are able to judge what must be the qualities of the majority of the individuals composing it. Thus the character of a nation is shown in its acts as a nation; not so much in the acts of its government, for those are much influenced by other causes, but in the current popular maxims, and other marks of the general direction of public opinion; in the character of the persons or writings that are held in permanent esteem or admiration; in laws and institutions, so far as they are the work of the nation itself, or are acknowledged and supported by it; and so forth. But even here there is a large margin of doubt and uncertainty. These things are liable to be influenced by many circumstances: they are partly determined by the distinctive qualities of that nation or body of persons, but partly also by external causes which would influence any other body of persons, in the same manner. In order, therefore, to make the experiment really complete, we ought to be able to try it without variation upon other nations: to try how Englishmen would act or feel if placed in the same circumstances in which we have supposed Frenchmen to be placed; to apply, in short, the Method of Difference as well as that of Agreement. Now these experiments we cannot try, nor even approximate to.

periment a much more satisfactory assurance of these generalisations than is really possible, they would still be only empirical laws. They would show, indeed, that there was some connection between the type of character formed and the circumstances existing in the case, but not what the precise connection was, nor to which of the peculiarities of those circumstances the effect was really owing. They could only, therefore, be received as results of causation, requiring to be resolved into the general laws of the causes: until the determination of which, we could not judge within what limits the derivative laws might serve as presumptions in cases yet unknown, or even be depended on as permanent in the very cases from which they were collected. The French people had, or were supposed to have, a certain national character; but they drive out their royal family and aristocracy, alter their institutions, pass through a series of extraordinary events for the greater part of a century, and at the end of that time their character is found to have undergone important changes. A long list of mental and moral differences are observed, or supposed to exist, between men and women; but at some future, and, it may be hoped, not distant period, equal freedom and an equally independent social position come to be possessed by both, and their differences of character are either removed or totally altered.

But if the differences which we think we observe between French and English, or between men and women, can be connected with more general laws;

if they be such as might be expected to be produced by the differences of government, former customs, and physical peculiarities in the two nations, and by the diversities of education, occupations, personal independence, and social privileges, and whatever original differences there may be in bodily strength and nervous sensibility between the two sexes,—then, indeed, the coincidence of the two kinds of evidence justifies us in believing that we have both reasoned rightly and observed rightly. Our observation, though not sufficient as proof, is ample as verification. And having ascertained not only the empirical laws, but the causes of the peculiarities, we need be under no difficulty in judging how far they may be expected to be permanent, or by what circumstances they would be modified or destroyed.

§ 4. Since, then, it is impossible to obtain really accurate propositions respecting the formation of character from observation and experiment alone, we are driven perforce to that which, even if it had not been the indispensable, would have been the most perfect, mode of investigation, and which it is one of the principal aims of philosophy to extend—namely, that which tries its experiments, not on the complex facts, but on the simple ones of which they are compounded; and after ascertaining the laws of the causes, the composition of which gives rise to the complex phenomena, then considers whether these will not explain and account for the approximate generalisations which have been framed empirically respecting the sequences of those complex phenomena. The laws of the formation of character are, in short, derivative laws, resulting from the general laws of mind, and are to be obtained by deducing them from those general laws by supposing any given set of circumstances, and then considering what, according to the laws of mind, will be the influence of those circumstances on the formation of character.

A science is thus formed, to which I would propose to give the name of Ethology, or the Science of Character, from ἦθος, a word more nearly corresponding to the term "character," as I here use it, than any other word in the same language. The name is perhaps etymologically applicable to the entire science of our mental and moral nature; but if, as is usual and convenient, we employ the name Psychology for the science of the elementary laws of mind, Ethology will serve for the ulterior science which determines the kind of character produced in conformity to those general laws, by any set of circumstances, physical and moral. According to this definition, Ethology is the science which corresponds to the art of education, in the widest sense of the term, including the formation of national or collective character as well as individual. It would indeed be vain to expect (however completely the laws of the formation of character might be ascertained) that we could know so accurately the circumstances of any given case as to be able positively to predict the character that would be produced in that case. But we must remember that a degree of knowledge far short of the power of actual prediction is often of much practical value. There may be great power of influencing phenomena, with a very imperfect knowledge of the causes by which they are in any given instance determined. It is enough that we know that certain means have a *tendency* to produce a given effect, and that others have a tendency to frustrate it. When the circumstances of an individual or of a nation are in any considerable degree under our control, we may, by our knowledge of tendencies, be enabled to shape those circumstances in a manner much more favourable to the ends we desire than the shape which they would of themselves assume. This is the limit of our power, but within this limit the power is a most important one.

This science of Ethology may be called the Exact Science of Human Nature; for its truths are not, like the empirical laws which depend on them, approximate generalisations, but real laws. It is, however (as in all cases of complex phenomena), necessary to the exactness of the propositions that they should be hypothetical only, and affirm tendencies, not facts. They must not assert that something will always or certainly happen, but only that such and such will be the effect of a given cause, so far as it operates uncounteracted. It is a scientific proposition that bodily strength tends to make men courageous; not that it always makes them so: that an interest on one side of a question tends to bias the judgment; not that it invariably does so: that experience tends to give wisdom; not that such is always its effect. These propositions, being assertive only of tendencies, are not the less universally true because the tendencies may be frustrated.

§ 5. While on the one hand Psychology is altogether, or principally, a science of observation and experiment, Ethology, as I have conceived it, is, as I have already remarked, altogether deductive. The one ascertains the simple laws of Mind in general, the other traces their operation in complex combinations of circumstances. Ethology stands to Psychology in a relation very similar to that in which the various branches of natural philosophy stand to mechanics. The principles of Ethology are properly the middle principles, the *axiomata media* (as Bacon would have said) of the science of mind: as distinguished, on the one hand, from the empirical laws resulting from simple observation, and on the other, from the highest generalisations.

And this seems a suitable place for a logical remark, which, though of general application, is of peculiar importance in reference to the present subject. Bacon has judiciously observed that the *axiomata media* of every science principally constitute its value. The lowest generalisations, until explained by and resolved into the middle principles of which they are the consequences, have only the imperfect accuracy of empirical laws; while the most general laws are *too* general, and include too few circumstances, to give sufficient indication of what happens in individual cases where the circumstances are almost always immensely numerous. In the importance, therefore, which Bacon assigns in every science to the middle principles, it is impossible not to agree with him. But I conceive him to have been radically wrong in his doctrine respecting the mode in which these *axiomata media* should be arrived at; though there is no one proposition laid down in his works for which he has been more extravagantly eulogised. He enunciates as an universal rule that induction should proceed from the lowest to the middle principles, and from those to the highest, never reversing that order, and consequently leaving no room for the discovery of new principles by way of deduction at all. It is not to be conceived that a man of his sagacity could have fallen into this mistake if there had existed in his time, among the sciences which treat of successive phenomena, one single instance of a deductive science, such as mechanics, astronomy, optics, acoustics, &c., now are. In those sciences it is evident that the higher and middle principles are by no means derived from the lowest, but the reverse. In some of them the very highest generalisations were those earliest ascertained with any scientific exactness—as, for example (in mechanics), the laws of motion. Those general laws had not indeed at first the acknowledged universality which they acquired after having been successfully employed to explain many classes of phenomena to which they were not originally seen to be applicable; as when the laws of motion were employed, in conjunction with other laws, to explain deductively the celestial phenomena. Still the fact remains that the propositions which were afterwards recognised as the most general truths of the science were, of all its accurate generalisations, those earliest arrived at. Bacon's greatest merit cannot, therefore, consist, as we are so often told that it did, in exploding the vicious method pursued by the ancients of flying to the highest generalisations first, and deducing the middle principles from them; since this is neither a vicious nor an exploded, but the universally accredited, method of modern science, and that to which it owes its greatest triumphs. The error of ancient speculation did not consist in making the largest generalisations first, but in making them without the aid or warrant of rigorous inductive methods, and applying them deductively without the needful use of that important part of the Deductive Method termed Verification.

The order in which truths of the various degrees of generality should be ascertained cannot, I apprehend, be prescribed by any unbending rule. I know of no maxim which can be laid down on the subject, but to obtain those first in respect to which the conditions of a real induction can be first and most completely realised. Now, wherever our means of investigation can reach causes, without stopping at the empirical laws of the effects, the simplest cases being those in which fewest causes are simultaneously concerned, will be most amenable to the inductive process; and these are the cases which elicit laws of the greatest comprehensiveness. In every science, therefore, which has reached the stage at which it becomes a science of causes, it will be usual, as well as desirable, first to obtain the highest generalisations, and then deduce the more special ones from them. Nor can I discover any foundation for the Baconian maxim, so much extolled by subsequent writers, except this: That before we attempt to explain deductively from more general laws any new class of phenomena, it is desirable to have gone as far as is practicable in ascertaining the empirical laws of those phenomena, so as to compare the results of deduction not with one individual instance after another, but with general propositions expressive of the points of agreement which have been found among many instances. For if Newton had been obliged to verify the theory of gravitation, not by deducing from it Kepler's laws, but by deducing all the observed planetary positions which had served Kepler to establish those laws, the Newtonian theory would probably never have emerged from the state of an hypothesis.*

* "To which," says Dr Whewell, "we may add, that it is certain from the history of the subject, that in that case the hypothesis would never have been framed at all."

Dr Whewell ('Philosophy of Discovery,' pp. 277-282) defends Bacon's rule against the preceding strictures. But his defence consists only in asserting and exemplifying a proposition which I had myself stated—viz., that though the largest generalisations may be the earliest made, they are not at first seen in their entire generality, but acquire it by degrees, as they are found to explain one class after another of phenomena. The laws of motion, for example, were not known to extend to the celestial regions until the motions of the celes-

The applicability of these remarks to the special case under consideration cannot admit of question. The science of the formation of character is a science of causes. The subject is one to which those among the canons of induction, by which laws of causation are ascertained, can be rigorously applied. It is, therefore, both natural and advisable to ascertain the simplest, which are necessarily the most general, laws of causation first, and to deduce the middle principles from them. In other words, Ethology, the deductive science, is a system of corollaries from Psychology, the experimental science.[1]

tial bodies had been deduced from them. This, however, does not in any way affect the fact that the middle principles of astronomy, the central force, for example, and the law of the inverse square, could not have been discovered if the laws of motion, which are so much more universal, had not been known first. On Bacon's system of step-by-step generalisation, it would be impossible in any science to ascend higher than the empirical laws; a remark which Dr Whewell's own Inductive Tables, referred to by him in support of his argument, amply bear out.

---

[1] 'System of Logic,' p. 143: "There are weighty scientific reasons for giving to every science as much of the character of a Deductive Science as possible; for endeavouring to construct the science from the fewest and the simplest possible inductions, and to make these, by any combinations, however complicated, suffice for proving even such truths, relating to complex cases, as could be proved, if we chose, by inductions from specific experience."

Ib., p. 210: "It may be affirmed as a general principle that all inductions, whether strong or weak, which can be connected by ratiocination, are confirmatory of one another; while any which lead deductively to consequences that are incompatible become mutually each other's test, showing that one or other must be given up, or at least more guardedly repressed. . . . If, then, a survey of the uniformities which have been ascertained to exist in nature should

§ 6. Of these, the earlier alone has been, as yet, really conceived or studied as a science; the other, Ethology, is still to be created. But its creation has at length become practicable. The empirical laws, destined to verify its deductions, have been formed in abundance by every successive age of humanity, and the premises for the deductions are now sufficiently complete. Excepting the degree of uncertainty which still exists as to the extent of the natural differences of individual minds, and the physical circumstances on which these may be dependent (considerations which are of secondary importance when we are considering mankind in the average, or *en masse*), I believe most competent judges will agree that the general laws of the different constituent elements of human nature are even now sufficiently understood to render it possible for a competent thinker to deduce from those laws, with a considerable approach to certainty, the particular type of character which would be formed in mankind generally by any assumed set of circumstances. A science of Ethology, founded on the laws of Psychology, is therefore possible, though little has yet been done, and that little not at all systematically, towards forming it. The progress of this important but most imperfect science will depend on a double process: first, that of deducing theoretically the ethological consequences of

point out some which, as far as any human purpose requires certainty, may be considered quite certain and quite universal, then by means of these uniformities we may be able to raise multitudes of other inductions to the same point in the scale."

particular circumstances of position, and comparing them with the recognised results of common experience; and secondly, the reverse operation—increased study of the various types of human nature that are to be found in the world, conducted by persons not only capable of analysing and recording the circumstances in which these types severally prevail, but also sufficiently acquainted with psychological laws to be able to explain and account for the characteristics of the type by the peculiarities of the circumstances, the residuum alone, when there proves to be any, being set down to the account of congenital predispositions.

For the experimental or *à posteriori* part of this process, the materials are continually accumulating by the observation of mankind. So far as thought is concerned, the great problem of Ethology is to deduce the requisite middle principles from the general laws of Psychology. The subject to be studied is, the origin and sources of all those qualities in human beings which are interesting to us, either as facts to be produced, to be avoided, or merely to be understood; and the object is to determine, from the general laws of mind, combined with the general position of our species in the universe, what actual or possible combinations of circumstances are capable of promoting or of preventing the production of those qualities. A science which possesses middle principles of this kind, arranged in the order, not of causes, but of the effects which it is desirable to produce or to prevent, is duly prepared to be the foundation of the corresponding Art. And when Ethology shall be thus prepared, practical education will be the mere transformation of those principles into a parallel system of precepts, and the adaptation of these to the sum total of the individual circumstances which exist in each particular case.[1]

It is hardly necessary again to repeat that, as in every other deductive science, verification *à posteriori* must proceed *pari passu* with deduction *à priori*. The inference given by theory as to the type of character which would be formed by any given circumstances must be tested by specific experience of those circumstances whenever obtainable; and the conclusions of the science as a whole must undergo a perpetual verification and correction from the general remarks afforded by common experience respecting human nature in our own age, and by history respecting times gone by. The conclusions of theory cannot be trusted, unless confirmed by observation; nor those of observation, unless they can be affiliated to theory, by deducing them from the laws of human nature, and from a close analysis of the circumstances of the particular

---

[1] Cf. 'Dissertations and Discussions,' vol. ii. p. 461: "Bentham was a moralist of another stamp. With him, the first use to be made of his ultimate principle was to erect on it, as a foundation, secondary or middle principles, capable of serving as premises for a body of ethical doctrine not derived from existing opinions, but fitted to be their test. Without such middle principles, an universal principle, either in science or in morals, serves for little but a thesaurus of commonplaces for the discussion of questions instead of a means of deciding them."

situation. It is the accordance of these two kinds of evidence separately taken—the consilience of *à priori* reasoning and specific experience — which forms the only sufficient ground for the principles of any science so "immersed in matter," dealing with such complex and concrete phenomena, as Ethology.

II. UTILITARIANISM

CHAPTER I

GENERAL REMARKS

THERE are few circumstances among those which make up the present condition of human knowledge, more unlike what might have been expected, or more significant of the backward state in which speculation on the most important subjects still lingers, than the little progress which has been made in the decision of the controversy respecting the criterion of right and wrong. From the dawn of philosophy, the question concerning the *summum bonum,* or, what is the same thing, concerning the foundation of morality, has been accounted the main problem in speculative thought, has occupied the most gifted intellects, and divided them into sects and schools, carrying on a vigorous warfare against one another. And after more than two thousand years the same discussions continue, philosophers are still ranged under the same contending banners, and neither thinkers nor mankind at large seem nearer to being unanimous on the subject than when the youth Socrates listened to the old Protagoras, and asserted (if Plato's dialogue be grounded on a real conversation) the theory of utilitarianism against the popular morality of the so-called sophist.

It is true that similar confusion and uncertainty, and in some cases similar discordance, exist respecting the first principles of all the sciences, not excepting that which is deemed the most certain of them, mathematics,—without much impairing, generally indeed without impairing at all, the trustworthiness of the conclusions of those sciences. An apparent anomaly, the explanation of which is, that the detailed doctrines of a science are not usually deduced from, nor depend for their evidence upon, what are called its first principles. Were it not so, there would be no science more precarious, or whose conclusions were more insufficiently made out, than algebra; which derives none of its certainty from what are commonly taught to learners as its elements, since these, as laid down by some of its most eminent teachers, are as full of fictions as English law, and of mysteries as theology. The truths which are ultimately accepted as the first principles of a science, are really the last results of metaphysical analysis, practised on the elementary notions with which the science is conversant; and their relation to the science is not that of foundations to an edifice, but of roots to a tree, which may perform their office equally well though they be never dug down to and exposed to light. But though in science the particular truths precede the general theory, the contrary might be expected to be the case with a practical art, such as morals or legislation. All action is for the sake of some end, and rules of action, it seems natural to suppose, must take their whole character and colour from the end to which they are subservient. When we engage in a pursuit, a clear and precise conception of what we are pursuing would seem to be the first thing we need, instead of the last we are to look forward to. A test of right and wrong must be the means, one would think, of ascertaining what is right or wrong, and not a consequence of having already ascertained it.[1]

The difficulty is not avoided by having recourse to the popular theory of a natural faculty, a sense or instinct, informing us of right and wrong. For—besides that the existence of such a moral instinct is itself one of the matters in dispute—those believers in it who have any pretensions to philosophy have been obliged to abandon the idea that it discerns what is right or wrong in the particular case in hand, as our other senses discern the sight or sound actually present. Our moral faculty, according to all those of its inter-

[1] 'Dissertations and Discussions,' vol. ii. p. 459: "We are as much for conscience, duty, rectitude as Dr Whewell. The terms, and all the feelings connected with them, are as much a part of the ethics of utility as of that of intuition. The point in dispute is, what acts are the proper objects of those feelings; whether we ought to take the feelings as we find them, as accident or design has made them, or whether the tendency of actions to promote happiness affords a test to which the feelings of morality should conform."

preters who are entitled to the name of thinkers, supplies us only with the general principles of moral judgments: it is a branch of our reason, not of our sensitive faculty; and must be looked to for the abstract doctrines of morality, not for perception of it in the concrete. The intuitive, no less than what may be termed the inductive, school of ethics, insists on the necessity of general laws. They both agree that the morality of an individual action is not a question of direct perception, but of the application of a law to an individual case. They recognise also, to a great extent, the same moral laws; but differ as to their evidence, and the source from which they derive their authority. According to the one opinion, the principles of morals are evident *à priori*, requiring nothing to command assent, except that the meaning of the terms be understood. According to the other doctrine, right and wrong, as well as truth and falsehood, are questions of observation and experience. But both hold equally that morality must be deduced from principles; and the intuitive school affirm as strongly as the inductive that there is a science of morals. Yet they seldom attempt to make out a list of the *à priori* principles which are to serve as the premises of the science; still more rarely do they make any effort to reduce those various principles to one first principle, or common ground of obligation. They either assume the ordinary precepts of morals as of *à priori* authority, or they lay down, as the common groundwork of those maxims, some generality much less obviously authoritative than the maxims themselves, and which has never succeeded in gaining popular acceptance. Yet to support their pretensions there ought either to be some one fundamental principle or law, at the root of all morality, or if there be several, there should be a determinate order of precedence among them;[1] and the one principle, or

[1] 'Dissertations and Discussions,' vol. i. p. 384 : "We think utility or happiness much too complex and indefinite an end to be sought except through the medium of various secondary ends, concerning which there may be, and often is, agreement among persons who differ in their ultimate standard ; and about which there does in fact prevail a much greater unanimity among thinking persons than might be supposed from their diametrical divergence on the great questions of moral metaphysics. As mankind are much more nearly of one nature than of one opinion about their own nature, they are more easily brought to agree in their intermediate principles, '*vera illa et media axiomata,*' as Bacon says, than in their first principles : and the attempt to make the bearings of actions upon the ultimate end more evident than they can be made by referring them to the intermediate ends, and to estimate their value by a direct reference to human happiness, generally terminates in attaching most importance not to those effects which are really the greatest, but to those which can most easily be pointed to and individually identified. Those who adopt utility as a standard can seldom apply it truly except through the secondary principles ; those who reject it generally do no more than erect these secondary principles into first principles. It is when two or more of the secondary principles conflict that a direct appeal to some first principle becomes necessary ; and then commences the practical importance of the utilitarian controversy ; which is in other respects a question of arrangement and logical subordination rather than of practice ; important principally in a purely scientific point of view, for the sake of the systematic unity and coherency of ethical philosophy. . . . Whether happiness be or be not the end to which morality should be referred—that it be referred to an *end* of some sort, and not left in the dominion of vague feeling or inexplicable internal conviction, that it be made a matter of reason and calculation, and not merely of sentiment, is essential to the very idea of moral philosophy ; is, in fact, what

the rule for deciding between the various principles when they conflict, ought to be self-evident.

To inquire how far the bad effects of this deficiency have been mitigated in practice, or to what extent the moral beliefs of mankind have been vitiated or made uncertain by the absence of any distinct recognition of an ultimate standard, would imply a complete survey and criticism of past and present ethical doctrine. It would, however, be easy to show that whatever steadiness or consistency these moral beliefs have attained, has been mainly due to the tacit influence of a standard not recognised. Although the non-existence of an acknowledged first principle has made ethics not so much a guide as a consecration of men's actual sentiments, still, as men's sentiments, both of favour and of aversion, are greatly influenced by what they suppose to be the effects of things upon their happiness, the principle of utility, or, as Bentham latterly called it, the greatest happiness principle, has had a large share in forming the moral doctrines even of those who most scornfully reject its authority.[1] Nor is

renders argument or discussion on moral questions possible. That the morality of actions depends on the consequences which they tend to produce is the doctrine of rational persons of all schools; that the good or evil of those consequences is measured solely by pleasure or pain is all of the doctrine of the school of utility, which is peculiar to it.

"In so far as Bentham's adoption of the principle of utility induced him to fix his attention upon the consequences of actions as the consideration determining their morality, so far he was indisputably in the right path."

[1] Compare with this Mill's statements as to the value of actual moral feelings, 'Liberty,' p. 4: "Among so many baser influences, the general and obvious interests of society have, of course,

there any school of thought which refuses to admit that the influence of actions on happiness is a most material and even predominant consideration in many of the details of morals, however unwilling to acknowledge it as the fundamental principle of morality, and the source of moral obligation. I might go much further, and say that to all those *à priori* moralists who deem it necessary to argue at all, utilitarian arguments are indispensable. It is not my present purpose to criticise these thinkers; but I cannot help referring, for illustration, to a systematic treatise by one of the most illustrious of them, the 'Metaphysics of Ethics,' by Kant. This remarkable man, whose system of thought will long remain one of the landmarks in the history

had a share, and a large one, in the direction of the moral sentiments: less however as a matter of reason, and on their own account, than as a consequence of the sympathies and antipathies which grew out of them: and sympathies and antipathies which had little or nothing to do with the interests of society, have made themselves felt in the establishment of moralities with quite as great force."

Essay on Whewell's Moral Philosophy, 'Dissertations and Discussions,' vol. ii. p. 453 : "His 'Elements of Morality' could be nothing better than a classification and systematising of the opinions which he found prevailing, among those who had been educated according to the approved methods of his own country; or, let us rather say, an apparatus for converting those prevailing opinions, on matters of morality, into reasons for themselves."

Ib., p. 499 : "But to pretend that any such antipathy, were it ever so general, gives the smallest guarantee of its own justice and reasonableness, or has any claim to be binding on those who do not partake in the sentiment, is as irrational as to adduce the belief in ghosts or witches as a proof of their real existence. I am not bound to abstain from an action because another person dislikes it, however he may dignify his dislike with the name of disapprobation."

of philosophical speculation, does, in the treatise in question, lay down an universal first principle as the origin and ground of moral obligation; it is this: "So act, that the rule on which thou actest would admit of being adopted as a law by all rational beings." But when he begins to deduce from this precept any of the actual duties of morality, he fails, almost grotesquely, to show that there would be any contradiction, any logical (not to say physical) impossibility, in the adoption by all rational beings of the most outrageously immoral rules of conduct. All he shows is that the *consequences* of their universal adoption would be such as no one would choose to incur.[1]

On the present occasion I shall, without further discussion of the other theories, attempt to contribute something towards the understanding and appreciation of the Utilitarian or Happiness theory, and towards such proof as it is susceptible of. It is evident that this cannot be proof in the ordinary and popular meaning of the term. Questions of ultimate ends are not amenable to direct proof. Whatever can be proved to be good, must be so by being shown to be a means to something admitted to be good without proof. The medical art is proved to be good, by its conducing to health; but how is it possible to prove that health is good? The art of music is good, for the reason, among

[1] 'Dissertations and Discussions,' vol. ii. p. 496: "Though Dr Whewell will not recognise the promotion of happiness as the ultimate principle, he deduces his secondary principles from it, and supports his propositions by utilitarian reasons as far as they will go."

others, that it produces pleasure; but what proof is it possible to give that pleasure is good? If, then, it is asserted that there is a comprehensive formula, including all things which are in themselves good, and that whatever else is good is not so as an end, but as a mean, the formula may be accepted or rejected, but is not a subject of what is commonly understood by proof. We are not, however, to infer that its acceptance or rejection must depend on blind impulse, or arbitrary choice. There is a larger meaning of the word proof, in which this question is as amenable to it as any other of the disputed questions of philosophy. The subject is within the cognisance of the rational faculty; and neither does that faculty deal with it solely in the way of intuition. Considerations may be presented capable of determining the intellect either to give or withhold its assent to the doctrine; and this is equivalent to proof.

We shall examine presently of what nature are these considerations; in what manner they apply to the case, and what rational grounds, therefore, can be given for accepting or rejecting the utilitarian formula. But it is a preliminary condition of rational acceptance or rejection, that the formula should be correctly understood. I believe that the very imperfect notion ordinarily formed of its meaning, is the chief obstacle which impedes its reception; and that could it be cleared, even from only the grosser misconceptions, the question would be greatly simplified, and a large proportion of its difficulties removed. Before, therefore, I attempt to enter into the philosophical grounds which can be given for assenting to the utilitarian standard, I shall offer some illustrations of the doctrine itself; with the view of showing more clearly what it is, distinguishing it from what it is not, and disposing of such of the practical objections to it as either originate in, or are closely connected with, mistaken interpretations of its meaning. Having thus prepared the ground, I shall afterwards endeavour to throw such light as I can upon the question, considered as one of philosophical theory.

CHAPTER II

WHAT UTILITARIANISM IS

A PASSING remark is all that needs be given to the ignorant blunder of supposing that those who stand up for utility as the test of right and wrong, use the term in that restricted and merely colloquial sense in which utility is opposed to pleasure. An apology is due to the philosophical opponents of utilitarianism, for even the momentary appearance of confounding them with any one capable of so absurd a misconception; which is the more extraordinary, inasmuch as the contrary accusation, of referring everything to pleasure, and that too in its grossest form, is another of the common charges against utilitarianism: and, as has been pointedly remarked by an able writer, the same sort of persons, and often the very same persons, denounce the theory "as impracticably dry when the word utility precedes the word pleasure, and as too practicably voluptuous when the word pleasure precedes the word utility." Those who know anything about the matter are aware that every writer, from Epicurus to Bentham, who maintained the theory of utility, meant by it, not something to be contradistinguished from pleasure, but pleasure itself, together with exemption from pain; and instead of opposing the useful to the agreeable or the ornamental, have always declared that the useful means these, among other things. Yet the common herd, including the herd of writers, not only in newspapers and periodicals, but in books of weight and pretension, are perpetually falling into this shallow mistake. Having caught up the word utilitarian, while knowing nothing whatever about it but its sound, they habitually express by it the rejection, or the neglect, of pleasure in some of its forms—of beauty, of ornament, or of amusement. Nor is the term thus ignorantly misapplied solely in disparagement, but occasionally in compliment; as though it implied superiority to frivolity and the mere pleasures of the moment. And this perverted use is the only one in which the word is popularly known, and the one from which the new generation are acquiring their sole notion of its meaning. Those who introduced the word, but who had for many years discontinued it as a distinctive appellation, may well feel themselves called upon to resume it, if by doing so they can hope to contribute anything towards rescuing it from this utter degradation.*

---

* The author of this essay has reason for believing himself to be the first person who brought the word utilitarian into use. He did not invent it, but adopted it from a passing expression in Mr Galt's 'Annals of the Parish.' After using it as a designation for several years, he and others abandoned it from a growing dislike to anything resembling a badge or watchword of sectarian distinction. But as a name for one single opinion, not a set of opinions—to denote the recognition of util-

The creed which accepts as the foundation of morals, Utility, or the Greatest Happiness Principle, holds that actions are right in proportion as they tend to promote happiness, wrong as they tend to produce the reverse of happiness. By happiness is intended pleasure, and the absence of pain; by unhappiness, pain, and the privation of pleasure. To give a clear view of the moral standard set up by the theory, much more requires to be said: in particular, what things it includes in the ideas of pain and pleasure; and to what extent this is left an open question. But these supplementary explanations do not affect the theory of life on which this theory of morality is grounded — namely, that pleasure, and freedom from pain, are the only things desirable as ends; and that all desirable things (which are as numerous in the utilitarian as in any other scheme) are desirable either for the pleasure inherent in themselves, or as means to the promotion of pleasure and the prevention of pain.

Now, such a theory of life excites in many minds, and among them in some of the most estimable in feeling and purpose, inveterate dislike. To suppose that life has (as they express it) no higher end than pleasure—no better and nobler object of desire and pursuit—they designate as utterly mean and grovelling; as a doctrine worthy only of swine, to whom the followers of Epicurus were, at a very early period,

---

ity as a standard, not any particular way of applying it—the term supplies a want in the language, and offers, in many cases, a convenient mode of avoiding tiresome circumlocution.

contemptuously likened; and modern holders of the doctrine are occasionally made the subject of equally polite comparisons by its German, French, and English assailants.

When thus attacked, the Epicureans have always answered that it is not they, but their accusers, who represent human nature in a degrading light; since the accusation supposes human beings to be capable of no pleasures except those of which swine are capable. If this supposition were true, the charge could not be gainsaid, but would then be no longer an imputation: for if the sources of pleasure were precisely the same to human beings and to swine, the rule of life which is good enough for the one would be good enough for the other. The comparison of the Epicurean life to that of beasts is felt as degrading, precisely because a beast's pleasures do not satisfy a human being's conceptions of happiness. Human beings have faculties more elevated than the animal appetites, and when once made conscious of them, do not regard anything as happiness which does not include their gratification. I do not, indeed, consider the Epicureans to have been by any means faultless in drawing out their scheme of consequences from the utilitarian principle. To do this in any sufficient manner, many Stoic as well as Christian elements require to be included. But there is no known Epicurean theory of life which does not assign to the pleasures of the intellect, of the feelings and imagination, and of the moral sentiments, a much higher value as pleasures than to those of mere sensation.[1] It must be admitted, however, that utilitarian writers in general have placed the superiority of mental over bodily pleasures chiefly in the greater permanency, safety, uncostliness, &c., of the former—that is, in their circumstantial advantages rather than in their intrinsic nature. And on all these points utilitarians have fully proved their case; but they might have taken the other, and, as it may be called, higher ground, with entire consistency. It is quite compatible with the principle of utility to recognise the fact, that some *kinds* of pleasure are more desirable and more valuable than others. It would be absurd that while, in estimating all other things, quality is considered as well as quantity, the estimation of pleasures should be supposed to depend on quantity alone.

If I am asked what I mean by difference of quality in pleasures, or what makes one pleasure more valuable than another, merely as a pleasure, except its being greater in amount, there is but one possible answer. Of two pleasures, if there be one to which all or almost all who have experience of both give a decided preference, irrespective of any feeling of moral obligation to prefer it, that is the more desirable pleasure. If one of the two is, by those who are competently acquainted with both, placed so far above the other that they prefer it, even though knowing it to be attended with a

---

[1] Cf. Mill's statement about his father, 'Autobiography,' p. 49: "He never varied in rating intellectual enjoyments above all others, even in value as pleasures, independently of their ulterior benefits. The pleasures of the benevolent affections he placed high in the scale."

greater amount of discontent, and would not resign it for any quantity of the other pleasure which their nature is capable of, we are justified in ascribing to the preferred enjoyment a superiority in quality, so far outweighing quantity as to render it, in comparison, of small account.[1]

Now it is an unquestionable fact that those who are equally acquainted with, and equally capable of appreciating and enjoying, both, do give a most marked preference to the manner of existence which employs their higher faculties. Few human creatures would consent to be changed into any of the lower animals, for a promise of the fullest allowance of a beast's pleasures;

---

[1] 'Liberty,' p. 6: "I regard utility as the ultimate appeal on all ethical questions; but it must be utility in the largest sense, grounded on the permanent interests of man as a progressive being."

This must be compared, however, with other statements, 'Liberty,' p. 34: "But it is the privilege and proper condition of a human being, arrived at the maturity of his faculties, to use and interpret experiences in his own way. It is for him to find out what part of recorded experience is properly applicable to his own circumstances and character. . . . Human nature is not a machine to be built after a model and set to do exactly the work prescribed for it, but a tree which requires to grow and develop itself on all sides, according to the tendency of the inward forces which make it a living thing."

P. 39: "If a person possesses any tolerable amount of common sense and experience, his own mode of laying out his existence is the best, not because it is the best in itself, but because it is his own mode."

P. 40: "Such are the differences among human beings in their sources of pleasure, their susceptibilities of pain, and the operation on them of different physical and moral agencies, that unless there is a corresponding diversity in their modes of life, they neither obtain their fair share of happiness, nor grow up to the mental, and moral, and æsthetic stature of which their nature is capable."

'Representative Government,' p. 123: "When we talk of the

no intelligent human being would consent to be a fool, no instructed person would be an ignoramus, no person of feeling and conscience would be selfish and base, even though they should be persuaded that the fool, the dunce, or the rascal is better satisfied with his lot than they are with theirs. They would not resign what they possess more than he, for the most complete satisfaction of all the desires which they have in common with him. If they ever fancy they would, it is only in cases of unhappiness so extreme, that to escape from it they would exchange their lot for almost any other, however undesirable in their own eyes. A being of higher faculties requires more to make him

interest of a body of men, or even of an individual man, as a principle determining their actions, the question what would be considered their interest by an unprejudiced observer is one of the least important parts of the whole matter. As Coleridge observes, the man makes the motive, not the motive the man. What it is the man's interest to do or refrain from, depends less on any outward circumstances than upon what sort of man he is. If you wish to know what is practically a man's interest, you must know the cast of his habitual feelings and thoughts. Everybody has two kinds of interests—interests which he cares for and interests which he does not care for. Everybody has selfish and unselfish interests, and a selfish man has cultivated the habit of caring for the former and not caring for the latter. Every one has present and distant interests, and the improvident man is he who cares for the present interests and does not care for the distant. It matters little that on any correct calculation the latter may be the more considerable, if the habits of his mind lead him to fix his thoughts on the former. . . . On the average, a person who cares for other people, for his country or for mankind, is a happier man than one who does not; but of what use is it to preach this doctrine to a man who cares for nothing but his own ease or his own pocket? He cannot care for other people if he would. It is like preaching to the worm who crawls on the ground how much better it would be for him if he were an eagle."

happy, is capable probably of more acute suffering, and is certainly accessible to it at more points, than one of an inferior type; but in spite of these liabilities, he can never really wish to sink into what he feels to be a lower grade of existence. We may give what explanation we please of this unwillingness: we may attribute it to pride, a name which is given indiscriminately to some of the most and to some of the least estimable feelings of which mankind are capable; we may refer it to the love of liberty and personal independence, an appeal to which was with the Stoics one of the most effective means for the inculcation of it; to the love of power, or to the love of excitement, both of which do really enter into and contribute to it. But its most appropriate appellation is a sense of dignity, which all human beings possess in one form or other, and in some, though by no means in exact, proportion to their higher faculties, and which is so essential a part of the happiness of those in whom it is strong, that nothing which conflicts with it could be, otherwise than momentarily, an object of desire to them. Whoever supposes that this preference takes place at a sacrifice of happiness — that the superior being, in anything like equal circumstances, is not happier than the inferior — confounds the two very different ideas, of happiness, and content. It is indisputable that the being whose capacities of enjoyment are low, has the greatest chance of having them fully satisfied; and a highly endowed being will always feel that any happiness which he can look for, as the world is constituted, is imperfect. But he can learn to bear its imperfections, if they are at all bearable; and they will not make him envy the being who is indeed unconscious of the imperfections, but only because he feels not at all the good which those imperfections qualify. It is better to be a human being dissatisfied than a pig satisfied; better to be Socrates dissatisfied than a fool satisfied. And if the fool, or the pig, is of a different opinion, it is because they only know their own side of the question. The other party to the comparison knows both sides.

It may be objected that many who are capable of the higher pleasures, occasionally, under the influence of temptation, postpone them to the lower. But this is quite compatible with a full appreciation of the intrinsic superiority of the higher. Men often, from infirmity of character, make their election for the nearer good, though they know it to be the less valuable; and this no less when the choice is between two bodily pleasures, than when it is between bodily and mental. They pursue sensual indulgences to the injury of health, though perfectly aware that health is the greater good. It may be further objected that many who begin with youthful enthusiasm for everything noble, as they advance in years sink into indolence and selfishness. But I do not believe that those who undergo this very common change, voluntarily choose the lower description of pleasures in preference to the higher. I believe that before they devote themselves exclusively to the one, they have already become incapable of the other. Capacity for the nobler feelings is in most natures a very tender plant, easily killed, not only by hostile influences, but by mere want of sustenance; and in the majority of young persons it speedily dies away if the occupations to which their position in life has devoted them, and the society into which it has thrown them, are not favourable to keeping that higher capacity in exercise. Men lose their high aspirations as they lose their intellectual tastes, because they have not time or opportunity for indulging them; and they addict themselves to inferior pleasures, not because they deliberately prefer them, but because they are either the only ones to which they have access, or the only ones which they are any longer capable of enjoying. It may be questioned whether any one who has remained equally susceptible to both classes of pleasures, ever knowingly and calmly preferred the lower; though many, in all ages, have broken down in an ineffectual attempt to combine both.

From this verdict of the only competent judges, I apprehend there can be no appeal. On a question which is the better worth having of two pleasures, or which of two modes of existence is the more grateful to the feelings, apart from its moral attributes and from its consequences, the judgment of those who are qualified by knowledge of both, or, if they differ, that of the majority among them, must be admitted as final. And there needs be the less hesitation to accept this judgment respecting the quality of pleasures, since there is no other tribunal to be referred to even on the question of quantity. What means are there of determining which is the acuter of two pains, or the intenser of two pleasurable sensations, except the general suffrage of those who are familiar with both? Neither pains nor pleasures are homogeneous, and pain is always heterogeneous with pleasure. What is there to decide whether a particular pleasure is worth purchasing at the cost of a particular pain, except the feelings and judgment of the experienced? When, therefore, those feelings and judgment declare the pleasures derived from the higher faculties to be preferable *in kind*, apart from the question of intensity, to those of which the animal nature, disjoined from the higher faculties, is susceptible, they are entitled on this subject to the same regard.

I have dwelt on this point, as being a necessary part of a perfectly just conception of Utility or Happiness, considered as the directive rule of human conduct. But it is by no means an indispensable condition to the acceptance of the utilitarian standard, for that standard is not the agent's own greatest happiness, but the greatest amount of happiness altogether; and if it may possibly be doubted whether a noble character is always the happier for its nobleness, there can be no doubt that it makes other people happier, and that the world in general is immensely a gainer by it. Utilitarianism, therefore, could only attain its end by the general cultivation of nobleness of character, even if each individual were only benefited by the nobleness of others, and his own, so far as happiness is concerned, were a sheer deduction from the benefit. But the bare enunciation of such an absurdity as this last renders refutation superfluous.

According to the Greatest Happiness Principle, as above explained, the ultimate end, with reference to and for the sake of which all other things are desirable (whether we are considering our own good or that of other people), is an existence exempt as far as possible from pain, and as rich as possible in enjoyments, both in point of quantity and quality; the test of quality, and the rule for measuring it against quantity, being the preference felt by those who, in their opportunities of experience, to which must be added their habits of self-consciousness and self-observation, are best furnished with the means of comparison. This, being, according to the utilitarian opinion, the end of human action, is necessarily also the standard of morality; which may accordingly be defined, the rules and precepts for human conduct, by the observance of which an existence such as has been described might be, to the greatest extent possible, secured to all mankind; and not to them only, but, so far as the nature of things admits, to the whole sentient creation.

Against this doctrine, however, rises another class of objectors, who say that happiness, in any form, cannot be the rational purpose of human life and action; because, in the first place, it is unattainable: and they contemptuously ask, What right hast thou to be happy? a question which Mr Carlyle clenches by the addition, What right, a short time ago, hadst thou even *to be?* Next, they say, that men can do *without* happiness; that all noble human beings have felt this, and could not have become noble but by learning the lesson of Entsagen, or renunciation; which lesson, thoroughly learnt and submitted to, they affirm to be the beginning and necessary condition of all virtue.

The first of these objections would go to the root of the matter were it well founded; for if no happiness is to be had at all by human beings, the attainment of it cannot be the end of morality, or of any rational conduct. Though, even in that case, something might still be said for the utilitarian theory, since utility includes not solely the pursuit of happiness, but the prevention or mitigation of unhappiness; and if the former aim be chimerical, there will be all the greater scope and more imperative need for the latter, so long at least as mankind think fit to live, and do not take refuge in the simultaneous act of suicide recommended under certain conditions by Novalis. When, however, it is thus positively asserted to be impossible that human life should be happy, the assertion, if not something like a verbal quibble, is at least an exaggeration. If by happiness be meant a continuity of highly pleasurable excitement, it is evident enough that this is impossible. A state of exalted pleasure lasts only moments, or in some cases, and with some intermissions, hours or days, and is the occasional brilliant flash of enjoyment, not its permanent and steady flame. Of this the philosophers who have taught that happiness is the end of life were as fully aware as those who taunt them. The happiness which they meant was not a life of rapture; but moments of such, in an existence made up of few and transitory pains, many and various pleasures, with a decided predominance of the active over the passive, and having, as the foundation of the whole, not to expect more from life than it is capable of bestowing. A life thus composed, to those who have been fortunate enough to obtain it, has always appeared worthy of the name of happiness. And such an existence is even now the lot of many, during some considerable portion of their lives. The present wretched education, and wretched social arrangements, are the only real hindrance to its being attainable by almost all.

The objectors perhaps may doubt whether human beings, if taught to consider happiness as the end of life, would be satisfied with such a moderate share of it. But great numbers of mankind have been satisfied with much less. The main constituents of a satisfied life appear to be two, either of which by itself is often found sufficient for the purpose—tranquillity, and excitement. With much tranquillity, many find that they can be content with very little pleasure: with much excitement, many can reconcile themselves to a considerable quantity of pain. There is assuredly no inherent impossibility in enabling even the mass of mankind to unite both; since the two are so far from being incompatible that they are in natural alliance, the prolongation of either being a preparation for, and exciting a wish for, the other. It is only those in whom indolence amounts to a vice, that do not desire excitement after an interval of repose; it is only those in whom the need of excitement is a disease, that feel the tranquillity which follows excitement dull and insipid, instead of pleasurable in direct proportion to the excitement which preceded it. When people who are tolerably fortunate in their outward lot do not find in life sufficient enjoyment to make it valuable to them, the cause generally is, caring for nobody but themselves. To those who have neither public nor private affections, the excitements of life are much curtailed, and in any case dwindle in value as the time approaches when all selfish interests must be terminated by death: while those who leave after them objects of personal affection, and especially those who have also cultivated a fellow-feeling with the collective interests of mankind, retain as lively an interest in life on the eve of death as in the vigour of youth and health. Next to selfishness, the principal cause which makes life unsatisfactory is want of mental cultivation. A cultivated mind—I do not mean that of a philosopher, but any mind to which the fountains of knowledge have been opened, and which has been taught, in any tolerable degree, to exercise its faculties—finds sources of inexhaustible interest in all that surrounds it: in the objects of nature, the achievements of art, the imaginations of poetry, the incidents of history, the ways of mankind past and present, and their prospects in the future. It is possible, indeed, to become indifferent to all this, and that too without having exhausted a thousandth part of it; but only when one has had from the beginning no moral or human interest in these things, and has sought in them only the gratification of curiosity.

Now there is absolutely no reason in the nature of things why an amount of mental culture sufficient to give an intelligent interest in these objects of contemplation, should not be the inheritance of every one born in a civilised country. As little is there an inherent necessity that any human being should be a selfish egotist, devoid of every feeling or care but those which centre in his own miserable individuality. Something far superior to this is sufficiently common even now, to give ample earnest of what the human species may be made. Genuine private affections, and a sincere interest in the public good, are possible, though in unequal degrees, to every rightly brought up human being. In a world in which there is so much to interest, so much to enjoy, and so much also to correct and improve, every one who has this moderate amount of moral and intellectual requisites is capable of an existence which may be called enviable; and unless such a person, through bad laws, or subjection to the will of others, is denied the liberty to use the sources of happiness within his reach, he will not fail to find this enviable existence, if he escape the positive evils of life, the great sources of physical and mental suffering—such as indigence, disease, and the unkindness, worthlessness, or premature loss of objects of affection. The main stress of the problem lies, therefore, in the contest with these calamities, from which it is a rare good fortune entirely to escape; which, as things now are, cannot be obviated, and often cannot be in any material degree mitigated. Yet no one whose opinion deserves a moment's consideration can doubt that most of the great positive evils of the world are in themselves removable, and will, if human affairs continue to improve, be in the end reduced within narrow limits. Poverty, in any sense implying suffering, may be completely extinguished by the wisdom of society, combined with the good sense and providence of individuals. Even that most intractable of enemies, disease, may be indefinitely reduced in dimensions by good physical and moral education, and proper control of noxious influences; while the progress of science holds out a promise for the future of still more direct conquests over this detestable foe. And every advance in that direction relieves us from some, not only of the chances which cut short our own lives, but, what concerns us still more, which deprive us of those in whom our happiness is wrapt up. As for vicissitudes of fortune, and other disappointments connected with worldly circumstances, these are principally the effect either of gross imprudence, of ill-regulated desires, or of bad or imperfect social institutions. All the grand sources, in short, of human suffering are in a great degree, many of them almost entirely, conquerable by human care and effort; and though their removal is grievously slow—

though a long succession of generations will perish in the breach before the conquest is completed, and this world becomes all that, if will and knowledge were not wanting, it might easily be made — yet every mind sufficiently intelligent and generous to bear a part, however small and unconspicuous, in the endeavour, will draw a noble enjoyment from the contest itself, which he would not for any bribe in the form of selfish indulgence consent to be without.

And this leads to the true estimation of what is said by the objectors concerning the possibility, and the obligation, of learning to do without happiness. Unquestionably it is possible to do without happiness: it is done involuntarily by nineteen-twentieths of mankind, even in those parts of our present world which are least deep in barbarism; and it often has to be done voluntarily by the hero or the martyr, for the sake of something which he prizes more than his individual happiness. But this something, what is it, unless the happiness of others, or some of the requisites of happiness? It is noble to be capable of resigning entirely one's own portion of happiness, or chances of it: but, after all, this self-sacrifice must be for some end; it is not its own end; and if we are told that its end is not happiness, but virtue, which is better than happiness, I ask, would the sacrifice be made if the hero or martyr did not believe that it would earn for others immunity from similar sacrifices? Would it be made, if he thought that his renunciation of happiness for himself would produce no fruit for any of his fellow-creatures, but to make their lot like his, and place them also in the condition of persons who have renounced happiness? All honour to those who can abnegate for themselves the personal enjoyment of life, when by such renunciation they contribute worthily to increase the amount of happiness in the world; but he who does it, or professes to do it, for any other purpose, is no more deserving of admiration than the ascetic mounted on his pillar. He may be an inspiriting proof of what men *can* do, but assuredly not an example of what they *should*.

Though it is only in a very imperfect state of the world's arrangements that any one can best serve the happiness of others by the absolute sacrifice of his own, yet so long as the world is in that imperfect state, I fully acknowledge that the readiness to make such a sacrifice is the highest virtue which can be found in man.[1] I will add, that in this condition of the world, paradoxical as the assertion may be, the conscious ability to do without happiness gives the best prospect of realising such happiness as is attainable.[2] For nothing

---

[1] 'Auguste Comte and Positivism,' p. 146: "It is as much a part of our scheme as of M. Comte's, that the direct cultivation of altruism, and the subordination of egoism to it, far beyond the point of absolute moral duty, should be one of the chief aims of education, both individual and collective. We even recognise the value, for this end, of ascetic discipline, in the original Greek sense of the word. We think with Dr Johnson, that he who has never denied himself anything which is not wrong, cannot be fully trusted for denying himself everything which is so."

[2] 'Autobiography,' p. 142: "I never indeed wavered in the conviction that happiness is the test of all rules of conduct, and the end of life. But I now thought that this end was only to be attained by not making it the direct end. Those only are happy (I thought)

except that consciousness can raise a person above the chances of life, by making him feel that, let fate and fortune do their worst, they have not power to subdue him: which, once felt, frees him from excess of anxiety concerning the evils of life, and enables him, like many a Stoic in the worst times of the Roman empire, to cultivate in tranquillity the sources of satisfaction accessible to him, without concerning himself about the uncertainty of their duration, any more than about their inevitable end.

Meanwhile, let utilitarians never cease to claim the morality of self-devotion as a possession which belongs by as good a right to them, as either to the Stoic or to the Transcendentalist. The utilitarian morality does recognise in human beings the power of sacrificing

who have their minds fixed on some object other than their own happiness: on the happiness of others, on the improvement of mankind, even on some art or pursuit, followed not as a means, but as itself an ideal end. Aiming thus at something else, they find happiness by the way. The enjoyments of life (such was now my theory) are sufficient to make it a pleasant thing, when they are taken *en passant* without being made a principal object. Once make them so, and they are immediately felt to be insufficient. They will not bear a scrutinising examination. Ask yourself whether you are happy, and you cease to be so. The only chance is to treat, not happiness, but some end external to it, as the purpose of life. Let your self-consciousness, your scrutiny, your self-interrogation exhaust themselves on that; and if otherwise fortunately circumstanced you will inhale happiness with the air you breathe, without dwelling on it or thinking about it, without either forestalling it in imagination or putting it to flight by fatal questioning. This theory now became the basis of my philosophy of life. And I still hold to it as the best theory for all those who have but a moderate degree of sensibility, and of capacity for enjoyment—that is, for the great majority of mankind."

their own greatest good for the good of others.[1] It only refuses to admit that the sacrifice is itself a good. A sacrifice which does not increase, or tend to increase, the sum total of happiness, it considers as wasted. The only self-renunciation which it applauds is devotion to the happiness, or to some of the means of happiness, of others; either of mankind collectively, or of individuals within the limits imposed by the collective interests of mankind.[2]

---

[1] 'Essays on Religion,' p. 109: "The essence of religion is the strong and earnest direction of the emotions and desires towards an ideal object, recognised as of the highest excellence; and as rightfully paramount over all selfish objects of desire. This condition is fulfilled by the Religion of Humanity."

'Auguste Comte and Positivism,' p. 135: "We join with him [Comte] in contemning, as equally irrational and mean, the conception of human nature as incapable of giving its love and devoting its existence to any object which cannot afford in exchange an eternity of personal enjoyment."

'Principles of Political Economy,' p. 127: "Mankind are capable of a far greater amount of public spirit than the present age is accustomed to suppose possible. History bears witness to the success with which large bodies of human beings may be trained to feel the public interest their own. And no soil could be more favourable to the growth of such a feeling than a Communist association, since all the ambition, and the bodily and mental activity, which are now exerted in the pursuit of separate and self-regarding interests, would require another sphere of employment, and would naturally find it in the pursuit of the general benefit of the community."

'Representative Government,' p. 55: "For my own part, not believing in universal selfishness, I have no difficulty in admitting that Communism would even now be practicable among the *élite* of mankind, and may become so among the rest."

[2] 'Auguste Comte and Positivism,' p. 145: "We do not conceive life to be so rich in enjoyments, that it can afford to forego the cultivation of all those which address themselves to what M. Comte terms the egoistic propensities. . . . The moralisation of the personal enjoyments we deem to consist, not in reducing them to

I must again repeat, what the assailants of utilitarianism seldom have the justice to acknowledge, that the happiness which forms the utilitarian standard of what is right in conduct is not the agent's own happiness, but that of all concerned. As between his own happiness and that of others, utilitarianism requires him to be as strictly impartial as a disinterested and benevolent spectator. In the golden rule of Jesus of Nazareth, we read the complete spirit of the ethics of utility. To do as one would be done by, and to love one's neighbour as oneself, constitute the ideal perfection of utilitarian morality. As the means of making the nearest approach to this ideal, utility would enjoin, first, that laws and social arrangements should place the happiness, or (as speaking practically it may be called) the interest, of every individual, as nearly as possible in harmony with the interest of the whole; and secondly, that education and opinion, which have so vast a power over human character, should so use that power as to establish in the mind of every individual an indissoluble association between his own happiness and the good of the whole; especially between his own happiness and the practice of such modes of conduct, negative and positive, as regard for the universal happiness prescribes: so that not only he may be unable to conceive the possibility of happiness to himself, consistently with conduct opposed to

the smallest possible amount, but in cultivating the habitual wish to share them with others, and with all others, and scorning to desire anything for oneself which is incapable of being so shared."

the general good, but also that a direct impulse to promote the general good may be in every individual one of the habitual motives of action, and the sentiments connected therewith may fill a large and prominent place in every human being's sentient existence. If the impugners of the utilitarian morality represented it to their own minds in this its true character, I know not what recommendation possessed by any other morality they could possibly affirm to be wanting to it; what more beautiful or more exalted developments of human nature any other ethical system can be supposed to foster, or what springs of action, not accessible to the utilitarian, such systems rely on for giving effect to their mandates.

The objectors to utilitarianism cannot always be charged with representing it in a discreditable light. On the contrary, those among them who entertain anything like a just idea of its disinterested character, sometimes find fault with its standard as being too high for humanity. They say it is exacting too much to require that people shall always act from the inducement of promoting the general interests of society. But this is to mistake the very meaning of a standard of morals, and to confound the rule of action with the motive of it. It is the business of ethics to tell us what are our duties, or by what test we may know them; but no system of ethics requires that the sole motive of all we do shall be a feeling of duty: on the contrary, ninety-nine hundredths of all our actions are done from other motives, and rightly so done, if the rule of duty does not condemn them. It is the more unjust to utilitarianism that this particular misapprehension should be made a ground of objection to it, inasmuch as utilitarian moralists have gone beyond almost all others in affirming that the motive has nothing to do with the morality of the action, though much with the worth of the agent. He who saves a fellow-creature from drowning does what is morally right, whether his motive be duty, or the hope of being paid for his trouble: he who betrays the friend that trusts him is guilty of a crime, even if his object be to serve another friend to whom he is under greater obligations.* But to speak only of actions done from the motive of duty, and in direct obedience to principle: it is a misapprehension of the utilitarian mode of thought, to conceive it as implying that people should fix their minds upon so wide a generality as the

* An opponent, whose intellectual and moral fairness it is a pleasure to acknowledge (the Rev. J. Llewelyn Davies), has objected to this passage, saying: "Surely the rightness or wrongness of saving a man from drowning does depend very much upon the motive with which it is done.. Suppose that a tyrant, when his enemy jumped into the sea to escape from him, saved him from drowning simply in order that he might inflict upon him more exquisite tortures, would it tend to clearness to speak of that rescue as 'a morally right action'? Or suppose again, according to one of the stock illustrations of ethical inquiries, that a man betrayed a trust received from a friend, because the discharge of it would fatally injure that friend himself or some one belonging to him, would utilitarianism compel one to call the betrayal 'a crime' as much as if it had been done from the meanest motive?"

I submit, that he who saves another from drowning in order to kill him by torture afterwards, does not differ only in motive from him who does the same thing from duty or benevolence; the act itself is different. The rescue of the man is, in the case supposed,

world, or society at large. The great majority of good actions are intended, not for the benefit of the world, but for that of individuals, of which the good of the world is made up; and the thoughts of the most virtuous man need not on these occasions travel beyond the particular persons concerned, except so far as is necessary to assure himself that in benefiting them he is not violating the rights—that is, the legitimate and authorised expectations—of any one else. The multiplication of happiness is, according to the utilitarian ethics, the object of virtue: the occasions on which any person (except one in a thousand) has it in his power to do this on an extended scale in other words, to be a public benefactor, are but exceptional; and on these occasions alone is he called on to consider public utility; in every other case, private utility, the interest or happiness of some few persons, is all he has to attend to. Those alone the influence of whose actions

only the necessary first step of an act far more atrocious than leaving him to drown would have been. Had Mr Davies said, "The rightness or wrongness of saving a man from drowning does depend very much"—not upon the motive, but—"upon the *intention*," no utilitarian would have differed from him. Mr Davies, by an oversight too common not to be quite venial, has in this case confounded the very different ideas of Motive and Intention. There is no point which utilitarian thinkers (and Bentham pre-eminently) have taken more pains to illustrate than this. The morality of the action depends entirely upon the intention—that is, upon what the agent *wills to do*. But the motive—that is, the feeling which makes him will so to do—when it makes no difference in the act, makes none in the morality; though it makes a great difference in our moral estimation of the agent, especially if it indicates a good or a bad habitual *disposition* —a bent of character from which useful, or from which hurtful, actions are likely to arise.

extends to society in general, need concern themselves habitually about so large an object. In the case of abstinences indeed—of things which people forbear to do, from moral considerations, though the consequences in the particular case might be beneficial — it would be unworthy of an intelligent agent not to be consciously aware that the action is of a class which, if practised generally, would be generally injurious, and that this is the ground of the obligation to abstain from it. The amount of regard for the public interest implied in this recognition is no greater than is demanded by every system of morals, for they all enjoin to abstain from whatever is manifestly pernicious to society.

The same considerations dispose of another reproach against the doctrine of utility, founded on a still grosser misconception of the purpose of a standard of morality, and of the very meaning of the words right and wrong. It is often affirmed that utilitarianism renders men cold and unsympathising; that it chills their moral feelings towards individuals; that it makes them regard only the dry and hard consideration of the consequences of actions, not taking into their moral estimate the qualities from which those actions emanate. If the assertion means that they do not allow their judgment respecting the rightness or wrongness of an action to be influenced by their opinion of the qualities of the person who does it, this is a complaint not against utilitarianism, but against having any standard of morality at all; for certainly no known ethical standard decides an action to be good or bad because it is done by a good or a bad man, still less because done by an amiable, a brave, or a benevolent man, or the contrary. These considerations are relevant, not to the estimation of actions, but of persons; and there is nothing in the utilitarian theory inconsistent with the fact that there are other things which interest us in persons besides the rightness and wrongness of their actions. The Stoics, indeed, with the paradoxical misuse of language which was part of their system, and by which they strove to raise themselves above all concern about anything but virtue, were fond of saying that he who has that has everything; that he, and only he, is rich, is beautiful, is a king. But no claim of this description is made for the virtuous man by the utilitarian doctrine. Utilitarians are quite aware that there are other desirable possessions and qualities besides virtue, and are perfectly willing to allow to all of them their full worth. They are also aware that a right action does not necessarily indicate a virtuous character, and that actions which are blameable often proceed from qualities entitled to praise. When this is apparent in any particular case, it modifies their estimation, not certainly of the act, but of the agent. I grant that they are, notwithstanding, of opinion, that in the long-run the best proof of a good character is good actions; and resolutely refuse to consider any mental disposition as good, of which the predominant tendency is to produce bad conduct.[1] This makes them unpopular with many people; but it is an unpopularity which they must share with every one who regards the distinction between right and wrong in a serious light, and the reproach is not one which a conscientious utilitarian need be anxious to repel.

If no more be meant by the objection than that many utilitarians look on the morality of actions, as measured by the utilitarian standard, with too exclusive a regard, and do not lay sufficient stress upon the other beauties of character which go towards making a human being loveable or admirable, this may be admitted. Utilitarians who have cultivated their moral feelings, but not their sympathies nor their artistic perceptions, do fall into this mistake;[2] and so do all

---

[1] Cf. Mill's statements about his father, 'Autobiography,' p. 49: "He blamed as severely what he thought a bad action, when the motive was a feeling of duty, as if the agents had been consciously evil-doers."

Ib., p. 50: "But though he did not allow honesty of purpose to soften his disapprobation of actions, it had its full effect on his estimation of characters."

[2] 'Autobiography,' p. 143: "I had now learnt by experience that the passive susceptibilities needed to be cultivated as well as the active capacities, and required to be nourished and enriched as well as guided."

Ib., p. 214: "In the conduct of the Review ['London and Westminster Review'] I had two principal objects. One was to free philosophic Radicalism from the reproach of sectarian Benthamism. I desired, while retaining the precision of expression, the definiteness of meaning, the contempt of declamatory phrases and vague generalities, which were so honourably characteristic both of Bentham and of my father, to give a wider basis and a more free and genial character to Radical speculations; to show that there was a Radical philosophy, better and more complete than Bentham's, while recognising and incorporating all of Bentham's which is permanently valuable."

Cf. also Appendix D.

other moralists under the same conditions. What can be said in excuse for other moralists is equally available for them, namely, that if there is to be any error, it is better that it should be on that side. As a matter of fact, we may affirm that among utilitarians, as among adherents of other systems, there is every imaginable degree of rigidity and of laxity in the application of their standard: some are even puritanically rigorous, while others are as indulgent as can possibly be desired by sinner or by sentimentalist. But, on the whole, a doctrine which brings prominently forward the interest that mankind have in the repression and prevention of conduct which violates the moral law is likely to be inferior to no other in turning the sanctions of opinion against such violations. It is true, the question, What does violate the moral law? is one on which those who recognise different standards of morality are likely now and then to differ. But difference of opinion on moral questions was not first introduced into the world by utilitarianism, while that doctrine does supply, if not always an easy, at all events a tangible and intelligible, mode of deciding such differences.

It may not be superfluous to notice a few more of the common misapprehensions of utilitarian ethics, even those which are so obvious and gross that it might appear impossible for any person of candour and intelligence to fall into them: since persons, even of considerable mental endowments, often give themselves so little trouble to understand the bearings of any opinion against which they entertain a prejudice, and men are in general so little conscious of this voluntary ignorance as a defect, that the vulgarest misunderstandings of ethical doctrines are continually met with in the deliberate writings of persons of the greatest pretensions both to high principle and to philosophy. We not uncommonly hear the doctrine of utility inveighed against as a *godless* doctrine. If it be necessary to say anything at all against so mere an assumption, we may say that the question depends upon what idea we have formed of the moral character of the Deity. If it be a true belief that God desires, above all things, the happiness of His creatures, and that this was His purpose in their creation, utility is not only not a godless doctrine, but more profoundly religious than any other. If it be meant that utilitarianism does not recognise the revealed will of God as the supreme law of morals, I answer that an utilitarian who believes in the perfect goodness and wisdom of God, necessarily believes that whatever God has thought fit to reveal on the subject of morals must fulfil the requirements of utility in a supreme degree. But others besides utilitarians have been of opinion that the Christian revelation was intended, and is fitted, to inform the hearts and minds of mankind with a spirit which should enable them to find for themselves what is right, and incline them to do it when found, rather than to tell them, except in a very general way, what it is: and that we need a doctrine of ethics, carefully followed out, to *interpret* to us the will of God.

Whether this opinion is correct or not, it is superfluous here to discuss; since whatever aid religion, either natural or revealed, can afford to ethical investigation, is as open to the utilitarian moralist as to any other. He can use it as the testimony of God to the usefulness or hurtfulness of any given course of action, by as good a right as others can use it for the indication of a transcendental law, having no connection with usefulness or with happiness.

Again, Utility is often summarily stigmatised as an immoral doctrine by giving it the name of Expediency, and taking advantage of the popular use of that term to contrast it with Principle. But the Expedient, in the sense in which it is opposed to the Right, generally means that which is expedient for the particular interest of the agent himself; as when a minister sacrifices the interest of his country to keep himself in place. When it means anything better than this, it means that which is expedient for some immediate object, some temporary purpose, but which violates a rule whose observance is expedient in a much higher degree. The Expedient, in this sense, instead of being the same thing with the useful, is a branch of the hurtful. Thus, it would often be expedient, for the purpose of getting over some momentary embarrassment, or attaining some object immediately useful to ourselves or others, to tell a lie. But inasmuch as the cultivation in ourselves of a sensitive feeling on the subject of veracity is one of the most useful and the enfeeblement of that feeling one of the most hurtful, things to which our conduct can be instrumental; and inasmuch as any, even unintentional, deviation from truth, does that much towards weakening the trustworthiness of human assertion, which is not only the principal support of all present social wellbeing, but the insufficiency of which does more than any one thing that can be named to keep back civilisation, virtue, everything on which human happiness on the largest scale depends,—we feel that the violation, for a present advantage, of a rule of such transcendent expediency, is not expedient, and that he who, for the sake of a convenience to himself or to some other individual, does what depends on him to deprive mankind of the good, and inflict upon them the evil, involved in the greater or less reliance which they can place in each other's word, acts the part of one of their worst enemies. Yet that even this rule, sacred as it is, admits of possible exceptions, is acknowledged by all moralists; the chief of which is when the withholding of some fact (as of information from a malefactor, or of bad news from a person dangerously ill) would preserve some one (especially a person other than oneself) from great and unmerited evil, and when the withholding can only be effected by denial. But in order that the exception may not extend itself beyond the need, and may have the least possible effect in weakening reliance on veracity, it ought to be recognised, and, if possible, its limits defined; and if the principle of utility is good for anything, it must be good for weighing these conflicting utilities against one another, and marking out the region within which one or the other preponderates.

Again, defenders of utility often find themselves called upon to reply to such objections as this—that there is not time, previous to action, for calculating and weighing the effects of any line of conduct on the general happiness. This is exactly as if any one were to say that it is impossible to guide our conduct by Christianity, because there is not time, on every occasion on which anything has to be done, to read through the Old and New Testaments. The answer to the objection is, that there has been ample time, namely, the whole past duration of the human species. During all that time mankind have been learning by experience the tendencies of actions; on which experience all the prudence, as well as all the morality, of life, is dependent. People talk as if the commencement of this course of experience had hitherto been put off, and as if, at the moment when some man feels tempted to meddle with the property or life of another, he had to begin considering for the first time whether murder and theft are injurious to human happiness. Even then I do not think that he would find the question very puzzling; but, at all events, the matter is now done to his hand. It is truly a whimsical supposition, that if mankind were agreed in considering utility to be the test of morality, they would remain without any agreement as to what *is* useful, and would take no measures for having their notions on the subject taught to the young, and enforced by law and opinion. There is no difficulty in proving any ethical standard whatever to work ill, if we suppose universal idiocy to be conjoined with it, but on any hypothesis short of that, mankind must by this time have acquired positive beliefs as to the effects of some actions on their happiness; and the beliefs which have thus come down are the rules of morality for the multitude, and for the philosopher until he has succeeded in finding better.[1] That philosophers might easily do this, even now, on many subjects; that the received code

---

[1] Cf. Mill's criticism of Bentham. 'Dissertations and Discussions,' vol. i. p. 351: "He did not heed, or rather the nature of his mind prevented it from occurring to him, that these generalities contained the whole unanalysed experience of the human race.

"Unless it can be asserted that mankind did not know anything until logicians taught it to them —that until the last hand has been put to a moral truth by giving it a metaphysically precise expression, all the previous rough-hewing which it has undergone by the common intellect at the suggestion of common wants and common experience is to go for nothing; it must be allowed, that even the originality which can, and the courage which dares, think for itself, is not a more necessary part of the philosophical character than a thoughtful regard for previous thinkers, and for the collective mind of the human race. What has been the opinion of mankind, has been the opinions of persons of all tempers and dispositions, of all partialities and prepossessions, of all varieties in position, in education, in opportunities of observation and inquiry. No one inquirer is all this; every inquirer is either young or old, rich or poor, sickly or healthy, married or unmarried, meditative or active, a poet or a logician, an ancient or a modern, a man or a woman; and, if a thinking person, has, in addition, the accidental peculiarities of his individual modes of thought. Every circumstance which gives a character to the life of a human being, carries with it its peculiar biases; its peculiar facilities for perceiving some things, and for missing or forgetting others. But, from points of view different from his, different things are perceptible; and none are more likely to have seen what he does not see, than those who do not see what he sees. The general opinion

of ethics is by no means of divine right; and that mankind have still much to learn as to the effects of actions on the general happiness, I admit, or rather, earnestly maintain.[1] The corollaries from the principle of utility, like the precepts of every practical art, admit of indefinite improvement, and, in a progressive state of the human mind, their improvement is perpetually going on. But to consider the rules of morality as improvable, is one thing; to pass over the intermediate generalisations entirely, and endeavour to test each individual action directly by the first prin-

of mankind is the average of the conclusions of all minds, stripped, indeed, of their choicest and most recondite thoughts, but freed from their twists and partialities: a net result, in which everybody's particular point of view is represented, nobody's predominant. The collective mind does not penetrate below the surface, but it sees all the surface; which profound thinkers, even by reason of their profundity, often fail to do: their intenser view of a thing in some of its aspects diverting their attention from others."

[1] 'Dissertations and Discussions,' vol. i. p. 333: "If the superstition about ancestorial wisdom has fallen into decay; if the public are grown familiar with the idea that their laws and institutions are in a great part not the product of intellect and virtue but of modern corruption grafted upon ancient barbarism; if the hardiest innovation is no longer scouted because it is an innovation—establishments no longer considered sacred because they are establishments—it will be found that those who have accustomed the public mind to these ideas have learnt them in Bentham's school, and that the assault on ancient institutions has been, and is, carried on for the most part with his weapons."

Ib., vol. ii. p. 472: "The contest between the morality which appeals to an external standard, and that which grounds itself on internal conviction, is the contest of progressive morality against stationary — of reason and argument against the deification of mere opinion and habit. The doctrine that the existing order of things is the natural order, and that, being natural, all innovation upon it is criminal, is as vicious in morals as it is now at last admitted to be in physics, and in society and government."

ciple, is another. It is a strange notion that the acknowledgment of a first principle is inconsistent with the admission of secondary ones. To inform a traveller respecting the place of his ultimate destination, is not to forbid the use of landmarks and direction-posts on the way. The proposition that happiness is the end and aim of morality, does not mean that no road ought to be laid down to that goal, or that persons going thither should not be advised to take one direction rather than another. Men really ought to leave off talking a kind of nonsense on this subject, which they would neither talk nor listen to on other matters of practical concernment. Nobody argues that the art of navigation is not founded on astronomy, because sailors cannot wait to calculate the Nautical Almanack. Being rational creatures, they go to sea with it ready calculated; and all rational creatures go out upon the sea of life with their minds made up on the common questions of right and wrong, as well as on many of the far more difficult questions of wise and foolish. And this, as long as foresight is a human quality, it is to be presumed they will continue to do. Whatever we adopt as the fundamental principle of morality, we require subordinate principles to apply it by: the impossibility of doing without them, being common to all systems, can afford no argument against any one in particular. But gravely to argue as if no such secondary principles could be had, and as if mankind had remained till now, and always must remain, without drawing any general conclusions from the experience of human life, is as high a pitch, I think, as absurdity has ever reached in philosophical controversy.[1]

The remainder of the stock arguments against utilitarianism mostly consist in laying to its charge the common infirmities of human nature, and the general difficulties which embarrass conscientious persons in shaping their course through life. We are told that an utilitarian will be apt to make his own particular case an exception to moral rules, and, when under temptation, will see an utility in the breach of a rule, greater than he will see in its observance. But is utility the only creed which is able to furnish us with excuses for evil-doing, and means of cheating our own conscience? They are afforded in abundance by all doctrines which recognise as a fact in morals the existence of conflicting considerations; which all doctrines do, that have been believed by sane persons. It is not the fault of any creed, but of the complicated nature of human affairs, that rules of conduct cannot be so framed as to require no exceptions, and that hardly any kind of action can safely be laid down as either always obligatory or always condemnable. There is no ethical creed which does not temper the rigidity of its laws, by giving a certain lati-

[1] 'Dissertations and Discussions,' vol. i. p. 142: "Some of the consequences of an action are accidental; others are its natural result, according to the known laws of the universe. The former, for the most part, cannot be foreseen; but the whole course of human life is founded upon the fact that the latter can. . . . The commonest person lives according to maxims of prudence wholly founded on foresight of consequences."

tude, under the moral responsibility of the agent, for accommodation to peculiarities of circumstances; and under every creed, at the opening thus made, self-deception and dishonest casuistry get in. There exists no moral system under which there do not arise unequivocal cases of conflicting obligation. These are the real difficulties, the knotty points both in the theory of ethics and in the conscientious guidance of personal conduct. They are overcome practically with greater or with less success according to the intellect and virtue of the individual; but it can hardly be pretended that any one will be the less qualified for dealing with them, from possessing an ultimate standard to which conflicting rights and duties can be referred.[1] If utility is the ultimate source of moral obligations, utility may be invoked to decide between them when their demands are incompatible. Though the application of the standard may be difficult, it is better than none at all: while in other systems, the moral laws all claiming independent authority, there is no common umpire entitled to interfere between them; their claims to precedence one over another rest on little better than

---

[1] 'Dissertations and Discussions,' vol. iii. p. 16 : "We should endeavour to set before ourselves the ideal conception of a perfect representative government, however distant, not to say doubtful, may be the hope of actually obtaining it: to the intent that whatever is now done may if possible be in the direction of what is best, and may bring the actual fact nearer, and not further off from the standard of right, at however great a distance it may still remain from that standard. Though we may be only sailing from the port of London to that of Hull, let us still guide our navigation by the North Star."

V. Note 1 on p. 83 and note 1 on p. 123.

sophistry, and unless determined, as they generally are, by the unacknowledged influence of considerations of utility, afford a free scope for the action of personal desires and partialities. We must remember that only in these cases of conflict between secondary principles is it requisite that first principles should be appealed to. There is no case of moral obligation in which some secondary principle is not involved; and if only one, there can seldom be any real doubt which one it is, in the mind of any person by whom the principle itself is recognised.

CHAPTER III

OF THE ULTIMATE SANCTION OF THE PRINCIPLE OF UTILITY

THE question is often asked, and properly so in regard to any supposed moral standard, What is its sanction? what are the motives to obey it? or more specifically, what is the source of its obligation? whence does it derive its binding force? It is a necessary part of moral philosophy to provide the answer to this question; which, though frequently assuming the shape of an objection to the utilitarian morality, as if it had some special applicability to that above others, really arises in regard to all standards. It arises, in fact, whenever a person is called on to *adopt* a standard or refer morality to any basis on which he has not been accustomed to rest it. For the customary morality, that which education and opinion have consecrated, is the only one which presents itself to the mind with the feeling of being *in itself* obligatory; and when a person is asked to believe that this morality *derives* its obligation from some general principle round which custom has not thrown the same halo, the assertion is to him a paradox; the supposed corollaries seem to have a more binding force than the original theorem; the superstructure seems to stand better without, than with, what is represented as its foundation. He says to himself, I feel that I am bound not to rob or murder, betray or deceive; but why am I bound to promote the general happiness? If my own happiness lies in something else, why may I not give that the preference?

If the view adopted by the utilitarian philosophy of the nature of the moral sense be correct, this difficulty will always present itself, until the influences which form moral character have taken the same hold of the principle which they have taken of some of the consequences—until, by the improvement of education, the feeling of unity with our fellow-creatures shall be (what it cannot be doubted that Christ intended it to be) as deeply rooted in our character, and to our own consciousness as completely a part of our nature, as the horror of crime is in an ordinarily well-brought-up young person. In the meantime, however, the difficulty has no peculiar application to the doctrine of utility, but is inherent in every attempt to analyse morality and reduce it to principles; which, unless the principle is already in men's minds invested with as much sacredness as any of its applications, always seems to divest them of a part of their sanctity.

The principle of utility either has, or there is no reason why it might not have, all the sanctions which belong to any other system of morals. Those sanctions are either external or internal. Of the external sanctions it is not necessary to speak at any length. They are, the hope of favour and the fear of displeasure from our fellow-creatures or from the Ruler of the Universe, along with whatever we may have of sympathy or affection for them or of love and awe of Him, inclining us to do His will independently of selfish consequences. There is evidently no reason why all these motives for observance should not attach themselves to the utilitarian morality, as completely and as powerfully as to any other. Indeed those of them which refer to our fellow-creatures are sure to do so, in proportion to the amount of general intelligence; for whether there be any other ground of moral obligation than the general happiness or not, men do desire happiness; and however imperfect may be their own practice, they desire and commend all conduct in others towards themselves, by which they think their happiness is promoted. With regard to the religious motive, if men believe, as most profess to do, in the goodness of God, those who think that conduciveness to the general happiness is the essence, or even only the criterion, of good, must necessarily believe that it is also that which God approves. The whole force therefore of external reward and punishment, whether physical or moral, and whether proceeding from God or from our fellow-men, together with all that the capacities of human nature admit, of disinterested devotion to either, become available to enforce the utilitarian morality, in proportion as that morality is recognised; and the more powerfully, the more the appliances of education and general cultivation are bent to the purpose.

So far as to external sanctions. The internal sanction of duty, whatever our standard of duty may be, is one and the same—a feeling in our own mind; a pain, more or less intense, attendant on violation of duty, which in properly cultivated moral natures rises, in the more serious cases, into shrinking from it as an impossibility. This feeling, when disinterested, and connecting itself with the pure idea of duty, and not with some particular form of it, or with any of the merely accessory circumstances, is the essence of Conscience; though in that complex phenomenon as it actually exists, the simple fact is in general all encrusted over with collateral associations, derived from sympathy, from love, and still more from fear; from all the forms of religious feeling; from the recollections of childhood and of all our past life; from self-esteem, desire of the esteem of others, and occasionally even self-abasement. This extreme complication is, I apprehend, the origin of the sort of mystical character which, by a tendency of the human mind of which there are many other examples, is apt to be attributed to the idea of moral obligation, and which leads people to believe that the idea cannot possibly attach itself to any other objects than those which, by a supposed mysterious law, are found in our present experience to excite it. Its binding force, however, consists in the existence of a mass of feeling which must be broken through in order to do what violates our standard of right, and which, if we do nevertheless violate that standard, will probably have to be encountered afterwards in the form of remorse. Whatever theory we have of the nature or origin of conscience, this is what essentially constitutes it.

The ultimate sanction, therefore, of all morality (external motives apart) being a subjective feeling in our own minds, I see nothing embarrassing to those whose standard is utility, in the question, what is the sanction of that particular standard? We may answer, the same as of all other moral standards—the conscientious feelings of mankind. Undoubtedly this sanction has no binding efficacy on those who do not possess the feelings it appeals to; but neither will these persons be more obedient to any other moral principle than to the utilitarian one. On them morality of any kind has no hold but through the external sanctions. Meanwhile the feelings exist, a fact in human nature, the reality of which, and the great power with which they are capable of acting on those in whom they have been duly cultivated, are proved by experience. No reason has ever been shown why they may not be cultivated to as great intensity in connection with the utilitarian, as with any other rule of morals.

There is, I am aware, a disposition to believe that a person who sees in moral obligation a transcendental fact, an objective reality belonging to the province of "Things in Themselves," is likely to be more obedient to it than one who believes it to be entirely subjective, having its seat in human consciousness only. But whatever a person's opinion may be on this point of Ontology, the force he is really urged by is his own subjective feeling, and is exactly measured by its strength. No one's belief that Duty is an objective reality is stronger than the belief that God is so; yet the belief in God, apart from the expectation of actual reward and punishment, only operates on conduct through, and in proportion to, the subjective religious feeling. The sanction, so far as it is disinterested, is always in the mind itself; and the notion, therefore, of the transcendental moralists must be, that this sanction will not exist *in* the mind unless it is believed to have its root out of the mind; and that if a person is able to say to himself, That which is restraining me, and which is called my conscience, is only a feeling in my own mind, he may possibly draw the conclusion that when the feeling ceases the obligation ceases, and that if he find the feeling inconvenient, he may disregard it, and endeavour to get rid of it. But is this danger confined to the utilitarian morality ? Does the belief that moral obligation has its seat outside the mind make the feeling of it too strong to be got rid of? The fact is so far otherwise, that all moralists admit and lament the ease with which, in the generality of minds, conscience can be silenced or stifled. The question, Need I obey my conscience ? is quite as often put to themselves by persons who never heard of the principle of utility, as by its adherents. Those whose conscientious feelings are so weak as to allow of their asking this question, if they answer it affirmatively, will not do so because they believe in the transcendental theory, but because of the external sanctions.

It is not necessary, for the present purpose, to decide whether the feeling of duty is innate or implanted. Assuming it to be innate, it is an open question to what objects it naturally attaches itself; for the philosophic supporters of that theory are now agreed that the intuitive perception is of principles of morality, and not of the details. If there be anything innate in the matter, I see no reason why the feeling which is innate should not be that of regard to the pleasures and pains of others. If there is any principle of morals which is intuitively obligatory, I should say it must be that. If so, the intuitive ethics would coincide with the utilitarian, and there would be no further quarrel between them. Even as it is, the intuitive moralists, though they believe that there are other intuitive moral obligations, do already believe this to be one; for they unanimously hold that a large *portion* of morality turns upon the consideration due to the interests of our fellow-creatures. Therefore, if the belief in the transcendental origin of moral obligation gives any additional efficacy to the internal sanction, it appears to me that the utilitarian principle has already the benefit of it.

On the other hand, if, as is my own belief, the moral feelings are not innate, but acquired, they are not for that reason the less natural. It is natural to man to speak, to reason, to build cities, to cultivate the ground, though these are acquired faculties. The moral feelings are not indeed a part of our nature, in the sense of being in any perceptible degree present in all of us; but this, unhappily, is a fact admitted by those who believe the most strenuously in their transcendental origin. Like the other acquired capacities above referred to, the moral faculty, if not a part of our nature, is a natural outgrowth from it; capable, like them, in a certain small degree, of springing up spontaneously; and susceptible of being brought by cultivation to a high degree of development. Unhappily it is also susceptible, by a sufficient use of the external sanctions and of the force of early impressions, of being cultivated in almost any direction: so that there is hardly anything so absurd or so mischievous that it may not, by means of these influences, be made to act on the human mind with all the authority of conscience. To doubt that the same potency might be given by the same means to the principle of utility, even if it had no foundation in human nature, would be flying in the face of all experience.[1]

---

[1] 'System of Logic,' p. 604: "As the strongest propensities of uncultivated or half-cultivated human nature (being the purely selfish ones, and those of a sympathetic character which partake most of the nature of selfishness) evidently tend in themselves to disunite mankind, not to unite them, to make them rivals, not confederates; social existence is only possible by the disciplining of these more powerful propensities, which consists in subordinating them to a common system of opinions. The degree of this subordination is the measure of the completeness of the social union, and the nature of the common opinions determines its kind."

'Principles of Political Economy,' p. 127: "And independently of the public motive, every member of the association would

But moral associations which are wholly of artificial creation, when intellectual culture goes on, yield by degrees to the dissolving force of analysis: and if the feeling of duty, when associated with utility, would

be amenable to the most universal, and one of the strongest of personal motives, that of public opinion. The force of this motive in deterring from any act or omission positively reproved by the community no one is likely to deny; but the power also of emulation, in exciting to the most strenuous exertions for the sake of the approbation and admiration of others, is borne witness to by experience in every situation in which human beings publicly compete with one another, even if it be in things frivolous or from which the public derive no benefit."

Ib., p. 226: "All experience shows that the mass of mankind never judge of moral questions for themselves, never see anything to be right or wrong until they have been frequently told it."

Ib., p. 227: "Those who think it hopeless that the labouring classes should be induced to practise a sufficient degree of prudence in regard to the increase of their families, because they have hitherto stopped short of that point, show an inability to estimate the ordinary principles of human action. Nothing more would probably be necessary to secure that result than an opinion generally diffused that it was desirable."

Ib., p. 228: "Any one who supposes that this state of opinion (*i.e.*, belief in the necessity of limiting the increase of population) would not have a great effect on conduct must be profoundly ignorant of human nature; can never have considered how large a portion of the motives which induce the generality of men to take care even of their own interests is derived from regard for opinion — from the expectation of being disliked or despised for not doing it. . . . Men are seldom found to brave the general opinion of their class, unless supported either by some principle higher than regard for opinion or by some strong body of opinion elsewhere."

Ib., p. 230: "An education directed to diffuse good sense among the people, with such knowledge as would qualify them to judge of the tendencies of their actions, would be certain, even without any direct inculcation, to raise up a public opinion by which intemperance and improvidence of every kind would be held discreditable, and the improvidence which overstocks the labour-market would be severely condemned as an offence against the common weal."

appear equally arbitrary; if there were no leading department of our nature, no powerful class of sentiments, with which that association would harmonise, which would make us feel it congenial, and incline us not only to foster it in others (for which we have abundant interested motives), but also to cherish it in ourselves; if there were not, in short, a natural basis of sentiment for utilitarian morality, it might well happen that this association also, even after it had been implanted by education, might be analysed away.

But there *is* this basis of powerful natural sentiment; and this it is which, when once the general happiness is recognised as the ethical standard, will constitute the strength of the utilitarian morality. This firm foundation is that of the social feelings of mankind; the desire to be in unity with our fellow-creatures, which is already a powerful principle in human nature, and happily one of those which tend to become stronger, even without express inculcation, from the influences of advancing civilisation.[1] The social state is at once so natural, so necessary, and so habitual to man, that, except in some unusual circumstances or by an effort of voluntary abstraction, he never conceives himself otherwise than as a member of a body; and this association is riveted more and more, as mankind are further removed from the state

---

[1] 'Essays on Religion,' p. 49: "I do not in any wise mean to deny that sympathy is natural also; I believe, on the contrary, that on that important fact rests the possibility of any cultivation of goodness and nobleness, and the hope of their ultimate entire ascendancy."

of savage independence. Any condition, therefore, which is essential to a state of society, becomes more and more an inseparable part of every person's conception of the state of things which he is born into, and which is the destiny of a human being. Now, society between human beings, except in the relation of master and slave, is manifestly impossible on any other footing than that the interests of all are to be consulted. Society between equals can only exist on the understanding that the interests of all are to be regarded equally. And since in all states of civilisation, every person, except an absolute monarch, has equals, every one is obliged to live on these terms with somebody; and in every age some advance is made towards a state in which it will be impossible to live permanently on other terms with anybody.[1] In this

---

[1] 'Subjection of Women,' p. 79: "The equality of married persons before the law is not only the sole mode in which that particular relation can be made consistent with justice to both sides, and conducive to the happiness of both, but it is the only means of rendering the daily life of mankind, in any high sense, a school of moral cultivation. Though the truth may not be felt or generally acknowledged for generations to come, the only school of genuine moral sentiment is society between equals. The moral education of mankind has hitherto emanated chiefly from the law of force, and is adapted almost solely to the relations which force creates. In the less advanced states of society, people hardly recognise any relation with their equals. To be an equal is to be an enemy. Society, from its highest place to its lowest, is one long chain, or rather ladder, where every individual is either above or below his nearest neighbour, and wherever he does not command he must obey. Existing moralities, accordingly, are mainly fitted to a relation of command and obedience. Yet command and obedience are but unfortunate necessities of human life: society in equality is its normal state. Already in modern life, and more

way people grow up unable to conceive as possible to them a state of total disregard of other people's interests. They are under a necessity of conceiving themselves as at least abstaining from all the grosser injuries, and (if only for their own protection) living in a state of constant protest against them. They are also familiar with the fact of co-operating with others, and proposing to themselves a collective, not an individual, interest, as the aim (at least for the time being) of their actions.[1] So long as they are co-operating,

and more as it progressively improves, command and obedience become exceptional facts in life, equal association its general rule. The morality of the first ages rested on the obligation to submit to power; that of the ages next following, on the right of the weak to the forbearance and protection of the strong. How much longer is one form of society and life to content itself with the morality made for another? We have had the morality of submission, and the morality of chivalry and generosity; the time is now come for the morality of justice. Whenever, in former ages, any approach has been made to society in equality, Justice has asserted its claims as the foundation of virtue. . . . We are entering into an order of things in which justice will again be the primary virtue; grounded as before on equal, but now also on sympathetic association; having its root no longer in the instinct of equals for self-protection, but in a cultivated sympathy between them; and no one being now left out, but an equal measure being extended to all."

Ib., p. 81: "But the true virtue of human beings is fitness to live together as equals; claiming nothing for themselves but what they as freely concede to every one else; regarding command of any kind as an exceptional necessity, and in all cases a temporary one: and preferring, whenever possible, the society of those with whom leading and following can be alternate and reciprocal."

Ib., p. 82: "The moral training of mankind will never be adapted to the conditions of the life for which all other human progress is a preparation until they practise in the family the same moral rule which is adapted to the normal constitution of human society."

[1] 'Principles of Political Economy,' p. 422: "One of the changes which most infallibly at-

their ends are identified with those of others ; there is at least a temporary feeling that the interests of others are their own interests. Not only does all strengthening of social ties, and all healthy growth of society, give to each individual a stronger personal

tend the progress of modern society is an improvement in the business capacities of the general mass of mankind. I do not mean that the practical sagacity of an individual human being is greater than formerly. I am inclined to believe that economical progress has hitherto had even a contrary effect. A person of good natural endowments, in a rude state of society, can do a greater number of things tolerably well, has a greater power of adapting means to ends, is more capable of extricating himself and others from an unforeseen embarrassment, than ninety-nine in a hundred of those who have known only what is called the civilised form of life. How far these points of inferiority of faculties are compensated, and by what means they might be compensated still more completely to the civilised man as an individual being, is a question belonging to a different inquiry from the present. But to civilised human beings collectively considered, the compensation is ample. What is lost in the separate efficiency of each, is far more than made up by the greater capacity of united action. In proportion as they put off the qualities of the savage, they become amenable to discipline ; capable of adhering to plans concerted beforehand, and about which they may not have been consulted ; of subordinating their individual caprice to a preconceived determination, and performing severally the parts allotted to them in a combined undertaking. . . . The peculiar characteristic, in short, of civilised beings, is the capacity of co-operation ; and this, like other faculties, tends to improve by practice, and becomes capable of assuming a constantly wider sphere of action."

'Dissertations and Discussions,' vol. i. p. 163 : "The most remarkable of those consequences of advancing civilisation which the state of the world is now forcing upon the attention of thinking minds is this: that power passes more and more from individuals, and small knots of individuals, to masses ; that the importance of the masses becomes constantly greater, that of individuals less."

Ib., p. 165 : "There is not a more accurate test of the progress of civilisation than the progress of the power of co-operation."

interest in practically consulting the welfare of others; it also leads him to identify his *feelings* more and more with their good, or at least with an ever greater degree of practical consideration for it. He comes, as though instinctively, to be conscious of himself as a being who *of course* pays regard to others. The good of others becomes to him a thing naturally and necessarily to be attended to, like any of the physical conditions of our existence.[1] Now, whatever amount of this feeling a person has, he is urged by the strongest

[1] 'Representative Government,' p. 68 : " He is made to feel himself one of the public, and whatever is for their benefit to be for his benefit. When this school of public spirit does not exist, scarcely any sense is entertained that private persons, in no eminent social situation, owe any duties to society, except to obey the laws and submit to the government. There is no unselfish sentiment of identification with the public. Every thought and feeling, either of interest or of duty, is absorbed in the individual and in the family. The man never thinks of any collective interest, of any objects to be pursued jointly with others, but only in competition with them, and in some measure at their expense. A neighbour not being an ally or an associate, since he is never engaged in any common undertaking for joint benefit, is therefore only a rival. Thus even private morality suffers, while public is actually extinct."

'Principles of Political Economy,' p. 461 : " And in the moral aspect of the question, which is still more important than the economical, something better should be aimed at as the goal of industrial improvement than to disperse mankind over the earth in single families, each ruled internally as families now are by a patriarchal despot, and having scarcely any community of interest, or necessary mental communion, with other human beings. . . . But if public spirit, generous sentiments, or true justice and equality are desired, association, not isolation, of interests, is the school in which these excellences are nurtured. The aim of improvement should be not solely to place human beings in a condition in which they will be able to do without one another, but to enable them to work with or for one another in relations not involving dependence."

motives both of interest and of sympathy to demonstrate it, and to the utmost of his power encourage it in others; and even if he has none of it himself, he is as greatly interested as any one else that others should have it. Consequently, the smallest germs of the feeling are laid hold of and nourished by the contagion of sympathy and the influences of education; and a complete web of corroborative association is woven round it, by the powerful agency of the external sanctions. This mode of conceiving ourselves and human life, as civilisation goes on, is felt to be more and more natural. Every step in political improvement renders it more so, by removing the sources of opposition of interest, and levelling those inequalities of legal privilege between individuals or classes, owing to which there are large portions of mankind whose happiness it is still practicable to disregard. In an improving state of the human mind, the influences are constantly on the increase, which tend to generate in each individual a feeling of unity with all the rest; which feeling, if perfect, would make him never think of, or desire, any beneficial condition for himself, in the benefits of which they are not included.[1] If we now

---

[1] 'Representative Government,' p. 29: "Whenever the general disposition of the people is such, that each individual regards those only of his interests which are selfish, and does not dwell on, or concern himself for, his share of the general interest, in such a state of things good government is impossible."

'Dissertations and Discussions,' vol. i. p. 467: "From the principle of the necessity of identifying the interest of the government with that of the people, most of the practical maxims of

suppose this feeling of unity to be taught as a religion, and the whole force of education, of institutions, and of opinion, directed, as it once was in the case of religion, to make every person grow up from infancy surrounded on all sides both by the profession and by the practice of it, I think that no one, who can realise this conception, will feel any misgiving about the sufficiency of the ultimate sanction for the Happiness morality. To any ethical student who finds the realisation difficult, I recommend, as a means of facilitating it, the second of M. Comte's two principal works, the 'Système de Politique Positive.' I entertain the strongest objections to the system of politics and morals set forth in that treatise; but I think it has superabundantly shown the possibility of giving to the service of humanity, even without the aid of belief in a Providence, both the physical power and the social efficacy of a religion; making it take hold of human life, and colour all thought, feeling, and action, in a manner of which the greatest ascendancy ever exercised by any religion may be but

a representative government are corollaries. All popular institutions are means towards rendering the identity of interests more complete. We say *more* complete, because (and this it is important to remark) perfectly complete it can never be."

Ib., p. 468 : "Identification of interest between the rulers and the ruled, being therefore in a literal sense impossible to be realised, ought not to be spoken of as a condition which a government must absolutely fulfil ; but as an end to be incessantly aimed at, and approximated to as nearly as circumstances render possible, and as is compatible with the regard due to other ends."

a type and foretaste; and of which the danger is, not that it should be insufficient, but that it should be so excessive as to interfere unduly with human freedom and individuality.

Neither is it necessary to the feeling which constitutes the binding force of the utilitarian morality on those who recognise it, to wait for those social influences which would make its obligation felt by mankind at large. In the comparatively early state of human advancement in which we now live, a person cannot indeed feel that entireness of sympathy with all others, which would make any real discordance in the general direction of their conduct in life impossible; but already a person in whom the social feeling is at all developed, cannot bring himself to think of the rest of his fellow-creatures as struggling rivals with him for the means of happiness, whom he must desire to see defeated in their object in order that he may succeed in his. The deeply rooted conception which every individual even now has of himself as a social being, tends to make him feel it one of his natural wants that there should be harmony between his feelings and aims and those of his fellow-creatures. If differences of opinion and of mental culture make it impossible for him to share many of their actual feelings—perhaps make him denounce and defy those feelings—he still needs to be conscious that his real aim and theirs do not conflict; that he is not opposing himself to what they really wish for, namely, their own good, but is, on the contrary, promoting it.[1] This feeling in most individuals is much inferior in strength to their selfish feelings, and is often wanting altogether. But to those who have it, it possesses all the characters of a natural feeling. It does not present itself to their minds as a superstition of education, or a law despotically imposed by the power of society, but as an attribute which it would not be well for them to be without. This conviction is the ultimate sanction of the greatest-happiness morality. This it is which makes any mind, of well-developed feelings, work with, and not against, the outward motives to care for others, afforded by what I have called the external sanctions; and when those sanctions are wanting, or act in an opposite direction, constitutes in itself a powerful internal binding force, in proportion to the sensitiveness and thoughtfulness of the character; since few but those whose mind is a moral blank, could bear to lay out their course of life on the plan of paying no regard to others except so far as their own private interest compels.

[1] 'Representative Government,' p. 207 : "It is a very superficial view of the utility of public opinion, to suppose that it does good only when it succeeds in enforcing a servile conformity to itself. To be under the eyes of others—to have to defend oneself to others—is never more important than to those who act in opposition to the opinion of others, for it obliges them to have sure ground of their own. Nothing has so steadying an influence as working against pressure."

CHAPTER IV

OF WHAT SORT OF PROOF THE PRINCIPLE OF UTILITY IS SUSCEPTIBLE

It has already been remarked, that questions of ultimate ends do not admit of proof, in the ordinary acceptation of the term. To be incapable of proof by reasoning is common to all first principles—to the first premises of our knowledge, as well as to those of our conduct. But the former, being matters of fact, may be the subject of a direct appeal to the faculties which judge of fact—namely, our senses, and our internal consciousness. Can an appeal be made to the same faculties on questions of practical ends? Or by what other faculty is cognisance taken of them?

Questions about ends are, in other words, questions what things are desirable. The utilitarian doctrine is, that happiness is desirable, and the only thing desirable, as an end; all other things being only desirable as means to that end. What ought to be required of this doctrine — what conditions is it requisite that the doctrine should fulfil — to make good its claim to be believed?

The only proof capable of being given that an object is visible, is that people actually see it. The only proof that a sound is audible, is that people hear it: and so of the other sources of our experience. In like manner, I apprehend, the sole evidence it is possible to produce that anything is desirable, is that people do actually desire it.[1] If the end which the utilitarian

---

[1] Compare with this the estimate which Mill elsewhere gives of the ethical worth of natural impulses and desires. 'Examination of Hamilton,' p. 171 : "On every theory of the divine government, it is carried on, intellectually as well as morally, not by the mere indulgence of our natural tendencies, but by the regulation and control of them."

'Principles of Political Economy,' p. 226 : "Civilisation in every one of its aspects is a struggle against the animal instincts. Over some, even of the strongest of them, it has shown itself capable of acquiring abundant control. It has artificialised large portions of mankind to such an extent that of many of their most natural inclinations they have scarcely a vestige or a remembrance left."

Ib., p. 575 : " But there are other things of the worth of which the demand of the market is by no means a test ; things of which the utility does not consist in ministering to inclinations, nor in serving the daily uses of life, and the want of which is least felt where the need is greatest. This is peculiarly true of those things which are chiefly useful as tending to raise the character of human beings. The uncultivated cannot be competent judges of cultivation. Those who most need to be made wiser and better usually desire it least, and if they desired it, would be incapable of finding the way to it by their own lights."

'Dissertations and Discussions,' vol. i. p. 28 : " Of all calamities, they (ignorance and want of culture) are those of which the persons suffering from them are apt to be least aware. Of their bodily wants and ailments mankind are generally conscious ; but the want of the mind, the want of being wiser and better, is, in the far greater number of cases, unfelt : some of its disastrous consequences are felt, but are ascribed to any imaginable cause except the true one."

'Essays on Religion,' p. 45 : "Life could not go on if it were not admitted that impulses must be controlled, and that reason ought to govern our actions."

Ib., pp. 46-50 : "Allowing every-

doctrine proposes to itself were not, in theory and in practice, acknowledged to be an end, nothing could ever convince any person that it was so. No reason can be given why the general happiness is desirable, except that each person, so far as he believes it to be attainable, desires his own happiness. This, however, being a fact, we have not only all the proof which the

thing to be an instinct which any one has ever asserted to be one, it remains true that nearly every respectable attribute of humanity is the result not of instinct, but of a victory over instinct ; and that there is hardly anything valuable in the natural man except capacities — a whole world of possibilities, all of them dependent upon eminently artificial discipline for being realised. . . . The truth is that there is hardly a single point of excellence belonging to human character which is not decidedly repugnant to the untutored feelings of human nature. . . . [Courage] is from first to last a victory achieved over one of the most powerful emotions of human nature. . . . Neither *cleanliness* nor the love of cleanliness is natural to man, but only the capacity of acquiring a love of cleanliness. . . . The commonest self-control for one's own benefit — that power of sacrificing a present desire to a distant object or a general purpose which is indispensable for making the actions of the individual accord with his own notions of his individual good ; even this is most unnatural to the undisciplined human being."

Ib., p. 54 : " The duty of man is the same in respect to his own nature as in respect to the nature of all other things—namely, not to follow but to amend it."

Ib., p. 55 : " If, as is the more religious theory, Providence intends not all which happens, but only what is good, then indeed man has it in his power, by his voluntary actions, to aid the intentions of Providence ; but he can only learn those intentions by considering what tends to promote the general good, and not what man has a natural inclination to. . . . The inclinations with which man has been endowed, as well as any of the other contrivances which we observe in Nature, may be the expression not of the divine will, but of the fetters which impede its free action ; and to take hints from these for the guidance of our own conduct may be falling into a trap laid by the enemy."

Cf. also Appendix C.

case admits of, but all which it is possible to require, that happiness is a good: that each person's happiness is a good to that person, and the general happiness, therefore, a good to the aggregate of all persons.[1] Happiness has made out its title as *one* of the ends of conduct, and consequently one of the criteria of morality.

But it has not, by this alone, proved itself to be the sole criterion. To do that, it would seem, by the same rule, necessary to show, not only that people desire happiness, but that they never desire anything else. Now it is palpable that they do desire things which, in common language, are decidedly distinguished from happiness. They desire, for example, virtue, and the absence of vice, no less really than pleasure, and the absence of pain. The desire of virtue is not as universal, but it is as authentic, a fact as the desire of happiness. And hence the opponents of the utilitarian standard deem that they have a right to infer that there are other ends of human action besides happiness, and that happiness is not the standard of approbation and disapprobation.

[1] Cf. 'Principles of Political Economy,' p. 583: "It is greatly the interest of the community collectively and individually not to rob or defraud one another: but there is not the less necessity for laws to punish robbery and fraud; because, though it is the interest of each that nobody should rob or cheat, it is not any one's interest to refrain from robbing and cheating others when all others are permitted to rob and cheat him. Penal laws exist at all, chiefly for this reason, because even an unanimous opinion, that a certain line of conduct is for the general interest, does not always make it people's individual interest to adhere to that line of conduct."

But does the utilitarian doctrine deny that people desire virtue, or maintain that virtue is not a thing to be desired? The very reverse. It maintains not only that virtue is to be desired, but that it is to be desired disinterestedly, for itself. ⸢Whatever may be the opinion of utilitarian moralists as to the original conditions by which virtue is made virtue; however they may believe (as they do) that actions and dispositions are only virtuous because they promote another end than virtue; yet this being granted, and it having been decided, from considerations of this description, which *is* virtuous, they not only place virtue at the very head of the things which are good as means to the ultimate end, but they also recognise as a psychological fact the possibility of its being, to the individual, a good in itself, without looking to any end beyond it; and hold that the mind is not in a right state, not in a state conformable to Utility, not in the state most conducive to the general happiness, unless it does love virtue in this manner — as a thing desirable in itself, even although, in the individual instance, it should not produce those other desirable consequences which it tends to produce, and on account of which it is held to be virtue. This opinion is not, in the smallest degree, a departure from the Happiness principle. The ingredients of happiness are very various, and each of them is desirable in itself, and not merely when considered as swelling an aggregate. The principle of utility does not mean that any given pleasure, as music, for instance, or any given exemption from pain, as, for example, health, are to be looked upon as means to a collective something termed happiness, and to be desired on that account. They are desired and desirable in and for themselves; besides being means, they are a part of the end. Virtue, according to the utilitarian doctrine, is not naturally and originally part of the end, but it is capable of becoming so; and in those who love it disinterestedly it has become so, and is desired and cherished, not as a means to happiness, but as a part of their happiness.

To illustrate this further, we may remember that virtue is not the only thing, originally a means, and which if it were not a means to anything else, would be and remain indifferent, but which by association with what it is a means to, comes to be desired for itself, and that too with the utmost intensity. What, for example, shall we say of the love of money? There is nothing originally more desirable about money than about any heap of glittering pebbles. Its worth is solely that of the things which it will buy—the desires for other things than itself, which it is a means of gratifying. Yet the love of money is not only one of the strongest moving forces of human life, but money is, in many cases, desired in and for itself; the desire to possess it is often stronger than the desire to use it, and goes on increasing when all the desires which point to ends beyond it, to be compassed by it, are falling off. It may then be said truly, that money is desired not for the sake of an end, but as part of the end. From being a means to happiness, it has come to be itself a principal ingredient of the individual's conception of happiness. The same may be said of the majority of the great objects of human life —power, for example, or fame; except that to each of these there is a certain amount of immediate pleasure annexed, which has at least the semblance of being naturally inherent in them—a thing which cannot be said of money. Still, however, the strongest natural attraction, both of power and of fame, is the immense aid they give to the attainment of our other wishes; and it is the strong association thus generated between them and all our objects of desire, which gives to the direct desire of them the intensity it often assumes, so as in some characters to surpass in strength all other desires. In these cases the means have become a part of the end, and a more important part of it than any of the things which they are means to. What was once desired as an instrument for the attainment of happiness, has come to be desired for its own sake. In being desired for its own sake it is, however, desired as *part* of happiness. The person is made, or thinks he would be made, happy by its mere possession; and is made unhappy by failure to obtain it. The desire of it is not a different thing from the desire of happiness, any more than the love of music, or the desire of health. They are included in happiness. They are some of the elements of which the desire of happiness is made up. Happiness is not an abstract idea, but a concrete whole; and these are some of its parts. And the utilitarian standard sanctions and approves their being so. Life would be a poor thing, very ill provided with sources of happiness, if there were not this provision of nature, by which things originally indifferent, but conducive to, or otherwise associated with, the satisfaction of our primitive desires, become in themselves sources of pleasure more valuable than the primitive pleasures, both in permanency, in the space of human existence that they are capable of covering, and even in intensity.

Virtue, according to the utilitarian conception, is a good of this description. There was no original desire of it, or motive to it, save its conduciveness to pleasure, and especially to protection from pain. But through the association thus formed, it may be felt a good in itself, and desired as such with as great intensity as any other good; and with this difference between it and the love of money, of power, or of fame, that all of these may, and often do, render the individual noxious to the other members of the society to which he belongs, whereas there is nothing which makes him so much a blessing to them as the cultivation of the disinterested love of virtue. And consequently, the utilitarian standard, while it tolerates and approves those other acquired desires, up to the point beyond which they would be more injurious to the general happiness than promotive of it, enjoins and requires the cultivation of the love of virtue up to the greatest strength possible, as being above all things important to the general happiness.[1]

It results from the preceding considerations, that there is in reality nothing desired except happiness.

---

[1] 'Liberty,' p. 34: "Among the works of man, which human life is rightly employed in perfecting and beautifying, the first in importance surely is man himself."

Ib., p. 37: "What more or better can be said of any condition of human affairs, than that it brings human beings themselves nearer to the best thing they can be? or what worse can be said of any obstruction to good, than that it prevents this?"

Ib., p. 44: "Human beings owe to each other help to distinguish the better from the worse, and encouragement to choose the former and avoid the latter. They should be for ever stimulating each other to increased exercise of their higher faculties, and increased direction of their feelings and aims towards wise instead of foolish, elevating instead of degrading, objects and contemplations."

'Representative Government,' p. 60: "The character which improves human life is that which struggles with natural powers and tendencies, not that which gives way to them. The self-benefiting qualities are all on the side of the active and energetic character; and the habits and conduct which promote the advantage of each individual member of the community, must be at least a part of those which conduce most in the end to the advancement of the community as a whole."

Ib., p. 64: "The people who think it a shame when anything goes wrong—who rush to the conclusion that the evil could and ought to have been prevented—are those who, in the long-run, do most to make the world better. If the desires are low placed, if they extend to little beyond physical comfort and the show of riches, the immediate results of the energy will not be much more than the continual extension of man's power over material objects; but even this makes room and prepares the mechanical appliances, for the greatest intellectual and social achievements; and while the energy is there, some persons will apply it and it will be applied more and more to the perfecting not of outward circumstances alone, but of man's inward nature."

'Principles of Political Economy,' p. 27: "No limit can be set to the importance, even in a purely productive and material point of view, of mere thought. . . . But when (as in political economy one should always be prepared to do) we shift our point of view, and consider not individ-

Whatever is desired otherwise than as a means to some end beyond itself, and ultimately to happiness, is desired as itself a part of happiness, and is not desired for itself until it has become so. Those who desire virtue for its own sake, desire it either because the consciousness of it is a pleasure, or because the consciousness of being without it is a pain, or for both reasons united; as in truth the pleasure and pain seldom exist separately, but almost always together, the same person feeling pleasure in the degree of virtue attained, and pain in not having attained more. If one of these gave him no pleasure, and the other no pain, he would not love or desire virtue, or would

ual acts, and the motives by which they are determined, but national and universal results, intellectual speculation must be looked upon as a most influential part of the productive labour of society, and the portion of its resources employed in carrying on and in remunerating such labour, as a highly productive part of its expenditure."

Ib., p. 115: "We may say the same of improvement in education. The intelligence of the workman is a most important element in the productiveness of labour. So low, in some of the civilised countries, is the present standard of intelligence, that there is hardly any source from which a more indefinite amount of improvement may be looked for in productive power than by endowing with brains those who now have only hands. The carefulness, economy, and general trustworthiness of labourers are as important as their intelligence. Friendly relations and a community of interest between labourers and employers are eminently so : I should rather say would be ; for I know not where any such sentiment of friendly alliance now exists. Nor is it only in the labouring class that improvement of mind and character operates with beneficial effect even on industry. In the rich and idle classes increased mental energy, more solid instruction and stronger feelings of conscience, public spirit or philanthropy, would qualify them to originate and promote the most valuable improvements both in the economical resources of their country and in its institutions and customs."

desire it only for the other benefits which it might produce to himself or to persons whom he cared for.

We have now, then, an answer to the question, of what sort of proof the principle of utility is susceptible. If the opinion which I have now stated is psychologically true—if human nature is so constituted as to desire nothing which is not either a part of happiness or a means of happiness—we can have no other proof, and we require no other, that these are the only things desirable. If so, happiness is the sole end of human action, and the promotion of it the test by which to judge of all human conduct; from whence it necessarily follows that it must be the criterion of morality, since a part is included in the whole.

And now to decide whether this is really so,—whether mankind do desire nothing for itself but that which is a pleasure to them, or of which the absence is a pain,—we have evidently arrived at a question of fact and experience, dependent, like all similar questions, upon evidence. It can only be determined by practised self-consciousness and self-observation, assisted by observation of others. I believe that these sources of evidence, impartially consulted, will declare that desiring a thing and finding it pleasant, aversion to it and thinking of it as painful, are phenomena entirely inseparable, or rather two parts of the same phenomenon; in strictness of language, two different modes of naming the same psychological fact: that to think of an object as desirable (unless for the sake of its consequences), and to think of it as pleasant, are one and the same thing; and that to desire anything, except in proportion as the idea of it is pleasant, is a physical and metaphysical impossibility.

So obvious does this appear to me, that I expect it will hardly be disputed: and the objection made will be, not that desire can possibly be directed to anything ultimately except pleasure and exemption from pain, but that the will is a different thing from desire; that a person of confirmed virtue, or any other person whose purposes are fixed, carries out his purposes without any thought of the pleasure he has in contemplating them, or expects to derive from their fulfilment; and persists in acting on them, even though these pleasures are much diminished, by changes in his character or decay of his passive sensibilities, or are outweighed by the pains which the pursuit of the purposes may bring upon him. All this I fully admit, and have stated it elsewhere, as positively and emphatically as any one. Will, the active phenomenon, is a different thing from desire, the state of passive sensibility, and though originally an offshoot from it, may in time take root and detach itself from the parent stock; so much so, that in case of an habitual purpose, instead of willing the thing because we desire it, we often desire it only because we will it. This, however, is but an instance of that familiar fact, the power of habit, and is nowise confined to the case of virtuous actions. Many indifferent things, which men originally did from a motive of some sort, they continue to do from habit. Sometimes this is done unconsciously, the consciousness coming only after the action: at other times with conscious volition, but volition which has become habitual, and is put into operation by the force of habit, in opposition perhaps to the deliberate preference, as often happens with those who have contracted habits of vicious or hurtful indulgence. Third and last comes the case in which the habitual act of will in the individual instance is not in contradiction to the general intention prevailing at other times, but in fulfilment of it; as in the case of the person of confirmed virtue, and of all who pursue deliberately and consistently any determinate end. The distinction between will and desire, thus understood, is an authentic and highly important psychological fact; but the fact consists solely in this —that will, like all other parts of our constitution, is amenable to habit, and that we may will from habit what we no longer desire for itself, or desire only because we will it. It is not the less true that will, in the beginning, is entirely produced by desire; including in that term the repelling influence of pain as well as the attractive one of pleasure. Let us take into consideration, no longer the person who has a confirmed will to do right, but him in whom that virtuous will is still feeble, conquerable by temptation, and not to be fully relied on; by what means can it be strengthened? How can the will to be virtuous, where it does not exist in sufficient force, be implanted or awakened ? Only by making the person *desire* virtue —by making him think of it in a pleasurable light, or of its absence in a painful one. It is by associating the doing right with pleasure, or the doing wrong with pain, or by eliciting and impressing and bringing home to the person's experience the pleasure naturally involved in the one or the pain in the other, that it is possible to call forth that will to be virtuous, which, when confirmed, acts without any thought of either pleasure or pain. Will is the child of desire, and passes out of the dominion of its parent only to come under that of habit. That which is the result of habit affords no presumption of being intrinsically good; and there would be no reason for wishing that the purpose of virtue should become independent of pleasure and pain, were it not that the influence of the pleasurable and painful associations which prompt to virtue is not sufficiently to be depended on for unerring constancy of action until it has acquired the support of habit. Both in feeling and in conduct, habit is the only thing which imparts certainty; and it is because of the importance to others of being able to rely absolutely on one's feelings and conduct, and to oneself of being able to rely on one's own, that the will to do right ought to be cultivated into this habitual independence. In other words, this state of the will is a means to good, not intrinsically a good; and does not contradict the doctrine that nothing is a good to human beings but in so far as it is either itself pleasurable, or a means of attaining pleasure or averting pain.

But if this doctrine be true, the principle of utility is proved. Whether it is so or not, must now be left to the consideration of the thoughtful reader.

CHAPTER V

ON THE CONNEXION BETWEEN JUSTICE AND UTILITY

IN all ages of speculation, one of the strongest obstacles to the reception of the doctrine that Utility or Happiness is the criterion of right and wrong, has been drawn from the idea of Justice. The powerful sentiment, and apparently clear perception, which that word recalls with a rapidity and certainty resembling an instinct, have seemed to the majority of thinkers to point to an inherent quality in things; to show that the Just must have an existence in Nature as something absolute —generically distinct from every variety of the Expedient, and, in idea, opposed to it, though (as is commonly acknowledged) never, in the long-run, disjoined from it in fact.

In the case of this, as of our other moral sentiments, there is no necessary connection between the question of its origin and that of its binding force. That a feeling is bestowed on us by Nature, does not necessarily legitimate all its promptings.[1] The feeling of justice might be a peculiar instinct, and might yet require,

[1] Cf. Appendix C.

like our other instincts, to be controlled and enlightened by a higher reason. If we have intellectual instincts, leading us to judge in a particular way, as well as animal instincts that prompt us to act in a particular way, there is no necessity that the former should be more infallible in their sphere than the latter in theirs; it may as well happen that wrong judgments are occasionally suggested by those, as wrong actions by these. But though it is one thing to believe that we have natural feelings of justice, and another to acknowledge them as an ultimate criterion of conduct, these two opinions are very closely connected in point of fact. Mankind are always predisposed to believe that any subjective feeling, not otherwise accounted for, is a revelation of some objective reality. Our present object is to determine whether the reality, to which the feeling of justice corresponds, is one which needs any such special revelation; whether the justice or injustice of an action is a thing intrinsically peculiar, and distinct from all its other qualities, or only a combination of certain of those qualities, presented under a peculiar aspect. For the purpose of this inquiry, it is practically important to consider whether the feeling itself, of justice and injustice, is *sui generis* like our sensations of colour and taste, or a derivative feeling, formed by a combination of others. And this it is the more essential to examine, as people are in general willing enough to allow, that objectively the dictates of justice coincide with a part of the field of General Expediency; but inasmuch as the subjective mental feeling of

Justice is different from that which commonly attaches to simple expediency, and, except in extreme cases of the latter, is far more imperative in its demands, people find it difficult to see, in Justice, only a particular kind or branch of general utility, and think that its superior binding force requires a totally different origin.

To throw light upon this question, it is necessary to attempt to ascertain what is the distinguishing character of justice, or of injustice: what is the quality, or whether there is any quality, attributed in common to all modes of conduct designated as unjust (for justice, like many other moral attributes, is best defined by its opposite), and distinguishing them from such modes of conduct as are disapproved, but without having that particular epithet of disapprobation applied to them. If, in everything which men are accustomed to characterise as just or unjust, some one common attribute or collection of attributes is always present, we may judge whether this particular attribute or combination of attributes would be capable of gathering round it a sentiment of that peculiar character and intensity by virtue of the general laws of our emotional constitution, or whether the sentiment is inexplicable, and requires to be regarded as a special provision of Nature. If we find the former to be the case, we shall, in resolving this question, have resolved also the main problem: if the latter, we shall have to seek for some other mode of investigating it.

To find the common attributes of a variety of objects

it is necessary to begin by surveying the objects themselves in the concrete. Let us therefore advert successively to the various modes of action, and arrangements of human affairs, which are classed, by universal or widely spread opinion, as Just or as Unjust. The things well known to excite the sentiments associated with those names are of a very multifarious character. I shall pass them rapidly in review, without studying any particular arrangement.

In the first place, it is mostly considered unjust to deprive any one of his personal liberty, his property, or any other thing which belongs to him by law. Here, therefore, is one instance of the application of the terms just and unjust in a perfectly definite sense, namely, that it is just to respect, unjust to violate, the *legal rights* of any one. But this judgment admits of several exceptions, arising from the other forms in which the notions of justice and injustice present themselves. For example, the person who suffers the deprivation may (as the phrase is) have *forfeited* the rights which he is so deprived of—a case to which we shall return presently. But also,

Secondly ; the legal rights of which he is deprived may be rights which *ought* not to have belonged to him ; in other words, the law which confers on him these rights may be a bad law. When it is so, or when (which is the same thing for our purpose) it is supposed to be so, opinions will differ as to the justice or injustice of infringing it. Some maintain that no law, however bad, ought to be disobeyed by an individual citizen; that his opposition to it, if shown at all, should only be shown in endeavouring to get it altered by competent authority. This opinion (which condemns many of the most illustrious benefactors of mankind, and would often protect pernicious institutions against the only weapons which, in the state of things existing at the time, have any chance of succeeding against them) is defended, by those who hold it, on grounds of expediency; principally on that of the importance, to the common interest of mankind, of maintaining inviolate the sentiment of submission to law. Other persons, again, hold the directly contrary opinion, that any law, judged to be bad, may blamelessly be disobeyed, even though it be not judged to be unjust, but only inexpedient; while others would confine the licence of disobedience to the case of unjust laws: but again, some say that all laws which are inexpedient are unjust; since every law imposes some restriction on the natural liberty of mankind, which restriction is an injustice, unless legitimated by tending to their good. Among these diversities of opinion, it seems to be universally admitted that there may be unjust laws, and that law, consequently, is not the ultimate criterion of justice, but may give to one person a benefit, or impose on another an evil, which justice condemns. When, however, a law is thought to be unjust, it seems always to be regarded as being so in the same ways in which a breach of law is unjust, namely, by infringing somebody's right; which, as it cannot in this case be a legal right, receives a different appellation, and is called a moral right. We may say, therefore, that a second case of injustice consists in taking or withholding from any person that to which he has a *moral right*.

Thirdly, it is universally considered just that each person should obtain that (whether good or evil) which he *deserves;* and unjust that he should obtain a good, or be made to undergo an evil, which he does not deserve. This is, perhaps, the clearest and most emphatic form in which the idea of justice is conceived by the general mind. As it involves the notion of desert, the question arises, what constitutes desert? Speaking in a general way, a person is understood to deserve good if he does right, evil if he does wrong; and in a more particular sense, to deserve good from those to whom he does or has done good, and evil from those to whom he does or has done evil. The precept of returning good for evil has never been regarded as a case of the fulfilment of justice, but as one in which the claims of justice are waived, in obedience to other considerations.

Fourthly, it is confessedly unjust to *break faith* with any one: to violate an engagement, either express or implied, or disappoint expectations raised by our own conduct, at least if we have raised those expectations knowingly and voluntarily. Like the other obligations of justice already spoken of, this one is not regarded as absolute, but as capable of being overruled by a stronger obligation of justice on the other side; or by such conduct on the part of the person concerned as is deemed to absolve us from our obligation to him, and to constitute a *forfeiture* of the benefit which he has been led to expect.

Fifthly, it is, by universal admission, inconsistent with justice to be *partial;* to show favour or preference to one person over another, in matters to which favour and preference do not properly apply. Impartiality, however, does not seem to be regarded as a duty in itself, but rather as instrumental to some other duty; for it is admitted that favour and preference are not always censurable, and indeed the cases in which they are condemned are rather the exception than the rule. A person would be more likely to be blamed than applauded for giving his family or friends no superiority in good offices over strangers, when he could do so without violating any other duty; and no one thinks it unjust to seek one person in preference to another as a friend, connection, or companion. Impartiality where rights are concerned is of course obligatory, but this is involved in the more general obligation of giving to every one his right. A tribunal, for example, must be impartial, because it is bound to award, without regard to any other consideration, a disputed object to the one of two parties who has the right to it. There are other cases in which impartiality means, being solely influenced by desert; as with those who, in the capacity of judges, preceptors, or parents, administer reward and punishment as such. There are cases, again, in which it means, being solely influenced by consideration for the public interest; as in making a selection among candidates for a Government employment. Impartiality, in short, as an obligation of justice, may be said to mean, being exclusively influenced by the considerations which it is supposed ought to influence the particular case in hand; and resisting the solicitation of any motives which prompt to conduct different from what those considerations would dictate.

Nearly allied to the idea of impartiality is that of *equality*, which often enters as a component part both into the conception of justice and into the practice of it, and, in the eyes of many persons, constitutes its essence. But in this, still more than in any other case, the notion of justice varies in different persons, and always conforms in its variations to their notion of utility. Each person maintains that equality is the dictate of justice, except where he thinks that expediency requires inequality. The justice of giving equal protection to the rights of all, is maintained by those who support the most outrageous inequality in the rights themselves. Even in slave countries it is theoretically admitted that the rights of the slave, such as they are, ought to be as sacred as those of the master; and that a tribunal which fails to enforce them with equal strictness is wanting in justice; while, at the same time, institutions which leave to the slave scarcely any rights to enforce, are not deemed unjust, because they are not deemed inexpedient. Those who think that utility requires distinctions of rank, do not consider it unjust that riches and social privileges should be unequally dispensed; but those who think this inequality inexpedient, think it unjust also. Whoever thinks that Government is necessary, sees no injustice in as much inequality as is constituted by giving to the magistrate powers not granted to other people. Even among those who hold levelling doctrines, there are as many questions of justice as there are differences of opinion about expediency. Some Communists consider it unjust that the produce of the labour of the community should be shared on any other principle than that of exact equality; others think it just that those should receive most whose needs are greatest; while others hold that those who work harder, or who produce more, or whose services are more valuable to the community, may justly claim a larger quota in the division of the produce. And the sense of natural justice may be plausibly appealed to in behalf of every one of these opinions.

Among so many diverse applications of the term Justice, which yet is not regarded as ambiguous, it is a matter of some difficulty to seize the mental link which holds them together, and on which the moral sentiment adhering to the term essentially depends. Perhaps, in this embarrassment, some help may be derived from the history of the word, as indicated by its etymology.

In most, if not in all, languages, the etymology of the word which corresponds to Just, points to an origin connected either with positive law, or with that which was in most cases the primitive form of law — authoritative custom. *Justum* is a form of *jussum*, that which has been ordered. *Jus* is of the same origin. Δίκαιον comes from δίκη, of which the principal meaning, at least in the historical ages of Greece, was a suit at law. Originally, indeed, it meant only the mode or *manner* of doing things, but it early came to mean the *prescribed* manner—that which the recognised authorities, patriarchal, judicial, or political, would enforce. *Recht*, from which came *right* and *righteous*, is synonymous with law. The original meaning, indeed, of *recht* did not point to law, but to physical straightness; as *wrong* and its Latin equivalents meant twisted or *tortuous:* and from this it is argued that right did not originally mean law, but on the contrary law meant right. But however this may be, the fact that *recht* and *droit* became restricted in their meaning to positive law, although much which is not required by law is equally necessary to moral straightness or rectitude, is as significant of the original character of moral ideas as if the derivation had been the reverse way. The courts of justice, the administration of justice, are the courts and the administration of law. *La justice*, in French, is the established term for judicature. There can, I think, be no doubt that the *idée mère*, the primitive element, in the formation of the notion of justice, was conformity to law. It constituted the entire idea among the Hebrews, up to the birth of Christianity; as might be expected in the case of a people whose laws attempted to embrace all subjects on which precepts were required, and who believed those laws to be a direct emanation from the Supreme Being. But other nations, and in particular the Greeks and Romans, who knew that their laws had been made originally, and still continued to be made, by men, were not afraid to admit that those men might make bad laws; might do, by law, the same things, and from the same motives, which, if done by individuals, without the sanction of law, would be called unjust. And hence the sentiment of injustice came to be attached, not to all violations of law, but only to violations of such laws as *ought* to exist, including such as ought to exist but do not; and to laws themselves, if supposed to be contrary to what ought to be law. In this manner the idea of law and of its injunctions was still predominant in the notion of justice, even when the laws actually in force ceased to be accepted as the standard of it.

It is true that mankind consider the idea of justice and its obligations as applicable to many things which neither are, nor is it desired that they should be, regulated by law. Nobody desires that laws should interfere with the whole detail of private life; yet every one allows that in all daily conduct a person may and does show himself to be either just or unjust. But even here, the idea of the breach of what ought to be law still lingers in a modified shape. It would always give us pleasure, and chime in with our feelings of fitness, that acts which we deem unjust should be punished, though we do not always think it expedient that this should be done by the tribunals. We forego that gratification on account of incidental inconveniences. We should be glad to see just conduct enforced and injustice repressed, even in the minutest details, if we were not, with reason, afraid of trusting the magistrate with so unlimited an amount of power over individuals. When we think that a person is bound in justice to do a thing, it is an ordinary form of language to say that he ought to be compelled to do it. We should be gratified to see the obligation enforced by anybody who had the power. If we see that its enforcement by law would be inexpedient, we lament the impossibility, we consider the impunity given to injustice as an evil, and strive to make amends for it by bringing a strong expression of our own and the public disapprobation to bear upon the offender. Thus the idea of legal constraint is still the generating idea of the notion of justice, though undergoing several transformations before that notion, as it exists in an advanced state of society, becomes complete.

The above is, I think, a true account, as far as it goes, of the origin and progressive growth of the idea of justice. But we must observe that it contains, as yet, nothing to distinguish that obligation from moral obligation in general. For the truth is, that the idea of penal sanction, which is the essence of law, enters not only into the conception of injustice, but into that of any kind of wrong. We do not call anything wrong, unless we mean to imply that a person ought to be punished in some way or other for doing it; if not by law, by the opinion of his fellow-creatures; if not by opinion, by the reproaches of his own conscience. This seems the real turning-point of the distinction between morality and simple expediency. It is a part of the notion of Duty in every one of its forms, that a person may rightfully be compelled to fulfil it. Duty is a thing which may be *exacted* from a person, as one exacts a debt. Unless we think that it might be exacted from him, we do not call it his duty. Reasons of prudence, or the interest of other people, may militate against actually exacting it; but the person himself, it is clearly understood, would not be entitled to complain. There are other things, on the contrary, which we wish that people should do, which we like or admire them for doing, perhaps dislike or despise them for not doing, but yet admit that they are not bound to do; it is not a case of moral obligation; we do not blame them—that is, we do not think that they are proper objects of punishment. How we come by these ideas of deserving and not deserving punishment will appear, perhaps, in the sequel; but I think there is no doubt that this distinction lies at the bottom of the notions of right and wrong; that we call any conduct wrong, or employ instead some other term of dislike or disparagement, according as we think that the person ought, or ought not, to be punished for it; and we say that it would be right to do so and so, or merely that it would be desirable or laudable, according as we would wish to see the person whom it concerns compelled, or only persuaded and exhorted, to act in that manner.*

This, therefore, being the characteristic difference which marks off, not justice, but morality in general, from the remaining provinces of Expediency and Worthiness, the character is still to be sought which distinguishes justice from other branches of morality. Now it is known that ethical writers divide moral duties into two classes, denoted by the ill-chosen expressions, duties of perfect and of imperfect obligation; the latter being those in which, though the act is obligatory, the particular occasions of performing it are left to our choice; as in the case of charity or beneficence, which we are indeed bound to practise, but not towards any definite person, nor at any prescribed time. In the more precise language of philosophic jurists, duties of perfect obligation are those duties in virtue of which a correlative *right* resides in some person or persons; duties of imperfect obligation are those moral obligations which do not give birth to any right. I think it will be found that this distinction exactly coincides with that which exists between justice and the other obligations of morality. In our survey of the various popular acceptations of justice, the term appeared generally to involve the idea of a personal right—a claim on the part of one or more individuals, like that which the law gives when it confers a pro-

* See this point enforced and illustrated by Professor Bain, in an admirable chapter (entitled "The Ethical Emotions, or the Moral Sense") of the second of the two treatises composing his elaborate and profound work on the Mind.

prietary or other legal right. Whether the injustice consists in depriving a person of a possession, or in breaking faith with him, or in treating him worse than he deserves, or worse than other people who have no greater claims, in each case the supposition implies two things—a wrong done, and some assignable person who is wronged. Injustice may also be done by treating a person better than others; but the wrong in this case is to his competitors, who are also assignable persons. It seems to me that this feature in the case—a right in some person, correlative to the moral obligation— constitutes the specific difference between justice, and generosity or beneficence. Justice implies something which it is not only right to do, and wrong not to do, but which some individual person can claim from us as his moral right. No one has a moral right to our generosity or beneficence, because we are not morally bound to practise those virtues towards any given individual. And it will be found, with respect to this as with respect to every correct definition, that the instances which seem to conflict with it are those which most confirm it. For if a moralist attempts, as some have done, to make out that mankind generally, though not any given individual, have a right to all the good we can do to them, he at once, by that thesis, includes generosity and beneficence within the category of justice. He is obliged to say that our utmost exertions are *due* to our fellow-creatures, thus assimilating them to a debt; or that nothing less can be a sufficient *return* for what society does for us, thus classing the case as one of gratitude; both of which are acknowledged cases of justice. Wherever there is a right the case is one of justice, and not of the virtue of beneficence; and whoever does not place the distinction between justice and morality in general where we have now placed it, will be found to make no distinction between them at all, but to merge all morality in justice.

Having thus endeavoured to determine the distinctive elements which enter into the composition of the idea of justice, we are ready to enter on the inquiry, whether the feeling, which accompanies the idea, is attached to it by a special dispensation of nature, or whether it could have grown up, by any known laws, out of the idea itself; and in particular, whether it can have originated in considerations of general expediency.

I conceive that the sentiment itself does not arise from anything which would commonly, or correctly, be termed an idea of expediency; but that, though the sentiment does not, whatever is moral in it does.

We have seen that the two essential ingredients in the sentiment of justice are, the desire to punish a person who has done harm, and the knowledge or belief that there is some definite individual or individuals to whom harm has been done.

Now it appears to me that the desire to punish a person who has done harm to some individual is a spontaneous outgrowth from two sentiments, both in the highest degree natural, and which either are or resemble instincts: the impulse of self-defence, and the feeling of sympathy.

It is natural to resent, and to repel or retaliate, any harm done or attempted against ourselves, or against those with whom we sympathise. The origin of this sentiment it is not necessary here to discuss. Whether it be an instinct or a result of intelligence, it is, we know, common to all animal nature; for every animal tries to hurt those who have hurt, or who it thinks are about to hurt, itself or its young. Human beings on this point only differ from other animals in two particulars. First, in being capable of sympathising, not solely with their offspring, or, like some of the more noble animals, with some superior animal who is kind to them, but with all human, and even with all sentient, beings. Secondly, in having a more developed intelligence, which gives a wider range to the whole of their sentiments, whether self-regarding or sympathetic. By virtue of his superior intelligence, even apart from his superior range of sympathy, a human being is capable of apprehending a community of interest between himself and the human society of which he forms a part, such that any conduct which threatens the security of the society generally is threatening to his own, and calls forth his instinct (if instinct it be) of self-defence. The same superiority of intelligence, joined to the power of sympathising with human beings generally, enables him to attach himself to the collective idea of his tribe, his country, or mankind, in such a manner that any act hurtful to them rouses his instinct of sympathy, and urges him to resistance.

The sentiment of justice, in that one of its elements which consists of the desire to punish, is thus, I conceive, the natural feeling of retaliation or vengeance, rendered by intellect and sympathy applicable to those injuries, that is, to those hurts, which wound us through, or in common with, society at large. This sentiment, in itself, has nothing moral in it; what is moral is, the exclusive subordination of it to the social sympathies, so as to wait on and obey their call.[1] For the natural feeling tends to make us resent indiscriminately whatever any one does that is disagreeable to us; but when moralised by the social feeling, it only acts in the directions conformable to the general good; just persons resenting a hurt to society, though not otherwise a hurt to themselves, and not resenting a hurt to themselves, however painful, unless it be of the kind which society has a common interest with them in the repression of.

It is no objection against this doctrine to say, that when we feel our sentiment of justice outraged, we are not thinking of society at large, or of any collective interest, but only of the individual case. It is

[1] 'Subjection of Women,' p. 8: "Laws and systems of polity always begin by recognising the relations they find already existing between individuals. They convert what was a mere physical fact into a legal right, give it the sanction of society, and principally aim at the substitution of public and organised means of asserting and protecting these rights, instead of the irregular and lawless conflict of physical strength."

Ib., p. 79: "The moral education of mankind has hitherto emanated chiefly from the law of force, and is adapted almost solely to the relations which force creates. . . . Yet command and obedience are but unfortunate necessities of human life: society in equality is its normal state."

common enough certainly, though the reverse of commendable, to feel resentment merely because we have suffered pain; but a person whose resentment is really a moral feeling, that is, who considers whether an act is blamable before he allows himself to resent it—such a person, though he may not say expressly to himself that he is standing up for the interest of society, certainly does feel that he is asserting a rule which is for the benefit of others as well as for his own. If he is not feeling this—if he is regarding the act solely as it affects him individually—he is not consciously just: he is not concerning himself about the justice of his actions. This is admitted even by anti-utilitarian moralists. When Kant (as before remarked) propounds as the fundamental principle of morals, " So act, that thy rule of conduct might be adopted as a law by all rational beings," he virtually acknowledges that the interest of mankind collectively, or at least of mankind indiscriminately, must be in the mind of the agent when conscientiously deciding on the morality of the act. Otherwise he uses words without a meaning; for, that a rule even of utter selfishness could not *possibly* be adopted by all rational beings—that there is any insuperable obstacle in the nature of things to its adoption — cannot be even plausibly maintained. To give any meaning to Kant's principle, the sense put upon it must be, that we ought to shape our conduct by a rule which all rational beings might adopt *with benefit to their collective interest.*

To recapitulate: the idea of justice supposes two things — a rule of conduct, and a sentiment which sanctions the rule. The first must be supposed common to all mankind, and intended for their good. The other (the sentiment) is a desire that punishment may be suffered by those who infringe the rule. There is involved, in addition, the conception of some definite person who suffers by the infringement; whose rights (to use the expression appropriated to the case) are violated by it. And the sentiment of justice appears to me to be, the animal desire to repel or retaliate a hurt or damage to oneself, or to those with whom one sympathises, widened so as to include all persons, by the human capacity of enlarged sympathy, and the human conception of intelligent self-interest. From the latter elements, the feeling derives its morality; from the former, its peculiar impressiveness, and energy of self-assertion.

I have, throughout, treated the idea of a *right* residing in the injured person, and violated by the injury, not as a separate element in the composition of the idea and sentiment, but as one of the forms in which the other two elements clothe themselves. These elements are, a hurt to some assignable person or persons on the one hand, and a demand for punishment on the other. An examination of our own minds, I think, will show, that these two things include all that we mean when we speak of violation of a right. When we call anything a person's right, we mean that he has a valid claim on society to protect him in the possession of it, either by the force of law, or by that of education and opinion. If he has what we consider a sufficient claim, on whatever account, to have something guaranteed to him by society, we say that he has a right to it. If we desire to prove that anything does not belong to him by right, we think this done as soon as it is admitted that society ought not to take measures for securing it to him, but should leave it to chance, or to his own exertions. Thus, a person is said to have a right to what he can earn in fair professional competition; because society ought not to allow any other person to hinder him from endeavouring to earn in that manner as much as he can. But he has not a right to three hundred a-year, though he may happen to be earning it; because society is not called on to provide that he shall earn that sum. On the contrary, if he owns ten thousand pounds three per cent stock he *has* a right to three hundred a-year; because society has come under an obligation to provide him with an income of that amount.

To have a right, then, is, I conceive, to have something which society ought to defend me in the possession of.[1] If the objector goes on to ask why it ought,

---

[1] 'Liberty,' p. 6: "The object of this essay is to assert one very simple principle, as entitled to govern absolutely the dealings of society with the individual in the way of compulsion and control, whether the means used be physical force in the form of legal penalties, or the moral coercion of public opinion. That principle is, that the sole end for which mankind are warranted, individually or collectively, in interfering with the liberty of action of any of

I can give him no other reason than general utility. If that expression does not seem to convey a sufficient feeling of the strength of the obligation nor to account for the peculiar energy of the feeling, it is because there goes to the composition of the sentiment, not a rational only but also an animal element, the thirst for retaliation; and this thirst derives its intensity, as well as its moral justification, from the extraordinarily important and impressive kind of utility which is concerned. The interest involved is that of security, to every one's feelings the most vital of all interests. Nearly all other earthly benefits are needed by one person, not needed by another; and many of them can, if necessary, be cheerfully foregone, or replaced by something else; but security no human being can possibly do without: on it we depend for all our immunity from evil, and for the whole value of all and every good, beyond the passing moment; since nothing but the gratification of the instant could be of any worth to us, if we could be deprived of everything the next instant by whoever was momentarily stronger than ourselves.[1] Now this most indispensable of all

their number, is self-protection. That the only purpose for which power can be rightfully exercised over any member of a civilised community, against his will, is to prevent harm to others."

[1] 'Political Economy,' p. 422: "Of this increased security, one of the most unfailing effects is a great increase both of production and of accumulation. Industry and frugality cannot exist, where there is not a preponderant probability that those who labour and spare will be permitted to enjoy. And the nearer this probability approaches to certainty, the more do industry and frugality become pervading qualities in a people. Experience has shown that a large

necessaries, after physical nutriment, cannot be had, unless the machinery for providing for it is kept unintermittingly in active play. Our notion, therefore, of the claim we have on our fellow-creatures to join in making safe for us the very groundwork of our existence, gathers feelings round it so much more intense than those concerned in any of the more common cases of utility, that the difference in degree (as is often the case in psychology) becomes a real difference

proportion of the results of labour and abstinence may be taken away by fixed taxation, without impairing, and sometimes even with the effect of stimulating, the qualities from which a great production and an abundant capital take their rise. But those qualities are not proof against a high degree of uncertainty. The government may carry off a part ; but there must be assurance that it will not interfere, nor suffer any one to interfere, with the remainder."

Ib., p. 531 : " The first of these [the functions of government] is the protection of person and property. There is no need to expatiate on the influence exercised over the economical interests of society by the degree of completeness with which this duty of government is performed. Insecurity of person and property, is as much as to say, uncertainty of the connection between all human exertion or sacrifice, and the attainment of the ends for the sake of which they are undergone. It means uncertainty whether they who sow shall reap, whether they who produce shall consume, and they who spare to-day shall enjoy to-morrow. It means not only that labour and frugality are not the road to acquisition, but that violence is. When person and property are to a certain degree insecure, all the possessions of the weak are at the mercy of the strong."

Ib., p. 591: " Even in the best state which society has yet reached, it is lamentable to think how great a proportion of all the efforts and talents in the world are employed in merely neutralising one another. It is the proper end of government to reduce this wretched waste to the smallest possible amount, by taking such measures as shall cause the energies now spent by mankind in injuring one another, or in protecting themselves against injury, to be turned to the legitimate employment of the human faculties, that of compelling the powers of nature to be more and more subservient to physical and moral good."

in kind. The claim assumes that character of absoluteness, that apparent infinity, and incommensurability with all other considerations, which constitute the distinction between the feeling of right and wrong and that of ordinary expediency and inexpediency. The feelings concerned are so powerful, and we count so positively on finding a responsive feeling in others (all being alike interested), that *ought* and *should* grow into *must*, and recognised indispensability becomes a moral necessity, analogous to physical, and often not inferior to it in binding force.

If the preceding analysis, or something resembling it, be not the correct account of the notion of justice; if justice be totally independent of utility, and be a standard *per se*, which the mind can recognise by simple introspection of itself; it is hard to understand why that internal oracle is so ambiguous, and why so many things appear either just or unjust, according to the light in which they are regarded.

We are continually informed that Utility is an uncertain standard, which every different person interprets differently, and that there is no safety but in the immutable, ineffaceable, and unmistakable dictates of Justice, which carry their evidence in themselves, and are independent of the fluctuations of opinion. One would suppose from this that on questions of justice there could be no controversy; that if we take that for our rule, its application to any given case could leave us in as little doubt as a mathematical demonstration. So far is this from being the fact, that there is as much difference of opinion, and as fierce discussion, about what is just, as about what is useful to society. Not only have different nations and individuals different notions of justice, but, in the mind of one and the same individual, justice is not some one rule, principle, or maxim, but many, which do not always coincide in their dictates, and in choosing between which, he is guided either by some extraneous standard, or by his own personal predilections.

For instance, there are some who say that it is unjust to punish any one for the sake of example to others; that punishment is just, only when intended for the good of the sufferer himself. Others maintain the extreme reverse, contending that to punish persons who have attained years of discretion, for their own benefit, is despotism and injustice, since if the matter at issue is solely their own good, no one has a right to control their own judgment of it; but that they may justly be punished to prevent evil to others, this being an exercise of the legitimate right of self-defence. Mr Owen, again, affirms that it is unjust to punish at all, for the criminal did not make his own character; his education, and the circumstances which surround him, have made him a criminal, and for these he is not responsible. All these opinions are extremely plausible; and so long as the question is argued as one of justice simply, without going down to the principles which lie under justice and are the source of its authority, I am unable to see how any of these reasoners can be refuted. For, in truth, every one of the three builds upon rules of justice confessedly true. The first appeals to the acknowledged injustice of singling out an individual, and making him a sacrifice, without his consent, for other people's benefit. The second relies on the acknowledged justice of self-defence, and the admitted injustice of forcing one person to conform to another's notions of what constitutes his good. The Owenite invokes the admitted principle, that it is unjust to punish any one for what he cannot help. Each is triumphant so long as he is not compelled to take into consideration any other maxims of justice than the one he has selected; but as soon as their several maxims are brought face to face, each disputant seems to have exactly as much to say for himself as the others. No one of them can carry out his own notion of justice without trampling upon another equally binding. These are difficulties; they have always been felt to be such; and many devices have been invented to turn rather than to overcome them. As a refuge from the last of the three, men imagined what they called the freedom of the will; fancying that they could not justify punishing a man whose will is in a thoroughly hateful state, unless it be supposed to have come into that state through no influence of anterior circumstances. To escape from the other difficulties, a favourite contrivance has been the fiction of a contract, whereby at some unknown period all the members of society engaged to obey the laws, and consented to be punished for any disobedience to them; thereby giving to their legislators the right, which it is assumed they would not otherwise have had, of punishing them, either for their own good or for that of society. This happy thought was considered to get rid of the whole difficulty, and to legitimate the infliction of punishment, in virtue of another received maxim of justice, *volenti non fit injuria;* that is not unjust which is done with the consent of the person who is supposed to be hurt by it. I need hardly remark, that even if the consent were not a mere fiction, this maxim is not superior in authority to the others which it is brought in to supersede. It is, on the contrary, an instructive specimen of the loose and irregular manner in which supposed principles of justice grow up. This particular one evidently came into use as a help to the coarse exigencies of courts of law, which are sometimes obliged to be content with very uncertain presumptions, on account of the greater evils which would often arise from any attempt on their part to cut finer. But even courts of law are not able to adhere consistently to the maxim, for they allow voluntary engagements to be set aside on the ground of fraud, and sometimes on that of mere mistake or misinformation.

Again, when the legitimacy of inflicting punishment is admitted, how many conflicting conceptions of justice come to light in discussing the proper apportionment of punishment to offences. No rule on this subject recommends itself so strongly to the primitive and spontaneous sentiment of justice as the *lex talionis,* an eye for an eye and a tooth for a tooth. Though this principle of the Jewish and of the Mahomedan law has been generally abandoned in Europe as a practical maxim, there is, I suspect, in most minds, a secret hankering after it; and when retribution accidentally falls on an offender in that precise shape, the general feeling of satisfaction evinced bears witness how natural is the sentiment to which this repayment in kind is acceptable. With many the test of justice in penal infliction is, that the punishment should be proportioned to the offence; meaning that it should be exactly measured by the moral guilt of the culprit (whatever be their standard for measuring moral guilt),—the consideration, what amount of punishment is necessary to deter from the offence, having nothing to do with the question of justice, in their estimation: while there are others to whom that consideration is all in all; who maintain that it is not just, at least for man, to inflict on a fellow-creature, whatever may be his offences, any amount of suffering beyond the least that will suffice to prevent him from repeating, and others from imitating, his misconduct.

To take another example from a subject already once referred to. In a co-operative industrial association, is it just or not that talent or skill should give a title to superior remuneration? On the negative side of the question it is argued, that whoever does the best he can, deserves equally well, and ought not in justice to be put in a position of inferiority for no fault of his own; that superior abilities have already advantages more than enough, in the admiration they excite, the personal influence they command, and the internal sources of satisfaction attending them, without adding to these a superior share of the world's goods; and that society is bound in justice rather to make compensation to the less favoured, for this unmerited inequality of advantages, than to aggravate it. On the contrary side it is contended, that society receives more from the more efficient labourer; that his services being more useful, society owes him a larger return for them; that a greater share of the joint result is actually his work, and not to allow his claim to it is a kind of robbery; that if he is only to receive as much as others, he can only be justly required to produce as much, and to give a smaller amount of time and exertion, proportioned to his superior efficiency. Who shall decide between these appeals to conflicting principles of justice? Justice has in this case two sides to it, which it is impossible to bring into harmony, and the two disputants have chosen opposite sides: the one looks to what it is just that the individual should receive, the other to what it is just that the community should give. Each, from his own point of view, is unanswerable; and any choice between them, on grounds of justice, must be perfectly arbitrary. Social utility alone can decide the preference.

How many, again, and how irreconcilable, are the standards of justice to which reference is made in discussing the repartition of taxation. One opinion is, that payment to the State should be in numerical proportion to pecuniary means. Others think that justice dictates what they term graduated taxation—taking a higher percentage from those who have more to spare.

In point of natural justice a strong case might be made for disregarding means altogether, and taking the same absolute sum (whenever it could be got) from every one: as the subscribers to a mess, or to a club, all pay the same sum for the same privileges, whether they can all equally afford it or not. Since the protection (it might be said) of law and government is afforded to, and is equally required by, all, there is no injustice in making all buy it at the same price. It is reckoned justice, not injustice, that a dealer should charge to all customers the same price for the same article, not a price varying according to their means of payment. This doctrine, as applied to taxation, finds no advocates, because it conflicts strongly with men's feelings of humanity and perceptions of social expediency; but the principle of justice which it invokes is as true and as binding as those which can be appealed to against it. Accordingly, it exerts a tacit influence on the line of defence employed for other modes of assessing taxation. People feel obliged to argue that the State does more for the rich than for the poor, as a justification for its taking more from them: though this is in reality not true, for the rich would be far better able to protect themselves, in the absence of law or government, than the poor, and indeed would probably be successful in converting the poor into their slaves. Others, again, so far defer to the same conception of justice, as to maintain that all should pay an equal capitation tax for the protection of their persons (these being of equal value to all) and an unequal tax for the protection of their property, which is unequal. To this others reply, that the all of one man is as valuable to him as the all of another. From these confusions there is no other mode of extrication than the utilitarian.

Is, then, the difference between the Just and the Expedient a merely imaginary distinction? Have mankind been under a delusion in thinking that justice is a more sacred thing than policy, and that the latter ought only to be listened to after the former has been satisfied? By no means. The exposition we have given of the nature and origin of the sentiment recognises a real distinction; and no one of those who profess the most sublime contempt for the consequences of actions as an element in their morality, attaches more importance to the distinction than I do. While I dispute the pretensions of any theory which sets up an imaginary standard of justice not grounded on utility, I account the justice which is grounded on utility to be the chief part, and incomparably the most sacred and binding part, of all morality. Justice is a name for certain classes of moral rules, which concern the essentials of human wellbeing more nearly, and are therefore of more absolute obligation, than any other rules for the guidance of life; and the notion which we have found to be of the essence of the idea of justice, that of a right residing in an individual, implies and testifies to this more binding obligation.

The moral rules which forbid mankind to hurt one another (in which we must never forget to include wrongful interference with each other's freedom) are more vital to human wellbeing than any maxims, however important, which only point out the best mode of managing some department of human affairs. They have also the peculiarity, that they are the main element in determining the whole of the social feelings of mankind. It is their observance which alone preserves peace among human beings; if obedience to them were not the rule, and disobedience the exception, every one would see in every one else a probable enemy, against whom he must be perpetually guarding himself. What is hardly less important, these are the precepts which mankind have the strongest and the most direct inducements for impressing upon one another. By merely giving to each other prudential instruction or exhortation, they may gain, or think they gain, nothing: in inculcating on each other the duty of positive beneficence they have an unmistakable interest, but far less in degree: a person may possibly not need the benefits of others; but he always needs that they should not do him hurt. Thus the moralities which protect every individual from being harmed by others, either directly or by being hindered in his freedom of pursuing his own good, are at once those which he himself has most at heart, and those which he has the strongest interest in publishing and enforcing by word and deed. It is by a person's observance of these, that his fitness to exist as one of the fellowship of human beings is tested and decided, for on that depends his being a nuisance or not to those with whom he is in contact. Now it is these moralities primarily, which compose the obligations of justice. The most marked cases of injustice, and those which give the tone to the feeling of repugnance which characterises the sentiment, are acts of wrongful aggression, or wrongful exercise of power over some one; the next are those which consist in wrongfully withholding from him something which is his due—in both cases, inflicting on him a positive hurt, either in the form of direct suffering, or of the privation of some good which he had reasonable ground, either of a physical or of a social kind, for counting upon.[1]

---

[1] 'Subjection of Women,' p. 148: ". . . the advantage of having the most universal and pervading of all human relations regulated by justice instead of injustice. The vast amount of this gain to human nature, it is hardly possible, by any explanation or illustration, to place in a stronger light than it is placed by the bare statement, to any one who attaches a moral meaning to words."

Ib., p. 152: "The example afforded and the education given to the sentiments, by laying the foundations of domestic existence upon a relation contradictory to the first principles of social justice, must, from the very nature of man, have a perverting influence of such magnitude, that it is hardly possible with our present experience to raise our imagination to the conception of so great a change for the better as would be made by its removal. All that education and civilisation are doing to efface the influences on character of the law of force, and replace them by those of justice, remains merely on the surface, as long as the citadel of the enemy is not attacked. The principle of the modern movement in morals and politics is that conduct, and conduct alone, entitles to respect: that not what men are, but what they do, constitutes their claim to deference; that, above all, merit and not birth is the only rightful claim to power and authority. If no authority, not in its nature temporary, were allowed to one human being over another, society would not be employed in building up propensities with one hand which it has to curb with the other. The child would really, for the first time in man's existence on earth, be

The same powerful motives which command the observance of these primary moralities, enjoin the punishment of those who violate them; and as the impulses of self-defence, of defence of others, and of vengeance, are all called forth against such persons, retribution, or evil for evil, becomes closely connected with the sentiment of justice, and is universally included in the idea. Good for good is also one of the dictates of justice; and this, though its social utility is evident, and though it carries with it a natural human feeling, has not at first sight that obvious connection with hurt or injury which, existing in the most elementary cases of just and unjust, is the source

trained in the way he should go, and when he was old there would be a chance that he would not depart from it. But so long as the right of the strong to power over the weak rules in the very heart of society, the attempt to make the equal right of the weak the principle of its outward actions will always be an uphill struggle; for the law of justice, which is also that of Christianity, will never get possession of men's inmost sentiments; they will be working against it even when bending to it."

Ib., p. 159: "The main foundations of the moral life of modern times must be justice and prudence; the respect of each for the rights of every other, and the ability of each to take care of himself."

Ib., p. 177: "The moral regeneration of mankind will only really commence, when the most fundamental of the social relations is placed under the rule of equal justice, and when human beings learn to cultivate their strongest sympathy with an equal in rights and in cultivation."

Ib., p. 180: "Whatever has been said or written from the time of Herodotus to the present, of the ennobling influence of free government—the nerve and spring which it gives to all the faculties, the larger and higher objects which it presents to the intellect and feelings, the more unselfish public spirit, and calmer and broader views of duty that it engenders, and the generally loftier platform on which it elevates the individual as a moral, spiritual, and social being—is every particle as true of women as of men."

of the characteristic intensity of the sentiment. But the connection, though less obvious, is not less real. He who accepts benefits, and denies a return of them when needed, inflicts a real hurt, by disappointing one of the most natural and reasonable of expectations, and one which he must at least tacitly have encouraged, otherwise the benefits would seldom have been conferred. The important rank, among human evils and wrongs, of the disappointment of expectation, is shown in the fact that it constitutes the principal criminality of two such highly immoral acts as a breach of friendship and a breach of promise. Few hurts which human beings can sustain are greater, and none wound more, than when that on which they habitually and with full assurance relied, fails them in the hour of need; and few wrongs are greater than this mere withholding of good: none excite more resentment, either in the person suffering or in a sympathising spectator. The principle, therefore, of giving to each what they deserve—that is, good for good, as well as evil for evil—is not only included within the idea of Justice as we have defined it, but is a proper object of that intensity of sentiment which places the Just, in human estimation, above the simply Expedient.

Most of the maxims of justice current in the world, and commonly appealed to in its transactions, are simply instrumental to carrying into effect the principles of justice which we have now spoken of. That a person is only responsible for what he has done voluntarily, or could voluntarily have avoided; that it is unjust to condemn any person unheard; that the punishment ought to be proportioned to the offence, and the like, are maxims intended to prevent the just principle of evil for evil from being perverted to the infliction of evil without that justification. The greater part of these common maxims have come into use from the practice of courts of justice, which have been naturally led to a more complete recognition and elaboration than was likely to suggest itself to others, of the rules necessary to enable them to fulfil their double function, of inflicting punishment when due, and of awarding to each person his right.

That first of judicial virtues, impartiality, is an obligation of justice, partly for the reason last mentioned; as being a necessary condition of the fulfilment of the other obligations of justice. But this is not the only source of the exalted rank, among human obligations, of those maxims of equality and impartiality which, both in popular estimation and in that of the most enlightened, are included among the precepts of justice. In one point of view, they may be considered as corollaries from the principles already laid down. If it is a duty to do to each according to its deserts, returning good for good as well as repressing evil by evil, it necessarily follows that we should treat all equally well (when no higher duty forbids) who have deserved equally well of us, and that society should treat all equally well who have deserved equally well of it, that is, who have deserved equally well absolutely. This is the highest abstract standard of social and distributive justice; towards which all institutions, and the efforts of all virtuous citizens, should be made in the utmost possible degree to converge. But this great moral duty rests upon a still deeper foundation, being a direct emanation from the first principle of morals, and not a mere logical corollary from secondary or derivative doctrines. It is involved in the very meaning of Utility, or the Greatest - Happiness Principle. That principle is a mere form of words without rational signification, unless one person's happiness, supposed equal in degree (with the proper allowance made for kind), is counted for exactly as much as another's. Those conditions being supplied, Bentham's dictum, "everybody to count for one, nobody for more than one," might be written under the principle of utility as an explanatory commentary.* The equal claim of everybody to happiness in

* This implication, in the first principle of the utilitarian scheme, of perfect impartiality between persons, is regarded by Mr Herbert Spencer (in his 'Social Statics') as a disproof of the pretensions of utility to be a sufficient guide to right ; since (he says) the principle of utility presupposes the anterior principle, that everybody has an equal right to happiness. It may be more correctly described as supposing that equal amounts of happiness are equally desirable, whether felt by the same or by different persons. This, however, is not a presupposition ; not a premise needful to support the principle of utility, but the very principle itself ; for what is the principle of utility, if it be not that "happiness" and "desirable" are synonymous terms ? If there is any anterior principle implied, it can be no other than this, that the truths of arithmetic are applicable to the valuation of happiness, as of all other measurable quantities.

[Mr Herbert Spencer, in a private communication on the subject of the preceding Note, objects to being considered an opponent of Utilitarianism, and states that he regards happiness as the ultimate end of morality ; but deems that end only partially attainable by empirical

the estimation of the moralist and the legislator, involves an equal claim to all the means of happiness, except in so far as the inevitable conditions of human life, and the general interest, in which that of every individual is included, set limits to the maxim; and those limits ought to be strictly construed. As every other maxim of justice, so this, is by no means applied or held applicable universally; on the contrary, as I have already remarked, it bends to every person's ideas of social expediency. But in whatever case it is deemed applicable to all, it is held to be the dictate of justice. All persons are deemed to have a *right* to equality of treatment, except when some recognised social expediency requires the reverse. And hence all social inequalities which have ceased to be considered expedient, assume the character not of simple inexpediency, but of injustice, and appear so tyrannical, that people are apt

generalisations from the observed results of conduct, and completely attainable only by deducing, from the laws of life and the conditions of existence, what kinds of action necessarily tend to produce happiness, and what kinds to produce unhappiness. With the exception of the word "necessarily," I have no dissent to express from this doctrine; and (omitting that word) I am not aware that any modern advocate of utilitarianism is of a different opinion. Bentham, certainly, to whom in the 'Social Statics' Mr Spencer particularly referred, is, least of all writers, chargeable with unwillingness to deduce the effect of actions on happiness from the laws of human nature and the universal conditions of human life. The common charge against him is of relying too exclusively upon such deductions, and declining altogether to be bound by the generalisations from specific experience which Mr Spencer thinks that utilitarians generally confine themselves to. My own opinion (and, as I collect, Mr Spencer's) is, that in ethics, as in all other branches of scientific study, the consilience of the results of both these processes, each corroborating and verifying the other, is requisite to give to any general proposition the kind and degree of evidence which constitutes scientific proof.]

to wonder how they ever could have been tolerated; forgetful that they themselves perhaps tolerate other inequalities under an equally mistaken notion of expediency, the correction of which would make that which they approve seem quite as monstrous as what they have at last learnt to condemn. The entire history of social improvement has been a series of transitions, by which one custom or institution after another, from being a supposed primary necessity of social existence, has passed into the rank of an universally stigmatised injustice and tyranny. So it has been with the distinctions of slaves and freemen, nobles and serfs, patricians and plebeians; and so it will be, and in part already is, with the aristocracies of colour, race, and sex.

It appears from what has been said, that justice is a name for certain moral requirements, which, regarded collectively, stand higher in the scale of social utility, and are therefore of more paramount obligation, than any others; though particular cases may occur in which some other social duty is so important, as to overrule any one of the general maxims of justice. Thus, to save a life, it may not only be allowable, but a duty, to steal, or take by force, the necessary food or medicine, or to kidnap, and compel to officiate, the only qualified medical practitioner. In such cases, as we do not call anything justice which is not a virtue, we usually say, not that justice must give way to some other moral principle, but that what is just in ordinary cases is, by reason of that other principle, not just in the particular case. By this useful accommodation of language, the character of indefeasibility attributed to justice is kept up, and we are saved from the necessity of maintaining that there can be laudable injustice.

The considerations which have now been adduced resolve, I conceive, the only real difficulty in the utilitarian theory of morals. It has always been evident that all cases of justice are also cases of expediency: the difference is in the peculiar sentiment which attaches to the former, as contradistinguished from the latter. If this characteristic sentiment has been sufficiently accounted for; if there is no necessity to assume for it any peculiarity of origin; if it is simply the natural feeling of resentment, moralised by being made coextensive with the demands of social good; and if this feeling not only does but ought to exist in all the classes of cases to which the idea of justice corresponds, — that idea no longer presents itself as a stumbling-block to the utilitarian ethics. Justice remains the appropriate name for certain social utilities which are vastly more important, and therefore more absolute and imperative, than any others are as a class (though not more so than others may be in particular cases); and which, therefore, ought to be, as well as naturally are, guarded by a sentiment not only different in degree, but also in kind; distinguished from the milder feeling which attaches to the mere idea of promoting human pleasure or convenience, at once by the more definite nature of its commands, and by the sterner character of its sanctions.

APPENDIX

APPENDIX A

CAUSALITY AND INDUCTION

'System of Logic,' p. 213: The only notion of a cause which the theory of induction requires, is such a notion as can be gained from experience. The law of Causation, the recognition of which is the main pillar of inductive science, is but the familiar truth, that invariability of succession is found by observation to obtain between every fact in nature, and some other fact which has preceded it, independently of all considerations respecting the ultimate mode of production of phenomena, and of every other question regarding the nature of "things in themselves."

Ib., p. 222: If there be any meaning which confessedly belongs to the term necessity, it is *unconditionalness*. That which is necessary, that which *must* be, means that which will be, whatever supposition we may make in regard to all other things. The succession of day and night evidently is not necessary in this sense. It is conditional on the occurrence of other antecedents. That which will be followed by a given consequent when, and only when, some third circumstance also exists, is not the cause, even although no case should have ever occurred in which the phenomenon took place without it.

Invariable sequence, therefore, is not synonymous with causation, unless the sequence, besides being invariable, is unconditional.

Ib., p. 369 : The validity of all the Inductive Methods depends on the assumption that every event, or the beginning of every phenomenon, must have some cause, some antecedent, on the existence of which it is invariably and unconditionally consequent.

'Auguste Comte and Positivism,' p. 57 : Comte has an objection to the *word* cause; he will only consent to speak of Laws of Succession : and depriving himself of the use of a word which has a Positive meaning, he misses the meaning it expresses. He sees no difference between such generalisations as Kepler's laws, and such as the theory of gravitation. He fails to perceive the real distinction between the laws of succession, and coexistence, which thinkers of a different school call Laws of Phænomena, and those of what they call the action of Causes : the former exemplified by the succession of day and night, the latter by the earth's rotation which causes it. The succession of day and night is as much an invariable sequence, as the alternate exposure of opposite sides of the earth to the sun. Yet day and night are not the causes of one another; why ? Because their sequence, though invariable in our experience, is not unconditionally so : those facts only succeed each other, provided that the presence and absence of the sun succeed each other, and if this alternation were to cease, we might have either day or night unfollowed by one another. There are thus two kinds of uniformities of succession, the one unconditional, the other conditional on the first : laws of causation, and other successions dependent on those laws. All ultimate laws are laws of causation, and the only universal law beyond the pale of mathematics is the law of universal causation—namely, that every phænomenon has a phænomenal cause; has some phænomenon other than itself, or some combination of phænomena, on which it is invariably and unconditionally consequent. It is on the universality of this law that the possibility rests of establishing a canon of Induction. A general proposition inductively obtained is only then proved to be true, when the instances on which it rests are such that if they have been correctly observed, the falsity of the generalisation would be inconsistent with the constancy of causation; with the universality of the fact that the phænomena of nature take place according to invariable laws of succession. It is probable, therefore, that M. Comte's determined abstinence from the word and the idea of Cause had much to do with his inability to conceive an Inductive Logic, by diverting his attention from the only basis upon which it could be founded.

'Dissertations and Discussions,' vol. iv. p. 172: True it is that all we can observe of physical phenomena is their constancies of coexistence, succession, and similitude. Berkeley had the merit of clearly discerning this fundamental truth, and handing down to his successors the true conception of that which alone the study of physical nature can consist in. He saw that the causation we think we see in nature is but uniformity of sequence. But this is not what he considers real causation to be. No physical phenomenon, he says, can be an efficient cause; but our daily experience proves to us that minds, by their volitions, can be, and are, efficient causes. Let us be thankful to Berkeley for the half of the truth which he saw, though the remainder was hidden from him by that mist of natural prejudice from which he had cleared so many other mental phenomena. No one, before Hume, ventured to think that this supposed experience of efficient causation by volitions is as mere an illusion as any of those which Berkeley exploded, and that what we really know of the power of our own volitions is only that certain facts (reducible, when analysed, to muscular movements) immediately follow them.

APPENDIX B

MILL'S THEORY OF THE SELF

'Examination of Hamilton,' p. 247: [Memories and expectations] are attended with the peculiarity, that each of them involves a belief in more than its own present existence.

Ib., p. 248: If therefore we speak of the Mind as a series of feelings, we are obliged to complete the statement by calling it a series of feelings which is aware of itself as past and future; and we are reduced to the alternative of believing that the mind or ego is something different from any series of feelings, or possibilities of them, or of accepting the paradox, that something which *ex hypothesi* is but a series of feelings, can be aware of itself as a series. . . . The true incomprehensibility perhaps is, that something which has ceased, or is not yet in existence, can still be, in a manner, present; that a series of feelings, the infinitely greater part of which is past or future, can be gathered up, as it were, into a single present conception, accompanied by a belief of reality.

Ib., p. 258: Expectation being one of these [postulated data], in so far as reference to an Ego is implied in Expectation, I do postulate an Ego.

Ib., p. 260: Certain of the attributes comprised in our notion of the Ego, and which are at the very foundation of it—namely, Memory and Expectation, have no equivalent in Matter, and cannot be reduced to any elements similar to those into which Matter is resolvable by the Psychological theory. Having stated these facts, as inexplicable by the Psychological theory, I left them to stand as facts, without any theory whatever: not adopting the Permanent Possibility hypothesis as a sufficient theory of Self in spite of the objections to it, as some of my critics have imagined, and have wasted no small amount of argument and sarcasm in exposing the untenability of such a position; neither on the other hand did I, as others have supposed, accept the common theory of Mind as a so-called Substance.

Ib., p. 262 : There seems no ground for believing, with Sir W. Hamilton and Mr Mansel, that the Ego is an original presentation of consciousness; that the mere impression on our senses involves, or carries with it, any consciousness of a Self, any more than I believe it to do of a Not-Self. . . . The inexplicable tie or law, the organic union (as Professor Masson calls it) which connects the present consciousness with the past one, of which it reminds me, is as near as I think we can get to a positive conception of Self. That there is something real in this tie, real as the sensations themselves, and not a mere product of the laws of thought, without any fact corresponding to it, I hold to be indubitable. . . . But this original element, which has no community of nature with any of the things answering to our names, and to which we cannot give any name but its own peculiar one without implying some false or ungrounded theory, is the Ego, or Self. As such, I ascribe a reality to the Ego—to my own Mind—different from that real existence as a Permanent Possibility, which is the only reality I acknowledge in Matter; and by fair experiential inference from that one Ego, I ascribe the same reality to other Egoes, or Minds.

Having thus, as I hope, more clearly defined my position in regard to the reality of the Ego, considered as a question of Ontology, I return to my first starting-point, the Relativity of human knowledge, and affirm (being here in entire accordance with Sir W. Hamilton) that whatever be the nature of the real existence we are compelled to acknowledge in Mind, the mind is only known to itself phænomenally, as the series of its feelings or consciousnesses. We are forced to apprehend every part of the series as linked with the other parts by something in common, which is not the feelings themselves, any more than the succession of the feelings is the feelings themselves; and as that which is the same in the first as in the second, in the second as in the third, in the third as in the fourth, and so on, must be the same in the first and in the fiftieth, this common element is a permanent element. But, beyond this, we can affirm nothing of it except the states of consciousness themselves. The feelings or consciousnesses which belong or have belonged to it, and its possibilities of having more, are the only facts there are to be asserted of Self—the only positive attributes, except permanence, which we can ascribe to it. In consequence of this, I occasionally use the words "mind" and "thread of consciousness" interchangeably, and treat Mind as existing, and Mind as known to itself, as convertible; but this is only for brevity, and the explanations which I have now given must always be taken as implied.

APPENDIX C

MILL'S THEORY OF THE RELATION OF MORALITY TO NATURE

'Essays on Religion,' p. 8: We must recognise at least two principal meanings in the word Nature. In one sense, it means all the powers existing in either the outer or the inner world and everything which takes place by means of these powers. In another sense, it means, not everything which happens, but only what takes place without the agency or without the voluntary and intentional agency of man.

Ib., p. 16: To bid people conform to the laws of nature, when they have no power but what the laws of nature give them—when it is a physical impossibility for them to do the smallest thing otherwise than through some law of nature, is an absurdity.

Ib., p. 19: While human action cannot help conforming to Nature in the one meaning of the term, the very aim and object of action is to alter and improve Nature in the other meaning.

Ib., p. 25: However offensive the proposition may appear to many religious persons, they should be willing to look in the face the undeniable fact, that the order of Nature, in so far as unmodified by man, is such as no being, whose attributes are justice and benevolence, would have made, with the intention that his rational creatures should follow it as an example. If made wholly by such a Being, and not partly by beings of very different qualities, it could only be as a designedly imperfect work, which man, in his limited sphere, is to exercise justice and benevolence in amending. The best persons have always held it to be the essence of religion, that the paramount duty of man upon earth is to amend himself: but all except monkish quietists have annexed to this in their inmost minds (though seldom willing to enunciate the obligation with the same clearness) the additional religious duty of amending the world and not solely the human part of it but the material: the order of physical nature.

Ib., p. 28 : In sober truth nearly all the things which men are hanged or imprisoned for doing to one another are Nature's everyday performances.

Ib., p. 37 : If the Maker of the world *can* all that he will, he wills misery, and there is no escape from the conclusion. . . .

If the Creator of mankind willed that they should all be virtuous, his designs are as completely baffled as if he had willed that they should all be happy : and the order of nature is constructed with even less regard to the requirements of justice than to those of benevolence. If the law of all creation were justice, and the Creator omnipotent, then in whatever amount suffering and happiness might be dispensed to the world, each person's share of them would be exactly proportioned to that person's good or evil deeds; no human being would have a worse lot than another, without worse deserts; accident or favouritism would have no part in such a world, but every human life would be the playing out of a drama constructed like a perfect moral tale. No one is able to blind himself to the fact that the world we live in is totally different from this.

Ib., p. 38 : The only admissible moral theory of creation is that the Principle of good *cannot* at once and altogether subdue the powers of evil, either physical or moral; could not place mankind in a world free from the necessity of an incessant struggle with the maleficent powers, or make them always victorious in that struggle, but could and did make them capable of carrying on the fight with vigour and with progressively increasing success. Of all the religious explanations of the order of nature, this alone is neither contradictory to itself, nor to the facts for which it attempts to account. According to it, man's duty would consist, not in simply taking care of his own interests by obeying irresistible power, but in standing forward a not ineffectual auxiliary to a Being of perfect beneficence; a faith which seems much better adapted for nerving him to exertion than a vague and inconsistent reliance on an author of good who is supposed to be also the author of evil.

Ib., p. 44 : Since what is done with deliberation seems more the man's own act, and he is held more completely responsible for it than for what he does from sudden impulse, the considerate part of human conduct is apt to be set down as man's share in the business, and the inconsiderate as God's. The result is the vein of sentiment so common in the modern world (though unknown to the philosophic ancients) which exalts instinct at the expense of reason; an aberration rendered still more mischievous by the opinion commonly held in conjunction with it, that every, or almost every, feeling or impulse which acts promptly without waiting to ask questions, is an instinct. Thus almost every variety of unreflecting and uncalculating impulse receives a kind of consecration, except those which, though unreflecting at the moment, owe their origin to previous habits of reflection : these, being evidently not instinctive, do not meet with the favour accorded to the rest; so that all unreflecting impulses are invested with authority over reason, except the only ones which are most probably right. I do not mean, of course, that this mode of judgment is even pretended to be consistently carried out : life could not go on if it were not admitted that impulses must be controlled, and that reason ought to govern our actions.

Ib., p. 46 : Allowing everything to be an instinct which anybody has ever asserted to be one, it remains true that nearly every respectable attribute of humanity is the result not of instinct, but of a victory over instinct; and that there is hardly anything valuable in the natural man except capacities—a whole world of possibilities, all of them dependent upon eminently artificial discipline for being realised. . . . The truth is that there is hardly a single point of excellence belonging to human character, which is not decidedly repugnant to the untutored feelings of human nature.

Ib., p. 54 : The duty of man is the same in respect to his own nature as in respect to the nature of all other things, namely, not to follow but to amend it.

Ib., p. 55 : The inclinations with which man has been endowed, as well as any of the other contrivances which we observe in Nature, may be the expression not of the Divine Will, but of the fetters which impede its free action, and to take hints from these for the guidance of our own conduct may be falling into a trap laid by the enemy.

Ib., p. 62 : Conformity to nature has no connection whatever with right and wrong. The idea can never be fitly introduced into ethical discussions at all, except, occasionally and partially, into the question of degrees of culpability. . . . But if an action or an inclination has been decided on other grounds to be blamable, it may be a circumstance in aggravation that it is unnatural, that is repugnant to some strong feeling usually found in human beings ; since the bad propensity, whatever it be, has afforded evidence of being both strong and deeply rooted, by having overcome that repugnance.

Ib., p. 64 : The word Nature has two principal meanings : it either denotes the entire system of things, with the aggregate of all their properties, or it denotes things as they would be, apart from human intervention.

In the first of these senses, the doctrine that man ought to follow nature is unmeaning; since man has no power to do anything else than follow nature ; all his actions are done through, and in obedience to, some one or many of nature's physical or mental laws. In the other sense of the term, the doctrine that man ought to follow nature, or in other words ought to make the spontaneous course of things the model of his voluntary actions, is equally irrational and immoral.

Irrational, because all human action whatever consists in altering, and all useful action in improving, the spontaneous course of nature:

Immoral, because the course of natural phenomena being replete with everything which when committed by human beings is most worthy of abhorrence, any one who endeavoured in his actions to imitate the natural course of things would be universally seen and acknowledged to be the wickedest of men.

APPENDIX D

MILL'S ESTIMATE OF BENTHAM

'Dissertations and Discussions,' vol. ii. p. 462 : It is by his *method* chiefly that Bentham, as we think, justly earned a position in Moral Science analogous to that of Bacon in Physical. It is because he was the first to enter into the right mode of working ethical problems, though he worked many of them, as Bacon did physical, on insufficient data.

'Dissertations and Discussions,' vol. i. p. 338 : They [other subversive thinkers] were purely negative thinkers, he [Bentham] was positive. They only assailed error, he made it a point of conscience not to do so until he could plant instead the corresponding truth. Their character was exclusively analytic, his was synthetic. They took for their starting-point the received opinion on any subject, dug round it with their logical implements, pronounced its foundations defective, and condemned it : he began *de novo*, laid his own foundations deeply and firmly, built up his own structure and bade mankind compare the two ; it was when he had solved the problem himself, or thought that he had done so, that he declared all other solutions to be erroneous. Hence, what they produced will not last ; it must perish, much of it has already perished, with the errors which it exploded : what he did has its own value, by which it must outlast all errors to which it is opposed. Though we may reject, as we often must, his practical conclusions, yet his premises, the collections of facts and observations from which his conclusions were drawn, remain for ever a part of the materials of philosophy.

Ib., p. 339 : If we were asked to say in the fewest possible words, what we conceive to be Bentham's place among these great intellectual benefactors of humanity ; what he was, and what he was not ; what kind of service he did and did not render to truth ; we should say—he was not a great philosopher, but he was a great reformer in Philosophy. He brought into Philosophy something which it greatly needed, and for want of which it was at a stand. It was not his doctrines which did this, it was his mode of arriving at them. He introduced into morals and politics those habits of thought and modes of investigation, which are essential to the idea of science, and the absence of which made those departments of inquiry, as Physics had been before Bacon, a field of interminable discussion, leading to no result. It was not his opinions, in short, but his method, that constituted the novelty and the value of what he did ; a value beyond all price, even though we should reject the whole, as we unquestionably must a large part, of the opinions themselves.

Bentham's method may be shortly described as the Method of Detail ; of treating wholes by separating them into their parts, abstractions, by resolving them into things, —classes and generalities by distinguishing them into the individuals of which they are made up ; and breaking every question into pieces before attempting to solve it.

Ib., p. 341 : It is a sound maxim, and one which all close thinkers have felt, but which no one before Bentham ever so consistently applied, that error lurks in generalities : that the human mind is not capable of embracing a complex whole, until it has surveyed and catalogued the parts of which that whole is made up; that abstractions are not realities *per se*, but an abridged mode of expressing facts, and that the only practical mode of dealing with them is to trace them back to the facts (whether of experience or of consciousness) of which they are the expression.

Ib., p. 345: It is the introduction into the Philosophy of human conduct of this method of detail—of this practice of never reasoning about wholes till they have been resolved into their parts, nor about abstractions till they have been translated into realities—that constitutes the originality of Bentham in Philosophy and makes him the great reformer of the moral and political branch of it.

Ib., p. 346: The application of a real inductive Philosophy to the problems of ethics is as unknown to the Epicurean moralists as to any of the other schools; they never take a question to pieces and join issue on a definite point. Bentham certainly did not learn his sifting and anatomising method from them.

Ib., p. 348: By the practice of it his speculations are rendered eminently systematic and consistent; no question with him is ever an insulated one; he sees every subject in connection with all the other subjects with which, in his view, it is related, and from which it requires to be distinguished.

Ib., p. 349: But to build either a philosophy or anything else there must be materials. For the philosophy of matter, the materials are the properties of matter; for moral and political philosophy, the properties of man, and of man's position in the world. The knowledge which any inquirer possesses of these properties, constitutes a limit beyond which, as a moralist or a political philosopher, whatever be his powers of mind, he cannot reach. Nobody's synthesis can be more complete than his analysis. If in his survey of human nature and life he has left any element out, then, wheresoever that element exerts any influence, his conclusions will fail more or less in their application. If he has left out many elements, and those very important, his labours may be highly valuable; he may have largely contributed to that body of partial truths which, when completed and corrected by one another, constitute practical truth; but the applicability of his system to practice in its own proper shape will be of an exceedingly limited range.

Human nature and human life are wide subjects, and whoever would embark in an enterprise requiring a thorough knowledge of them, has need both of large stores of his own, and of all aids and appliances from elsewhere. His qualifications for success will be proportional to two things: the degree in which his own nature and circumstances furnish him with a correct and complete picture of man's nature and circumstances; and his capacity of deriving light from other minds.

Ib., p. 355: He had never been made alive to the unseen influences which were acting on himself, nor consequently on his fellow-creatures. Other ages and other nations were a blank to him for purposes of instruction. He measured them but by one standard—their knowledge of facts, and their capability to take correct views of utility, and merge all other objects in it. His own lot was cast in a generation of the leanest and barrenest men whom England had yet produced, and he was an old man when a better race came in with the present century. He saw accordingly in man little but what the vulgarest eye can see; recognised no diversities of character but such as he who runs may read. Knowing so little of human feelings, he knew still less of the influences by which these feelings are formed: all the more subtle workings both of the mind upon itself, and of external things upon the mind, escaped him; and no one probably, who, in a highly instructed age, ever attempted to give a rule to all human conduct, set out with a more limited conception either of the agencies by which human conduct *is*, or of those by which it *should* be, influenced.

Ib., p. 356: The bad part of his writings is his resolute denial of all that he does not see, of all truths but those which he recognises. By that alone has he exercised any bad influence upon his age; by that he has, not created a school of deniers, for this is an ignorant prejudice, but put himself at the head of the school which exists always, though it does not always find a great man to give it the sanction of philosophy: thrown the mantle of intellect over the natural tendency of men in all ages to deny or disparage all feelings and mental states of which they have no consciousness in themselves.

Ib., p. 359 : Man is never recognised by him as a being capable of pursuing spiritual perfection as an end; of desiring, for its own sake, the conformity of his own character to his standard of excellence, without hope of good or fear of evil from other source than his own inward consciousness. Even in the more limited form of conscience, this great fact in human nature escapes him. Nothing is more curious than the absence of recognition in any of his writings of the existence of conscience as a thing distinct from philanthropy, from affection for God or man, and from self-interest in this world or in the next. There is a studied abstinence from any of the phrases which, in the mouths of others, import the acknowledgment of such a fact. If we find the words "Conscience," "Principle," "Moral Rectitude," "Moral Duty," in his Table of the Springs of Action, it is among the synonyms of the "love of reputation," with an intimation as to the two former phrases, that they are also sometimes synonymous with the *religious* motive, or the motive of *sympathy*. The feeling of moral approbation or disapprobation properly so called, either towards ourselves or our fellow-creatures, he seems unaware of the existence of ; and neither the word *self-respect*, nor the idea to which that word is appropriated, occurs even once, so far as our recollection serves us, in his whole writings.

Nor is it only the moral part of man's nature, in the strict sense of the term—the desire of perfection, or the feeling of an approving or of an accusing conscience—that he overlooks; he but faintly recognises as a fact in human nature the pursuit of any other ideal end for its own sake. The sense of *honour* and personal dignity—that feeling of personal exaltation and degradation which acts independently of other people's opinion, or even in defiance of it ; the love of *beauty*, the passion of the artist; the love of *order*, of congruity, of consistency in all things, and conformity to their end; the love of *power*, not in the limited form of power over other human beings, but abstract power —the power of making our volitions effectual; the love of *action*, the thirst for movement and activity, a principle scarcely of less influence in human life than its opposite, the love of ease,—none of these powerful constituents of human nature are thought worthy of a place among the "Springs of Action"; and though there is possibly no one of them of the existence of which an acknowledgment might not be found in some corner of Bentham's writings, no conclusions are ever founded on the acknowledgment. Man, that most complex being, is a very simple one in his eyes. Even under the head of *sympathy*, his recognition does not extend to the more complex forms of the feeling —the love of loving, the need of a sympathising support, or of objects of admiration and reverence. If he thought at all of any of the deeper feelings of human nature, it was but as idiosyncrasies of taste, with which the moralist no more than the legislator had any concern, further than to prohibit such as were mischievous among the actions to which they might chance to lead. To say either that man should, or that he should not, take pleasure in one thing, displeasure in another, appeared to him as much an act of despotism in the moralist as in the political ruler.

Ib., p. 363: It [Bentham's theory] will do nothing for the conduct of the individual, beyond prescribing some of the more obvious dictates of worldly prudence and outward probity and beneficence. There is no need to expatiate on the deficiencies of a system of ethics which does not pretend to aid individuals in the formation of their own character; which recognises no such wish as that of self-culture, we may even say no such power as existing in human nature; and if it did recognise, would furnish little assistance to that great duty, because it overlooks the existence of about half of the whole number of mental feelings which human beings are capable of, including all those of which the direct objects are states of their own mind.

Morality consists of two parts. One of these is self-education; the training by the human being himself, of his affections and will. That department is a blank in Bentham's system. The other and coequal part, the regulation of his outward actions, must be altogether halting and imperfect without the first: for how can we judge in what manner many an action will affect even the worldly interests of ourselves or others, unless we take in, as part of the question, its influence on the regulation of our, or their, affections and desires? A moralist, on Bentham's principles, may get as far as this, that he ought not to slay, burn, or steal; but what will be his qualifications for regulating the nicer shades of human behaviour, or for laying down even the greater moralities as to those facts in human life which are liable to influence the depths of the character quite independently of any influence on worldly circumstances—such, for instance, as the sexual relations, or those of family in general, or any other social and sympathetic connections of an intimate kind? The moralities of these questions depend essentially on considerations which Bentham never so much as took into the account; and when he happened to be in the right, it was always, and necessarily, on wrong or insufficient grounds.

Ib., p. 365: It [Bentham's theory of Life] will enable a society which has attained a certain state of spiritual development, and the maintenance of which in that state is otherwise provided for, to prescribe the rules by which it may protect its material interests. It will do nothing (except sometimes as an instrument in the hands of a higher doctrine) for the spiritual interests of society; nor does it suffice of itself even for the material interests. That which alone causes any material interests to exist, which alone enables any body of human beings to exist as a society, is national character: *that* it is which causes one nation to succeed in what it attempts, another to fail; one nation to understand and aspire to elevated things, another to grovel in mean ones; which makes the greatness of one nation lasting, and dooms another to early and rapid decay. . . . A philosophy of laws and institutions, not founded on a philosophy of national character, is an absurdity. But what could Bentham's opinion be worth on national character? How could he, whose mind contained so few and so poor types of individual character, rise to that higher generalisation? All he can do is but to indicate means by which, in any given state of the national mind, the material interests of society can be protected; saving the question of which others must judge, whether the use of those means would have, on the national character, any injurious influence.

Ib., p. 366: He committed the mistake of supposing that the business part of human affairs was the whole of them, —all at least that the legislator and the moralist had to do with. Not that he disregarded moral influences when he perceived them; but his want of imagination, small experience of human feelings, and ignorance of the filiation and connection of feelings with one another, made this rarely the case.

Ib., p. 386: It [the error] is that of treating the *moral* view of actions and characters, which is unquestionably the first and most important mode of looking at them, as if it were the sole one: whereas it is only one of three, by all of which our sentiments towards the human being may be, ought to be, and, without entirely crushing our own nature, cannot but be, materially influenced. Every human action has three aspects: its *moral* aspect, or that of its *right* and *wrong;* its *æsthetic* aspect, or that of its *beauty;* its *sympathetic* aspect, or that of its *lovableness*. The first addresses itself to our reason and conscience; the second to our imagination; the third to our human fellow-feeling. According to the first, we approve or disapprove; according to the second, we admire or despise; according to the third, we love, pity, or dislike. The morality of an action depends on its foreseeable consequences; its beauty and its lovableness, or the reverse, depend on the qualities which it is evidence of.

Ib., p. 388: It is not possible for any sophistry to confound these three modes of viewing an action; but it is very possible to adhere to one of them exclusively, and lose sight of the rest. Sentimentality consists in setting the last two of the three above the first; the error of moralists in general, and of Bentham, is to sink the two latter entirely. This is pre-eminently the case with Bentham: he both wrote and felt as if the moral standard ought not only to be paramount (which it ought), but to be alone; as if it ought to be the sole master of all our actions, and even of all our sentiments; as if either to admire or like, or despise or dislike a person for any action which neither does good nor harm, or which does not do a good or a harm proportioned to the sentiment entertained, were an injustice, and a prejudice.

INDEX

A

Altruism and Egoism—Comte on, 107 note 1, 109 notes 1 and 2.
Analysis—is the function of Psychology, lii, liii—is not complete explanation, liii ff.—implies the idea of system, liv ff.
Approximate generalisations about human nature—are sufficient for social science, 32—must be connected deductively with laws of nature from which they result, 33.
Association of ideas—Hartley on, xxxi, xxxii, 45—produces direct desire for means originally desired only for the sake of the end, 23—laws of, 42 ff. —James Mill on, 42—Bain on, 42—its relation to belief, 46, 47—its relation to desire, 48.
Axiomata media—constitute the principal value of every science, 70—are often discovered deductively from higher generalisations, 71 ff.

B

Bacon—his view of Axiomata media, 70 ff., 83 note 1—his position in physical science, 214, 215.
Bain—on the laws of Association, 42, 43.
Beneficence—is distinguished from Justice by the absence of a definite right, 174-176.
BENTHAM—his political Utilitarianism, xxi, xxvii—importance of his method, xvi, xxi, xxii, 77 note 1, 83 note 1, 84, 214-216—his Utilitarianism and Political Economy, xxvi—on the distinction of pleasures, lxix, 89—and Moral Experience, 122 note 1, 123 note 1—on impartiality, 197—narrowness of his conception of human nature, 216 ff.—the inadequacy of his ethical theory, 219 ff.
Berkeley, xlii, xliii—on Causality, 205.
Brown, 13.

C

Carlyle—on Renunciation, 100.
CAUSALITY—presupposed in Inductive Methods, 7 note 1, 203-205—its application to

human actions is the question at issue in the Free Will controversy, xxiii, 9—is generally supposed to mean more than mere constancy of succession, and is thus thought inapplicable to volition, 12—but does not really involve more than unconditional sequence, xxiv, 13, 203-205—Comte on, 204—Berkeley on, 205—Hume on, 205.

CHARACTER—is partly formed by a man himself, since his desire to alter it is a circumstance which influences it though only indirectly, 17—the desire to alter it is mainly due to experience, 18 — the power of altering it, is what is meant by moral freedom, 20, 21—its confirmation consists in the development of purposes independent of feelings of pleasure or pain, 24—there are universal laws of its formation which must be studied by the Deductive Method, 60 ff.—its cultivation is essential to the general happiness which is the utilitarian end, lxvii, 99, 100, 154 note 1.

Choice—is the act which chiefly develops human faculties, 17 note 1.

Christ—and the feeling of Unity with our fellow-creatures, 129.

Christian elements in morality, 92.

COLERIDGE — his influence on Mill, lxxiv, lxxviii—his relation to Hartley, lxxiv, lxxv—his relation to Kant and Schelling, lxxiv, lxxv — his distinction of Reason and Understanding, lxxiv, lxxv—his ethical Idealism, lxxv, lxxvi — inadequacy of his Idealism, lxxvi, lxxvii — on Motives, 94 note 1.

Compulsion—its propriety is implied in Morality, 172-174.

COMTE—his influence on Mill, lxxiii—reduces Psychology to Physiology, 37, 39—his neglect of the study of mental peculiarities, 52—on Altruism, 107 note 1, 109 note 1—on Egoism, 109 note 2—on the power of Social Feeling, 143 — on Causality, 204.

Condillac, 45 note 1.

Conscience—is a feeling attendant on violation of Duty, 131.

D

Davies, J. Llewelyn, on Motives and Morality, 112 note.

DEDUCTIVE METHOD—is essential to the Science of Human Nature, xliv, 33 — is the method of investigating the laws of the formation of character, xliv, xlv, 61 ff.—is the general Method of Science, xliv, 70-73, 74 note 1—requires Verification, xlv, 77.

Desert—and Justice, 166.

DESIRE—its object is determined by the nature of knowledge, xlii, xliii—the nature of its object determines the moral end, xl, 146 ff.—its relation to the real good of individuals, 147 note 1—seems to have other objects besides Happiness, *e.g.*, virtue, money, power, fame, 149 ff. — has really no object but Happiness, everything else being only desired as a means to, or part of, Happiness, xl ff, 154 ff.—is distinct from Will, but

Will, though amenable to habit, is originally produced by Desire and can only be altered by changing it, 157 ff.

Determinism. See Necessity.

De Tocqueville, 6 note 1.

Dignity — sense of, determines the preference for higher pleasures, 96.

Distribution—of profits can only be regulated by social utility, 188, 189.

E

EMPIRICAL LAWS — depend on more general conditions, xliv, 54, 55, 57 ff.—of human nature, xlv, 55-57, 75.

END—must be the basis of Moral Science, 81—questions of ultimate ends are incapable of direct proof although open to rational discussion, xxxix, 86, 87, 146 — the method of its realisation is the problem of Moral Science, 122-125— requires Sanctions, 128, 129— means what is desirable, 146 —utilitarian doctrine is that Happiness is the Moral End, 146 ff.—moral, and inclination, 147, 148 and note, 212.

Engagements—and Justice, 166, 167.

Epicureans—92—did not apply scientific methods to Ethics, 216.

Epicurus, 89, 91.

Equality—its moral importance, 138—and Justice, 168, 169— and Utility, 168, 169.

ETHOLOGY — consists of derivative laws resulting deductively from the general Laws of Mind, xliv, xlv, 68 ff.—is the science which corresponds to the Art of Education, 68, 69, 76, 77 —may be called the Exact Science of Human Nature, 69 —its propositions must be hypothetical, 69—its principles are the Axiomata Media of the Science of Mind, 70—has still to be created but has now been made practicable by the discovery of empirical laws, 75.

Expectation—implies Self, 206, 207.

Expediency—and Morality, 119, 120—does not excite the same feeling as Justice, 162, 163— is distinct from Justice, 191.

Experience—produces the wish to alter character, 18—is the source of the conceptions which are used in methodical thinking, 18 note 1—and Morality, 121-125.

External Sanctions—see Sanctions.

F

Fatalism—and Necessitarianism, 16, 17—its depressing effect depends on a wish to do what it represents as impossible, 20.

Feeling of Unity with others— 129—is natural to man and grows with the development of society, 137, 145—and punishment, 177.

FREEDOM OF WILL—Mill's interest in, xlix—is not inconsistent with the divine foreknowledge of actions, nor with prediction in general, 11— means only the power of altering our own character, 20, 21—this meaning gives the idea its practical usefulness, 22.

G

Gall—his phrenology untenable, 53.
Golden Rule — corresponds to Utilitarianism, 110.

H

Habit — is a frequent cause of voluntary action and brings about development of purposes and confirmed character, 23, 24.
Hamilton—on the Knowledge of Mind, 35 — on unconscious mental modifications, xxxv, 39, 40—on Self, 207.
HAPPINESS — is the utilitarian criterion, xviii ff., 91, 146 ff. —cultivation of Character essential to general Happiness, lxvii ff., 99, 100 — in what sense it is the standard of Morality, 100 ff.—how far it is attainable, 100 ff. — the chief obstacles to its realisation are selfishness and want of culture, together with evils such as poverty, disease, and other misfortunes which may be largely removed, 102-105 — may be derived from conflict with evils, 106—may be done without, but should only be resigned for the happiness of others, 106, 107—is best realised by the conscious ability to do without it, 107, 108—is proved to be desirable by being desired, xxxix, xl, 147 ff.—appears not to be the only object of Desire, 149—other objects are desired as means to it before being thought good in themselves, 150 ff. — is really the only object of Desire, 154 ff.
HARTLEY — and Determinism, xxx ff.—on Mental Association, xxxi, xxxii, 42—his doctrine of Vibrations, xxxii-xxxv — and Coleridge, lxxiv, lxxv—on the question of Complex Ideas, 45.
Hedonism. See Happiness, Pleasure, Utilitarianism.
Helvetius—on Education, 63.
Hume—on the criterion of Morality, xix, xlii, xliii, 13—on Impression and Idea, 42—on Causality, 205.

I

Impartiality—and Justice, 167, 168—is an obligation of Justice founded on Utility, 196 ff.—Bentham on, 197—Spencer on, 197 note.
Inclination—and Morality, 147, 148 and note, 212.
INDUCTIVE METHODS—can only be applied to Morality when it is considered to depend upon consequences of action, xxii, 123, note 1—imply Causality, xxiii, xxiv, 7 note 1, 203-205 —their use in Psychology, 46 ff.—cannot be applied to the problem of the formation of Character either by experiment or observation, xlv, 62 ff.—their application to Moral Science introduced by Bentham, 215, 216.
Instinct—and Morality, 211.
Internal Sanctions. See Sanctions.
INTUITIONISM — recognises the necessity of Moral Science, xvi, 82 — fails to give a

scientific ground for moral principles, xvii, xviii, 82 ff.—depends on Utilitarian arguments, 85, 86—and the Utilitarian principle, 134.

J

Jesus—in his Golden Rule we read the complete spirit of the Ethics of Utility, 110.
Johnson — on Self-denial, 107 note 1.
JUSTICE—and Utility, 161 ff., 191 ff.—might be instructive and yet require to be controlled, 161, 162 — is distinguished from Expediency by the feeling connected with it, 162, 163—involves respect for Legal Rights, 164 — involves respect for Moral Rights, 164 - 166 — involves respect for Desert, 166—involves respect for Engagements, 166 — involves Impartiality, 167, 168—involves Equality, 168, 169 — the derivation of the name connects it with positive Law, 170—is considered to apply to things not regulated by Law, 171, 172 — directly or indirectly implies the idea of legal restraint, 172 — shares the implication of Compulsion with Morality in general, 172-174 — is distinguished from Beneficence by the existence of a definite Right, 174-176 — sentiment of, consists of desire to punish and belief that some one has been injured, 176—apart from Utility gives no moral guidance as to the legitimacy or amount of punishment, or the Distribution of goods or taxation, 184-191—is really distinct from Expediency, 192—is a name for certain essential Moral Rules which protect mankind from injury or interference, 191-193—is the most sacred and binding part of Morality, 191.

K

Kant, xlv—and Coleridge, lxxiv —and Utilitarianism, 85, 179.
Kepler, 73.

L

LAWS OF MIND — are laws of mental phenomena, xlvi ff., 34 —are sometimes supposed to be merely derivative from laws of body, 36, 37—are directly discoverable, 38 — cannot always be deduced from physiological laws, 38—their relation to physiological laws is an important question for Psychology, 39 note 1, 48, 49, 52, 53—neglect of them produces serious errors in Social Science, 39—that every mental *impression* has its *idea*, 40-42—the laws of Association, 42—are ascertained experimentally, 43—the simpler give rise to more complex laws by composition and by a process akin to chemical combination, 43, 44 — their relation to mental peculiarities has been neglected, 51 ff.
Lex talionis, 187, 188.
Locke, xlii, xliii, 45 note 1.
Love of Money, Power, and

Fame—developed out of their experienced relation to Happiness, 151 ff.

M

Malthus, xxviii.
Mansel—on Self, 207.
Martineau—on Priestley, 50—on the psychological importance of Sensations, 50, 51.
Masson—on Self, 207.
Memory — implies Self, 206, 207.
Methods of Argument and Difference—their use in Psychology, 46.
Mill, James—on the Laws of Association, 42, 45 note 1—his preference for the pleasures of Intellect and Benevolence, 93 note 1.
Mind. See Laws of Mind.
MORAL FEELING—is the ultimate sanction of Morality, 131-134 —whether innate or acquired is natural to Man, 134, 135— may be cultivated in almost any direction and may thus support Utilitarianism, 135.
MORAL OBLIGATION—Paley's doctrine of, xx—does not depend for its authority upon a belief in its transcendental reality, 132, 134—perfect and imperfect, 174.
MORAL SCIENCE—Mill's interest in, xvii, xviii—inadequacy of psychological methods for, xlvi ff.—may include various inquiries about Morality, but is primarily a study of the grounds of Morality, lxiv ff.—is essential to Philosophy only in so far as it is an account of Moral Experience, lxv, lxvi—difference of opinion as to its Method, 3 ff., 79—must follow the method of the Natural Sciences, 5, 6 note 1—depends on the recognition of a Moral End, 81, 83 note 1—is not rendered unnecessary by Moral Sense, 81—is recognised by Intuitionism, 82—is not rendered unnecessary by Religion, 118—and Morality, lxiii ff., 122-125 — Bentham on the method of, xvi, 77 note 1, 83 note 1, 84, 214-216.
Moral Sense—idea of, does not solve the problem of Moral Science, 81 ff.
MORALITY—Hume on the criterion of, xix—is personal and social, lvi ff. — has various meanings, lxiii, lxiv—can be studied in different ways, lxiv, lxv—is concerned with Actions and not with Motives, 112, 113 —and Expediency, 119, 120 —and Experience, 121 - 125 —and Moral Science, 122-125—requires Sanctions whenever its obligation is referred to an end, 128, 129—its ultimate Sanction is Moral Feeling, whether this be believed to have objective validity or not, 131-134—is natural to Man, 134 ff. — develops with the growth of Social Relations, lxxii, lxxiii, 138-145 — and Inclination, 147, 148 and note, 212—is distinguished from Expediency by giving a ground for Compulsion, 172-174—is not found in Nature, 209-213 —is not instinctive in Man, 211, 212.
MOTIVE—does not always mean the anticipation of Pleasure or Pain, 23 — its strength

means its strength in relation to Pleasure and Pain, 23 note 1—Coleridge on, 94 note 1—and Morality, 112.

N

NATURE — Man's relation to, xxiii—in what sense Morality belongs to it, 135 ff., 209-213—is not the ground of Morality, 161, 162, 209-213—requires to be amended by human action, 209-213—does not manifest an Omnipotent Benevolence, 209-211.

NECESSITY OF HUMAN ACTIONS—implied in Science of Human Nature, xxv, 7—and Political Economy, xxviii-xxx — and Hartley's Psychology, xxx ff. —means only the possibility of predicting them, xxiv, 10 —is generally misunderstood even by those who maintain it, since it is supposed to mean more than the possibility of Prediction, 13 ff.—is an inappropriate and misleading phrase, since Necessity generally means uncontrollableness which does not apply to human actions, 14-16, 21—does not involve Fatalism though many Necessitarians are Fatalists, since they believe a man's Character to be made *for* and not *by* him, 16, 17.

Newton, xxiii, 73.

Novalis—on character, 24—on suicide, 101.

O

Owen—on Character and Circumstances, 18—on Punishment, 185.

P

Paley — his doctrine of Moral Obligation, xx—his Utilitarianism, xx.

Pelagius, 9.

Personality — is the source of voluntary action, 1 ff.

Physiology. See Psychology.

Plato, 80.

PLEASURE —- Bentham on the quality of, lxix — distinction of Kind among Pleasures implies the use of a non-hedonistic criterion, lxviii-lxxi—is the Utilitarian criterion, 91— nature of the superiority of mental over bodily Pleasures, 93—James Mill's estimate of various pleasures, 93 note 1— qualitative superiority of one Pleasure to another means its preference by those acquainted with both, lxviii ff., 93, 94— higher Pleasures universally preferred by those who have experience of them, 94 ff.—abandonment of higher for lower Pleasures is due to loss of the capacity for higher Pleasures, 97, 98—has no standard except the preference of experienced persons, 99—the only object of Desire, 147 ff.

Political Economy—and Utilitarianism, xxvi ff. — and the consequences of action, xxvii, xxviii—and the determination of conduct, xxviii-xxx.

PREDICTION OF HUMAN ACTIONS —its possibility is what is affirmed in the doctrine of Philosophical Necessity, xxiv,

10—its possibility is borne out by universal Experience, 11—does not conflict with Freedom of Action, 11.

Proof—of ultimate ends, 86, 87.

Protagoras, 80.

PSYCHOLOGY — and Philosophy, xlii, xlvii ff.—its account of Volition is incomplete, xlix ff.—its relation to the Theory of Conduct, lii ff.—the analytical character of its method limits its use as an explanation of Conduct, liii ff. — is an insufficient basis for Ethics, xlvi ff. — is distinct from though closely connected with Physiology, xxxv, xxxvi, 36 ff.—has to do with the laws of mental succession, xlvi, 40—is an Observational Science, xlvi ff., 34 ff., 70—is the foundation of Ethology, xliv, 70—cannot give a complete account of the Mind, xlix ff., 206-208 —*vide* Laws of Mind.

Public Opinion—its influence on Conduct, 135 note 1.

PUNISHMENT — desire for, depends on impulse of Self-defence and feeling of Sympathy, 176 ff.—its legitimacy and apportionment cannot be decided on grounds of Justice apart from Utility, 185-188—Owen on, 185 — and Social Contract, 186.

Purposes—are habits of Willing, 24.

R

Reid, xlv.

Religion — and Moral Science, 118.

Renunciation — is possible and constitutes the highest virtue, though only justified by increasing Happiness, 106, 107.

Retaliation—as an element in Punishment, 146 ff.—an impulse common to Man and Animals, 177—differentiated in Man by Sympathy and Intelligence, 177.

Ricardo — his economics and Utilitarianism, xxvi.

RIGHTS—legal, and Justice, 164 —moral, and Justice, 164-166 — mean something which Society ought to defend and are thus founded on Utility, 180 ff.

Rosseau—on Education, 63.

S

St Simon—his influence on Mill, lxxiii.

SANCTION—must be found for Moral Rules whenever Morality is referred to an End or Standard, 128, 129—external, consisting of hope of favour or fear of displeasure of God or men is available for Utilitarianism, 130—internal, consisting of Moral Feeling, may support Utilitarianism as readily as any other moral rule, 131, 132—internal, does not depend on a particular theory of Moral Obligation, 132-134.

Schelling—and Coleridge, lxxiv, lxxv.

SCIENCE OF HUMAN NATURE—its possibility depends on the existence of constant laws in Human Nature, xxv, 26—it may be compared in respect of exactness with Astronomy or Tidology, being less exact than the former but on a level with the latter, 27 - 30 — it would be ideally perfect if it enabled us to foretell the whole conduct of an individual, but it falls short of this, not only because we cannot foresee all the circumstances, but also because of the complexity of Human Character ; the necessary data are thus never fully accessible, 30, 31—the predominant importance of general causes enables this science to arrive at general propositions, which are almost always true, and which, for the purposes of Political and Social Science, are equivalent to Universal Propositions, 31, 32 —exists in proportion as its approximate truths can be deduced from Universal Laws of Human Nature, 33—*vide* Ethology.

Security—is the vital interest involved in Justice, 182-184.

SELF—implied in Volition, 1 ff.— incapable of complete psychological Explanation but implied in Experience, xlvii, xlix, 206-208—implied in Memory and Expectation, 206 — Hamilton on, 207—Mansell on, 207— Masson on, 207.

Sensation—is a state of mind, 35.

Social Contract — and Punishment, 186.

SOCIAL FEELING—is the basis of Utilitarianism, 137 ff. — develops along with Social Relations, 138-145—Comte on its influence, 143—is implied in the feeling of Justice, 177 ff.

Social Science—can make universal use of approximate propositions about Human Nature, 32—is dependent on the science of individual character, xxxix, 32, 39 note 1, 60.

Society—its conditions determine Morality and Moral Feeling, and its development must bring about a growth of sympathy, lxxii, lxxiii, 137-145—is implied in the idea of Rights, 180, 181.

Socrates—and Utilitarianism, 80 —dissatisfied, 97.

Spencer—on laws of Association, 43—on Impartiality, 197 note —on Utilitarianism, 197 note.

Stoicism — and Morality, 92— and Independence, 96.

Sympathy—and Retaliation, 177.

System—the idea of, is implied in Explanation, liv ff. — involved in Relation, lv, lvi.

T

Taxation—its incidence can only be regulated by Utility, 189, 190.

U

Unconscious mental states, xxxv, xlvii ff., 39 note 1.

Unhappiness — its principal causes, 102 ff.

Unity with others—see Feeling of.

UTILITARIANISM — in Hume, xix —in Paley, xx—in Bentham, xxi—and Political Economy, xxvi ff.—Mill's modification of, lxiii ff.—does not distinguish Utility from Pleasure, 89 ff.— origin of the name, 90 note— makes Happiness or Pleasure the criterion of Conduct, 91—

is attacked as a degrading theory, but this criticism assumes human beings to be capable only of degrading Pleasures, 91-93—requires the cultivation of virtuous character, lxvii, 99, 100, 150 ff.—justifies Self-devotion as a means to Happiness, 108, 109—prescribes the general Happiness as the Moral End and thus satisfies the moral consciousness, 110, 111—is sometimes criticised as too exacting, but this criticism confounds the Rule of Action with the Motive of it, 111 ff.—affirms that the Motive has nothing to do with the Morality of the Action, though much with the worth of the Agent, 112—makes the good of Society the End, but not the Motive, of Action, 113, 114—is affirmed to make men unsympathetic because it considers only the *Consequences* of their Actions; but it does not deny the value of good Character although many Utilitarians underrate qualities of Character, which do not affect the Consequences of Actions, 114-117—is often inveighed against as a godless doctrine, but is not inconsistent with a religious interpretation of Morality, 118, 119—is often stigmatised as immoral by calling it a doctrine of Expediency; but Expediency, in the sense in which it is immoral, is hurtful and contrary to the Utilitarian Principle, 119, 120—is often said to be an impracticable doctrine on the ground that there is not time before actions to calculate their effects, but this objection ignores the accumulated Experience of Mankind, 121 ff.—is objected to on the ground that it is apt to furnish excuses for neglect of Moral Rules; but in this respect it is better than other ethical theories, 125-127—may have all the Sanctions that belong to any other moral system, 129 ff.—has whatever support Intuition or Moral Feeling may give, 134, 135—might lose the support of Moral Feeling if it had not a natural basis in the Social Feelings of Mankind; but the growth of these Feelings is inseparable from Human Development, 136-145 — is proved by the fact that Happiness is the only object of Desire, xxxix, 156—affords a principle for deciding questions of Justice, 184 ff.—makes Justice depend upon Utility, 191 ff. — and Punishment, 194, 195—and Impartiality, 196 ff.—Spencer on, 197 note—and Equality, 198, 199—recognises the distinctness and supremacy of Justice, 200.

Utility—has had great influence in the formation of ordinary moral opinion, 84—is used as an argument by *à priori* moralists such as Kant and Whewell, 85, 86—means Pleasure in the Utilitarian Theory, 89 ff.—and Justice, 161 ff., 191 ff.—determines the application of the principle of Equality, 168, 169, 197-199 — determines the moral element in the feeling of Justice, 176, 178—is the basis of Rights, 182 ff.—and security of person

INDEX

and property, 182-184, 191 ff.
—is criticised as an uncertain standard, 184 — is the real ground for deciding questions of Justice in the case of Punishment, Distribution of Profits, and Taxation, 185 ff.— and retributive Justice, 194, 195—is the ground of Impartiality, 197, 198.

V

Verification—essential to the use of Deductive Method, 77.
VIRTUE—its cultivation is enjoined by Utilitarianism, lxvii, 99, 100, 150 ff.—is capable of being desired in and for itself as a part of Happiness, lxvii, 150, 151—from being originally desired as a means to Happiness, it comes to be felt good in itself and desired as part of Happiness, lxvii, 151-153.
VOLITION—is a function of self-conscious Personality, 1 ff.— can only be influenced indirectly, *i.e.*, by change of circumstances, 17 note 1 — becomes habitual, 23, 24—is distinct from Desire since it is amenable to Habit, but is originally produced by Desire and can only be influenced through it, 157 ff.

W

Whewell — his conception of Moral Science, xvi, xvii—on Bacon's Theory of Axiomata Media, 73 note — and Utilitarianism, 86 note 1.
Will. See Volition.
Wordsworth—his influence on Mill, lxxiv, lxxvi.

Reprint Publishing

For People Who Go For Originals.

This book is a facsimile reprint of the original edition. The term refers to the facsimile with an original in size and design exactly matching simulation as photographic or scanned reproduction.

Facsimile editions offer us the chance to join in the library of historical, cultural and scientific history of mankind, and to rediscover.

The books of the facsimile edition may have marks, notations and other marginalia and pages with errors contained in the original volume. These traces of the past refers to the historical journey that has covered the book.

ISBN 978-3-95940-169-2

Facsimile reprint of the original edition
Copyright © 2016 Reprint Publishing
All rights reserved.

www.reprintpublishing.com

www.ingramcontent.com/pod-product-compliance
Lightning Source LLC
Chambersburg PA
CBHW070717160426
43192CB00009B/1221